W9-BKM-903

tear here

Seven Rules for Success with Your Lawn

- ➤ Water thoroughly to promote deep rooting.
- ➤ Fertilize on schedule for consistent nutrition.
- ➤ Mow often with a sharp blade for clean cuts.
- ➤ Keep objects, toys, and vehicles off the lawn.
- ➤ Topdress with humus at least once every year.
- ➤ Aerate soil if compacted and resisting water.
- ➤ Inspect grass closely and often for signs of pests.

Secrets to the Art of the Mow

- ➤ Keep mower blades sharp for a clean cut.
- ➤ Avoid mowing when it's wet or muddy.
- ➤ Mow at the proper setting for grass type.
- ➤ Mow in a different pattern each time.
- ➤ Mow extra-long grass in stages.
- ➤ Mow at a higher level in very hot summer.

America's Best Turf Grasses

Cool-Season Regions
- ➤ Kentucky Blue Grass
- ➤ Perennial Rye
- ➤ Fescues

Warm-Season Regions
- ➤ St. Augustine
- ➤ Bermuda
- ➤ Zoysia
- ➤ Centipede
- ➤ Bahia

Native Grasses
- ➤ Buffalo Grass
- ➤ Blue Gamma

alpha
books

Water Conservation Tips

➤ Water only at night or early morning.

➤ Turn off water when runoff begins.

➤ Avoid watering in windy weather.

➤ Repair broken pipes and sprinkler heads immediately.

➤ Adjust heads to avoid watering paved surfaces.

➤ Fine-tune "day" and "duration" of automatic systems.

➤ Aerate soil to increase water penetration.

The Most Common Causes of Lawn Problems

➤ The wrong turf grass variety for your climate.

➤ Too much shade for turf grass to grow.

➤ Sparse lawns invite weed invasions.

➤ Compacted soils prevent water penetration.

➤ Improper mowing habits weaken grass plants.

➤ Too much nitrogen stimulates excessive growth.

➤ Overwatering rots roots and invites fungal diseases.

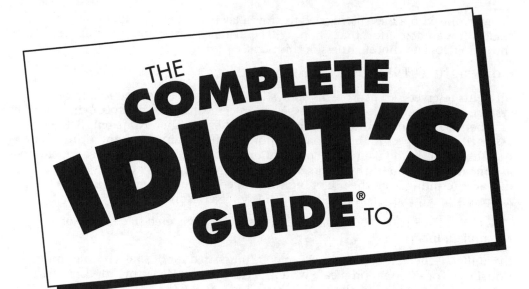

THE COMPLETE IDIOT'S GUIDE® TO

A Beautiful Lawn

by Maureen Gilmer

alpha books

A Division of Macmillan General Reference
A Pearson Education Macmillan Company
1633 Broadway, New York, NY 10019-6785

To everyone who has ever struggled to grow a lawn and been disappointed by the results. It is a noble effort that I hope will be made far easier and more successful by the simplicity and thoroughness of this book.

Copyright © 1999 by Maureen Gilmer

All rights reserved. No part of this book shall be reproduced, stored in a retrieval system, or transmitted by any means, electronic, mechanical, photocopying, recording, or otherwise, without written permission from the publisher. No patent liability is assumed with respect to the use of the information contained herein. Although every precaution has been taken in the preparation of this book, the publisher and author assume no responsibility for errors or omissions. Neither is any liability assumed for damages resulting from the use of information contained herein. For information, address Alpha Books, 1633 Broadway, 7th Floor, New York, NY 10019-6785.

THE COMPLETE IDIOT'S GUIDE TO and design are registered trademarks of Macmillan, Inc.

Macmillan General Reference books may be purchased for business or sales promotional use. For information please write: Special Markets Department, Macmillan Publishing USA, 1633 Broadway, New York, NY 10019-6785.

International Standard Book Number: 0-02-863008-4
Library of Congress Catalog Card Number is available from the publisher.

01 00 99   8 7 6 5 4 3 2 1

Interpretation of the printing code: the rightmost number of the first series of numbers is the year of the book's printing; the rightmost number of the second series of numbers is the number of the book's printing. For example, a printing code of 99-1 shows that the first printing occurred in 1999.

Printed in the United States of America

Note: This publication contains the opinions and ideas of its author. It is intended to provide helpful and informative material on the subject matter covered. It is sold with the understanding that the author and publisher are not engaged in rendering professional services in the book. If the reader requires personal assistance or advice, a competent professional should be consulted.

The author and publisher specifically disclaim any responsibility for any liability, loss or risk, personal or otherwise, which is incurred as a consequence, directly or indirectly, of the use and application of any of the contents of this book.

Alpha Development Team

Executive Editor
Anne Ficklen

Managing Editor
Cindy Kitchel

Marketing Brand Manager
Felice Primeau

Editor
Barbara Berger

Development Editor
Claudine Curry

Production Team

Production Editor
Sharon Lee

Copy Editor
Geneil Breeze

Cover Designer
Mike Freeland

Photo Editor
Richard H. Fox

Illustrators
Brian Moyer
Laura Robbins

Book Designers
Scott Cook and Amy Adams of DesignLab

Indexer
Laura Ogar

Layout/Proofreading
Jerry Cole
Laura Goetz
Marie Kristine Parial-Leonardo

Contents at a Glance

Contents

19 Pets and Wildlife and Your Lawn 271

22 Thatch: Not the Kind for Huts   319

Foreword

The rain has ended, and you're ready to head to work. If you hurry, you can run the bills to your mailbox and still make it to the office on time. You grab the stack of envelopes, dash out the door—and sink in the mud up to your ankles.

That's what life would be like if you didn't have a lawn.

It's easy to overlook the obvious, and turf is obvious. It's everywhere: home lawns, parks, roadsides, building grounds, and more. People forget that the main purpose of turf is to hold soil in place and offer solid footing. The beauty of turf overpowers its function.

Going beyond function, you may step into the sometimes competitive ranks of those desiring a beautiful lawn. If the dark green, luscious turf in your neighbor's yard or the sea of perfectly manicured grounds on a televised golf tournament stirs an inner desire for your lawn to look as good, you've planted the proverbial seed for grass that's "always greener on the other side."

But achieving the perfect lawn is not as easy as planting the seed and standing back. You have to know which grasses are best adapted to your particular site; how to fertilize, mow, irrigate, and control damaging turf pests; as well as a host of other topics. This book will get you started.

Maureen Gilmer takes you through all the things you'll need to know to have a beautiful lawn. She begins with a discussion on the origin of turf grasses and a description of the grasses from which you will choose, and she ends with an overview of turf pests you might encounter and how to control them. The author has written this book in well-organized, witty prose that is both informative and entertaining. Her comprehensive coverage of the subject will surely serve to answer all your questions about lawn care.

I must say that I was skeptical about this book when the publisher first approached me to write this foreword. I've worked on a golf course for 10 years, conducted turf research, taught Turf Management at the University of Maryland, and served as editor-in-chief of the leading professional turf-care magazine, *Grounds Maintenance,* for the last 10 years, and I didn't know how I could benefit from *The Complete Idiot's Guide to a Beautiful Lawn.* But upon reading this book, the benefits became obvious. In my job, it's easy to get caught up in the technical jargon, and it was refreshing to read the author's very practical approach to the subject of lawn care. Maureen Gilmer puts herself in your shoes and leads you through the basics of lawn care. You'll find your questions answered before you ask them. That's the mark of a good writer. Enjoy!

Mark S. Welterlen, Ph.D.
Editor-in-Chief
Grounds Maintenance
Intertec Publishing, A PRIMEDIA Company
Overland Park, Kansas

Introduction

Lawns need a lot of love, yet they are often seen as the poor stepchild of the home landscape because they aren't particularly colorful nor do they change over time. No other plant in the landscape will reward your efforts on such a large scale as the lawn. To prove this, simply look at any beautiful landscape of trees, shrubs, and flowers arranged around a lawn. They may look fabulous, but if the lawn is yellow and patchy, even the greatest garden suffers a black eye.

You'll be surprised at just how easy it is to take care of your grass after you learn a few basics. You don't have to know all about turf grass, just about the kind of grass in your lawn. You don't have to know all about fertilizers, just the brand you choose for your lawn. And you don't need to understand the complexities of mowing because you'll never mow any other lawn but your own. In short, learn just about what you have, and you are guaranteed emerald green success you can be proud of.

In *The Complete Idiot's Guide to a Beautiful Lawn*, you will be able to browse through virtually every aspect of turf grass science and craft. Each chapter builds on the information provided in the chapter preceding it. You begin with basic botany of grass, then move on to how grass is planted, and then learn about the care and feeding the lawn will need later on. This sequence is designed so that you need not learn more advanced aspects of lawn care until you have a firm foundation.

How to Use This Book

There is a method to the madness of how these chapters are laid out for you.

In Part 1, you get "A Thorough Grounding in Grass Family Culture." It helps you to understand Mother Nature's appreciation of grasses and the family tree of wild grasses scientifically bred into citified turf grasses. It also shows you why grass preferred in Florida is undesirable in Maine. After all, grasses are plants, and all plants draw a line in the sand when it comes to how much heat or cold they can stand.

Part 2, "Civilized Grasses for Your Yard," gives the rundown on how and why we put turf grass in a landscape. Your front yard lawn may be strictly to look at, whereas the grass in the back yard may take a beating as a family recreation area. You'll also learn ways to buy your grass, such as instant-gratification sod lawns. But if you're a budget-conscious gardener, it might take a lot longer to reach your finished lawn when a limited budget demands you start from seeds or plugs.

The basics of gardening are emphasized in Part 3, "The Nuts and Bolts of Grass Roots Gardening." The need for soil, water, sunlight, and oxygen is common to all plants, and turf grasses in particular. Pay special attention to the chapter on soils because this is the most important part of growing plants successfully. You'll also find out whether you're a push-mower type, a riding mower type, or somewhere in between.

In Part 4, "Creating a Green Carpet," you'll learn all about sowing and growing. These are the step-by-step instructions to get your new lawn off on the right foot so that it's bound to be successful. But there's also a helpful chapter on groundcover plants that are real lifesavers where there isn't enough sun or the ground is too rough to plant a turf grass lawn.

Part 5, "Please Feed the Grass," is all about tending your lawn whether it's new or old. It introduces a strict diet of health foods to ensure that you enjoy peak color and beauty. It's also a guide to identification and repair of the least expected sources of lawn damage caused by wear and tear. In addition, you'll find solutions to more obvious problems related to pet damage.

Part 6, "Old Lawn Makeovers," is the most important part of the book. It teaches you the process of aeration and renovation of lawns. It is the most beneficial aspect of lawn care and the most often neglected as well. Yet aeration is easy to do and makes a huge difference in how much water and fertilizer it takes to make the grass look great.

Part 7, "In Search of Small Game and Green Invaders," is your guide to problem pests, be they plant or animal. It walks you through some of the strange but wonderful connections that are consistently overlooked.

This book holds all the secrets of professional lawn care written in an easy-to-understand language. It not only helps you get started but will aid your efforts during the coming years when the lawn needs an occasional makeover. Turf grass, like other plants, doesn't ask for much, just food, water, air, sunlight, and an occasional haircut. In turn, it provides a soothing emerald field that will make your entire neighborhood green with envy.

Extras

Whenever there's something we don't want you to miss, you'll find it in these helpful boxes:

Turf Tip

These labor-saving ideas and short cuts help you get things done faster, easier, and for less money.

Turf Talk

There are many terms used in lawn care that you should know and understand.

The Grass Is Always Greener

Grasses are a big family with many facts and stories that make them more meaningful, and these help you get to know them better.

Turf Caveat

Caveat is a legal term meaning "beware." These warnings help you avoid the most common mistakes and costly errors in lawn care.

Acknowledgments

An author is only as good as her editor and agents, so I want to first thank Barbara Berger for bringing me on board and helping to develop the book in its early stages. At the other end, I am indebted to Claudine Curry who made sure that I got all the materials submitted correctly; and I wish to thank Cindy Kitchel and Sharon Lee, who both directed the final editorial process.

I also want to thank Brian Moyer and Laura Robbins for illustrating the book, and the Turf Resource Center for color photography, because pictures are indeed worth a thousand words.

Finally, I want to thank my literary agent, Jeanne Fredericks, who has worked tirelessly on my behalf to introduce me to *The Complete Idiot's Guide* series and this book project.

Part 1
A Thorough Grounding in Grass Family Culture

If all you know about grass is that you see it on TV football fields, then you'll really benefit from this section. Grass is actually a simple plant with simple needs that you'll understand if you see it in the wild. You'll need to know some special words, such as differences between grasses that run, those that walk, and some that just sit there. You'll also need to know which grasses like the Sun Belt and which ones prefer cold winters and snow.

This is also your first view into just one branch of the family of grasses. Because all grass types aren't suited to lawns, you'll find out that some make better fishing poles than play fields. After you discover the featured types, then you'll be able to identify which members of their family are best for you and your family.

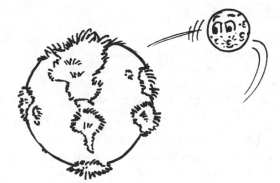

Chapter 1

Grass Goes Global

In This Chapter

➤ An overview of grasses around the world

➤ The vital roles of wild grasses

➤ Debunking turf grass myths

➤ When a grass is not a grass

No other plant is more routinely stomped and butchered and stabbed than the grasses. Yet, despite such savagery, their resilience is undeniable . . . that is until we try to grow a lawn. Then we see them as difficult and temperamental, yet we love them dearly and torture ourselves to make them grow. Why? Because green pastoral places are beautiful to behold and offer us a cool, natural outdoor living space.

Preoccupation with creating a perfect lawn is not always rational given that there are a series of tasks required to ensure that it looks its best. But grasses are remarkably adaptable, and even the novice gardener can be successful, particularly with so many new labor-saving products and equipment at our disposal. You, too, can cultivate a yard that sets the standard for the rest of the neighborhood.

> *Grasses there are, stout and higher than one's head, and grasses so slender that their dying stems among the wayside weeds are like threads of gold; grasses whose panicles of bloom are more than a half yard in length, and of a color which only midsummer sun can burn into August fields; grasses so stiff that winter's snow leaves them unbroken; and grasses so tiny that their highest flower is raised but a few inches from the soil.*

—Prof. Hi W. Staten, *Grasses and Grassland Farming*

The Meek Shall Inherit the Earth

Grasses are naturally multicultural and used by people of every nationality on earth. The grass family is called the *Gramnaceae*. It claims members on virtually every continent and in every climate except the extreme polar regions and the lowest points of Death Valley. No matter how hard you try, you can't put boundaries on grasses, because they're so adaptable. For example, bamboos are grasses that grow like timber, whereas tiny mosslike species of grasses inhabit the arctic tundra.

Savannas are grasslands that separate tropical forests from deserts around the world. Savannas are among the most nutritious habitats for herbivores. The great wildlife migrations of East Africa, which draw thousands of tourists each year to view the spectacle, are dictated by the condition of the grasses in Kenya. Savannas occur in many parts of sub-Saharan Africa from Tanzania to South Africa.

Our northern hemisphere tall grass prairies, which were grazed by the buffalo, are matched in the southern hemisphere by the pampas, expansive treeless plains of Argentina and neighboring countries. These ranges, like ours, host an enormous cattle industry.

Grasses are dominant in Asia, too. More cold-hardy varieties cloak the steppes, providing fodder for the musk ox and for the herds and flocks of pastoral Mongolian nomads. Farther south, thrive the bamboos, which grow like lawn grass on steroids. Ranging from short, ground-hugging species to timber bamboo, bamboo is not only forage for panda bears, it's also the major source of construction material in many cultures. Bamboo has long been used in China as a pulp for paper, and today it is being resurrected as a sustainable alternative to tree-produced pulp.

How Grasses Work in Nature

The grasses are some of Mother Nature's hardest workers, but their roles are so subtle that they are rarely appreciated for all they do. Practically every ecosystem includes one grass or another in its vital plant communities.

The most famous grasses are those that once dominated the plains of the American Midwest. Over many eons, they built up a thick layer of dead leaves and stems collectively called *sod*, which protected the fertile prairie soils that lay beneath. After the pioneer farmers stripped off the sod, these soils were exposed, and serious erosion occurred, peaking during the Dust Bowl, a drought that hit the American Midwest just before the Great Depression.

Grasses also play an important role on the coastal sand dune communities. Their extensive fibrous root systems are the first to take hold in the ever-shifting sand dunes. After dunes are colonized, the sand becomes stabilized, and, as seasons pass, the dead leaves and roots of the grasses enrich the sand and turn it into soil.

Around the edges of rivers, lakes, and ponds, entirely different grasses find a home. These are capable of surviving the rise and fall of water levels that can leave them completely submerged for weeks on end.

The Incredible Edible

Did you know that last night's pasta dinner comes from grasses? Wheat is one of our most important grass crops in the world. Dairy and meat products also come indirectly from grasses. Your breakfast oatmeal is a grass too. Many believe that grasses were the very first plants to be grown for food by human beings and that our most common cereal grains originated in ancient Middle Asia and Ethiopia.

Rice is a unique water grass cultivated on land that is too wet to sustain traditional grains. Rice has become the most valuable staple food for much of the world's hungriest populations.

In the hands of man, common grass has been manipulated to produce food in incredible quantities. A plant known as *Teosinte* has been bred repeatedly since ancient times to produce our modern corn, which is so different that you would never suspect that the two are related. Wheat, millet, barley, and rye are all grasses that feed the world and provide a bonus crop of useful straw.

Rice

Wheat and Rye

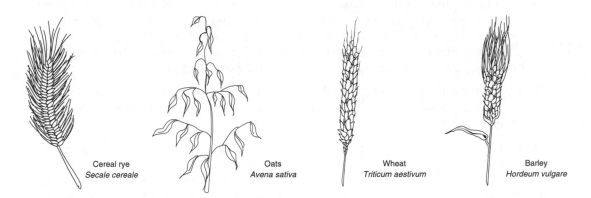

Cereal rye
Secale cereale

Oats
Avena sativa

Wheat
Triticum aestivum

Barley
Hordeum vulgare

Amazing Titanic Grasses

Titanic grasses display remarkable growth rates and adaptability combined with enormous size. It's fun to ponder their relationships to our tiny turf grasses, but it's also essential that you learn about them because they can be difficult to remove after they become established in your yard.

The family of bamboos is enormous—some members grow 100 feet tall—and has supported entire cultures. Bamboos behave much like our more invasive, smaller running grasses, which grow at lightning speed and have taken over entire homesites. The only difference is that the fibers of bamboo are more stiff and woody. Treat all bamboo as you would weeds and don't believe anyone who wants to sell or give you a "clumping" bamboo. These don't run—but they walk REALLY FAST.

A native grass of the South American pampas is known in the United States as pampas grass, or technically: *Cortaderia selloana*. This is an elephant of a grass that grows into huge clumps up to 10 feet wide and nearly as tall. It flowers out of the center on long, slender rods topped with big, fluffy, feather-dusterlike structures. This is a beautiful grass made popular in the 1960s; the flower heads were once the rage for decorating Victorian parlors.

The problem with pampas grass is that it is extremely difficult to get rid of because of the huge ball of stems and roots at its center. People burn it, dynamite it, and use wood-chopping axes to get rid of it, which shows just how well adapted some exotic grasses can be in our milder North American climate.

Another unusually large grass, which was planted on farms wherever the climate allowed, is called *Arundo donax.* This fast-growing reed was the primary source of fishing poles in the nineteenth century, and today is an undesirable invader of drainage ditches. With such great size and rapid spread, the grass can seriously reduce drainage capacity to such an extent that surrounding lands become susceptible to flooding.

Pampas Grass

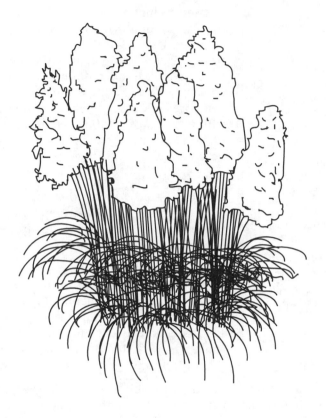

What Is Grass?

Without throwing a lot of botanical mumbo jumbo at you, all grasses simply have stems with solid joints. At the joint is a leaf, which fits around the stem like a split tube, and a blade, which is commonly long and narrow. No other plant family shares this particular structure. Grab a magnifying glass and check it out for yourself.

All grasses are wind pollinated, which means that they don't need flowers or bees to reproduce. Their modified structures for producing and catching pollen are borne on stems that rise up above the plants. However, some grasses reproduce asexually, meaning that pieces of the plant root easily when they are placed in contact with soil. This can be a good thing or a bad thing, depending on whether you want that grass in your lawn.

Turf Talk

You can roughly divide all plants into two categories. The first group is defined by woody trunks and stems, like trees. The second group is *herbaceous*, which means that the plants' parts are soft and green and have a high water content. Herbaceous plants are vulnerable to extreme cold, and hard freezes will cause most of the plant to die back to ground level. *Cold-hardy herbaceous plants* such as prairie grasses don't die entirely, because the roots are still alive and protected underground.

When Grass Gangs Up

Grasses are highly communal plants that like to grow together naturally in meadows and prairies. They form an inviting setting for other kinds of plants. Two centuries ago, before settlement of the midwestern prairies, the land looked much different than it does today. Our most extensive and important grasslands were originally composed of dense populations of tall grasses combined with a variety of wildflowers. In spring and summer, the prairies burst into color with a huge assortment of flowers that bloomed together with the grasses.

Wild grasses that are long lived can be divided into two categories—*sod grasses* and *bunch grasses*. Sod grasses tend to spread out and develop a carpetlike mass. Bunch grasses grow in tufts that gradually become larger but do not spread.

Like all herbaceous plants, prairie grasses shed their dead leaves with the advent of winter, and this material builds up around the plants. Combined with the network of roots, it accumulates into a thick layer called sod that gradually decomposes from the bottom up. The sod holds the soil in place and provides insulation for the roots during very cold or hot weather.

In the wild, you can gauge the depth of the soil by noting where trees and grass choose to grow. Grasses become dominant where there is deep soil, and, because they are so plentiful, they crowd out seedlings of trees and shrubs. Grasses are also part of *succession*. This is an environmental process that begins with a lake or pond where water gathers in the low spots. Over time, water weeds and sediment gradually fill the pond until it becomes a "wet meadow" and supports bog plants. The pord gradually fills until it becomes a dry meadow composed primarily of grasses and wildflowers.

Native Prairie and Meadow Grasses of the United States

Name	Habit
Big bluestem	Bunch
Yellow bluestem	Bunch
Forked silver beard bluestem	Bunch
Silver beard	Bunch
Buffalo	Sod
Curly mesquite	Sod

Name	Habit
Side-oats gama	Bunch
Black gama	Semibunch
Indian	Bunch
Joint grass	Bunch
Salt grass	Sod
Switch	Bunch
Sand love	Bunch
Weeping love	Bunch

Many American wildflowers, such as Black-eyed Susan and Phlox, grow with grasses in meadows and prairies and bloom at varying times from late spring to autumn.

Now that you understand where and how grasses live in the wild, it's much easier to see what's behind a lawn. Whereas a prairie or meadow can be considered a rural community of grasses, a lawn is a high-density apartment complex. Like its wild ancestors, the lawn needs deep, rich soil to grow well.

Unlike the wild ones, some cultivated lawns are composed of just one type of grass, whereas others are an integrated mixture of grasses. Lawns are trimmed short to make all the grass plants the same height, much as the buffalo and prairie fires once controlled the height of our wild grasslands. Lawn mowers are used to keep the grasses short and encourage them to spread out.

Turf Talk

The *meristem* of a grass plant is the part that produces new leaves from its center. The cells located there divide rapidly during the growing season. The meristems of sod grasses are located much closer to the ground than those of bunch grasses. If a grass has a high meristem, it simply can't tolerate mowing; thus, it is not a suitable turf grass.

From Tall Grass to Turf Grass

Each and every grass used in lawns today has a wild ancestor. These forebears evolved to live in certain climates with no assistance from man. They survived droughts, floods, winds, heat, and extreme cold. These native grasses were rugged individualists that populated not only America but also most of the world.

Through natural selection, the grasses with the greatest tendency to root deeply became most successful. They could access moisture from deep in the soil during prolonged drought cycles.

Turf Talk

Turf grass is a general term used to describe grasses suitable for lawns because of their growth habit and tolerance of regular mowing.

They developed dense, mounding habits that put enough of the plant above the soil to escape rotting in saturated soils due to excessive rain or flooding. These grasses could also grow quickly after a wildfire burned through, which allowed them to regrow in just a few months amidst the ashes.

This survivability was attractive to ranchers who first worked with the wild grasses to create managed pastures for their livestock. From the wild species, they chose those with the greatest vigor, drought tolerance, and resistance to rot. Over time, the grasses became a regular crop grown for pasture and orchard grass seed.

During ancient European times, grasses were appreciated because meadows gave people a place to gather outdoors that wasn't muddy or dusty. In fact, the word *lawn* is derived from the Celtic word *lann*, which means enclosed land. Lawns were often planted from cut sod in medieval times, and, in the monastic traditions, were called *viridarium* in Latin.

The greatest moment in the evolution of cultivated grasses was the advent of the lawn mower. The industrial revolution and assembly lines reduced costs so that anyone who could afford to buy one enjoyed a manicured, clipped lawn without servants to cut it or livestock to graze it down naturally. The market demanded there be new grasses that looked better, felt better, and grew into a more even mat than the lumpy pasture species. Out of the labs and breeding grounds came the ornamental grasses labeled "turf grass," due to their sole use in lawns.

Equal Rights for Grasses

In the last few decades, turf grass lawns have become the standard of beauty for residential homes. Tens of millions of American families maintain a front and/or a backyard lawn. An enormous industry has grown up around lawn creation and care.

In recent years, increased environmental awareness has taken its toll on the American lawn. The organic gardening movement is quick to point out that lawns are guzzling chemicals and commercial fertilizers and thus threaten our environment by polluting runoff and groundwater. We also hear a lot of accusations about the water consumption of lawns compared to other types of planting. This is particularly common in the west where the water supply is having a hard time keeping up with population growth.

There is also pressure regarding the potential for pollution by exhaust from gasoline-driven lawn care equipment such as mowers and trimmers. Some communities are threatening to enforce smog equipment on gas-fired lawn mowers or to outlaw them entirely in favor of electric mowers.

The reality is that lawns offer as many benefits to the environment as they do liabilities. The anti-lawn people tend to make blanket statements about the problems without a thorough consideration of the alternatives. These turn into media horror stories that are nowhere near the truth behind the issue. Be aware of the other side of the argument so that you can grow and enjoy a beautiful home lawn without guilt.

Most of the pollution stories you hear are caused by uninformed or irresponsible lawn owners—because you bought this book, I know you aren't one of them. Let's look at some of the most common myths, explore why they exist, and then compare them with the truths of responsible lawn care.

Myth #1: Lawns and lawn care pollute the environment with equipment exhaust, pesticides, herbicides, and nitrates.

You've seen lawn owners out on a windy day with a gun on the end of their garden hoses spraying their lawns with huge amounts of chemicals, most of which ends up blowing away or into the neighbors' yards. Or maybe they avoid an extra fee at the landfill by pouring excess garden chemicals into the gutter.

The truth is that when chemical pesticides, herbicides, and fertilizers are used properly, they are safe for the environment. As a responsible lawn owner, you view these products as food and medicine to use strictly according to doctor-manufacturer's instructions. You would never dream of disposing of excess product in an unsafe manner either.

Myth #2: Lawns gobble too much precious water that's already in short supply.

Ever see people's sprinklers running in the rain? How about a sprinkler that waters the driveway? Maybe you've followed the runoff three blocks away from somebody's rock-hard, worn-out lawn that is no more able to absorb water than a piece of sheet metal.

The truth is that plants don't waste water, people do. The reality is that a well-tended lawn, particularly when planted with more-efficient, modern turf grasses, absorbs water quickly and holds it for a long time. As a responsible lawn owner, you are always keenly aware of how much water is delivered at all times.

Myth #3: All grass clippings end up clogging our landfills.

Lawn owners gather up everything from the yard—leaves, grass clippings, and all sorts of rubbish—stuff it in a plastic bag and send it to the landfill.

The truth is that responsible lawn owners know that not all organic waste is the same. Just as you separate household disposables into their own recycling bins, you also separate yard junk. First stop is the compost heap for leaves and clippings, second stop is the fireplace for potential firewood, and third stop is the garbage can for whatever's left.

Reasons to Believe . . . in Lawns

Lawns, like their wild ancestors in grasslands, act as filters for rain runoff. The roots of sod in lawns and meadows form a dense layer capable of catching sediment and pollutants, allowing water to be cleaned before it percolates down into the water table.

The prairie sod keeps the fertile soils of the Corn Belt from drying out and blowing away in the persistent wind or washing out in heavy thunderstorms. The faster water flows across bare land, the more soil particles are picked up and carried away. Water flowing across that same land covered with grass must slow down as it winds its way through, thus reducing the erosion potential. Lawns also protect soil around your home from water and wind erosion in the same way, with a thick layer of sod.

Lawns grow well even where there is smog, dust, or other types of air pollution. As each grass plant breathes, it takes in carbon dioxide and expels oxygen through the leaves. This exchange filters the air 24 hours a day, extracting pollution and releasing the pure oxygen so vital to human life. Scientists proved that 2,500 square feet of lawn can absorb carbon dioxide from the atmosphere and release each day enough oxygen to supply a family of four.

Lawn as Urban Oasis

The suburban and urban environments we live in are not always comforting places to be. In fact, it can be downright challenging to find a nice quiet place to spend a few minutes and renew ourselves at the end of the day. There is no better place to recover from the daily grind than in a garden amidst a beautiful green lawn. Rather than a verdant oasis surrounded by dry desert, our lawns become a living oasis surrounded by urban sprawl.

Studies tell us that on a hot summer day the ambient air temperature around the lawn is up to 30 degrees cooler than that around pavement. We also know that a lawn has the capability to absorb harsh sounds, making our homes more quiet and peaceful. The softness of the lawn surface is a far safer place for children to play. We all have known these things for a long time, but only now are we discovering just how important lawns are to our state of mind. Lawns are more than aesthetic . . . they're therapeutic!

When Is a Grass Not a Grass . . . When It's a Sedge

The *sedges* are not grasses and are not even members of the *Gramnaceae* family, but they appear so similar that you may not be able to tell a grass from a sedge just by looking at them. The sedge family is called *Cyperaceae* and comprises more than 2,000 species. You probably know of its most famous member, Papyrus.

Papyrus grows on the banks of the River Nile, and its fibers were used to make the first paper. The habitat of Papyrus gives us a clue to reasons why sedges are different. First, they really like wet ground, which makes them the most hated weed among rice growers worldwide. Second, they are very fibrous, which makes them tough to mow.

If you live in low-lying land or in the southern states where sedges thrive, you should know how to tell a sedge from a grass. The best way is to touch them because the old phrase "sedges have edges" points to the serrated edges of all sedge leaves. Simply run your hand down the edge of the leaves, and if it's toothy like an emery board or a hacksaw blade, then it's a sedge. If it's smooth, it's a grass.

Turf Talk

Any plant that grows where you don't want it to is considered a *weed*. Grass growing in the lawn is turf. If the same plant grows outside the lawn edge, it becomes a weed.

Sedge Leaf

Sedges are among the most tenacious and dangerous weeds in the garden and are often brought in with nice fertile river-bottom topsoil. One nut sedge plant, the most common species, can produce 90,000 seeds in a single season. Because they look like turf grass, they often gain a foothold in lawns and spread from there. Sedges differ from grasses in another respect as well—their roots produce little potatolike tubers. Each mature plant can produce almost 7,000 new tubers in a soil area only 7 feet in diameter.

That's why control is so difficult—because you must dig up the *entire rootball* to eradicate the plant and all its root tubers. Plus, sedges are somewhat resistant to the more common garden herbicides as well. Know your sedges and keep them out of your lawn and garden from day one, and you will be sedge-free forever.

The Least You Need to Know

➤ Grasses are our most universal plants.

➤ Grasses fill many different roles in the wild from erosion control to wildlife grazing.

➤ Bunch grasses grow differently than turf grasses.

➤ Sedges look identical to grasses, but they are a very different plant altogether.

Chapter 2

Beginner's Botany

In This Chapter

➤ Understanding the language of grass

➤ How anatomy influences how we use grass

➤ The reproductive processes of grasses

➤ Growing grasses *au naturel*

Imagine a little bespectacled scientist in his laboratory using genetic engineering to produce a perfect turf grass for all the lawn junkies in America. The beauty of all his work is that you, the neophyte lawnowner, may brutalize your futuristic lawn grass with minimal ill effects.

Don't feel left out if you can't tell one grass from another. You're not alone. In fact, most homeowners know very little about their own yards except how to start the lawn mower. Yet knowing the plants in your landscape is as important as reading the fine print on a binding contract, because it is only then that you really understand what's going on in the lawn.

The best way to get up close and personal with your lawn is to get down on your hands and knees. It's not uncommon to see a greenskeeper do this when concerned with a part of a golf course, because you really can't assess a plant without getting a close look at it. Why not get down and really study a lawn with a magnifying glass? As you learn more about grasses, this is the best way to verify what you read.

Don't Be Afraid of the Latin

They say Latin is a dead language, and unless you are old enough to remember the Latin mass, you've probably never heard it spoken. When the great scientific minds of ancient Greek and Roman civilizations wrote a new text, it was readable only by people of those cultures. Producing a handwritten book in more than one language was virtually impossible. Eventually, the language problem in the scientific realm was solved by designating one common language—Latin. This meant that a physician or botanist in Britain could read the same text as a scientist in Constantinople or Israel. Today, this common language still has one foot in the grave and the other deeply rooted in terminology used in medicine, biology, and, in terms of grasses, botany.

Don't worry, you don't have to learn the botanical names of lawn grasses, but it's helpful to know how the names relate to one another.

Latin plant names are like our names but in reverse. The last name comes first and the first name last, like "Smith, John." Plants, like human families, are grouped by their last names. The last name of all apples is *Malus*. The last name of all roses is *Rosa*. These last names are technically called the *genus*.

When we want to know the exact individual of a genus, we use the first name, called the *species*. A species of rose is *rugosa*, or in full, *Rosa rugosa*, just like the "John" in John Smith.

But what if there's more than one John Smith? Maybe they are cousins who both have the exact same name and belong to the same family. How do we tell them apart? Perhaps they have different middle names, or one is a Jr., or they are John Smith I and John Smith II.

This often happens when a certain species is artificially bred into a new size or color, but it remains the exact same species. This happens a lot with grasses and roses, too, because together they are the two most widely bred of all garden plants. To deal with this, we add a *cultivar name*. Often these cultivar names are combined with a common name, or actually *are* the common name.

To see how all this nomenclature relates to turf grasses, we'll use an example of a native American wild grass that has been altered considerably by special breeding. Kentucky bluegrass obviously comes from Kentucky. It got the name because of the bluish cast that appears when the seed heads are produced, but the leaves are just as emerald green as all the other grasses. The vigor and beauty of this grass is the reason why the region is world renowned for the racehorses bred there, which feed upon this rich, luxuriant grass.

The common name, Kentucky bluegrass, is generic. Its official last name, the genus, is *Poa*. The first name or species is *pratensis*. Dozens of cultivars of *Poa pratensis* were developed to make it a better grass for lawns, which experience continual, close mowing. Among these are Adelphi, Flyking, and True Blue.

Here's an example of how this name breaks down:

➤ All members of the bluegrass family share the last name, or genus, *Poa*.

➤ There are 5,000 bluegrass first names, or species, worldwide; the one used for turf grass is *pratensis*, which means "having rhizomes."

➤ More than 77 recognized cultivars of Kentucky bluegrass are on the market today.

The company that developed Adelphi may have exclusive rights to that name, which is protected just like any other trademark or patent. That does not mean that the company's competitor can't grow the very same strain; they just can't call it Adelphi. To get around this, the competitor will adopt its own name and sell the grass strain under that label. It's not uncommon for five different seed producers to sell identical strains of bluegrass, each marketed under its own trade name.

The Grass Is Always Greener

Don't be surprised if you find an oxymoron or two in turf grass names. My favorite is dwarf tall fescue. What began as tall fescue was bred to have shorter stature while maintaining its rooting depth. The result was a stunted version of one of our most drought-tolerant native grasses with enough root zone to survive periodic dry spells.

Nerd Words You Need to Know

When you read about grass names above, you may have noticed the word *rhizome*. This is just one of a few terms to learn that will help you better understand both the anatomy of your lawn and its good or bad habits. There's no need to memorize these terms, but remember the location of these definitions if you encounter them again later on.

Origination and Behavior Terms

➤ *Native:* A grass that originates in your region, nation, or continent; for example, bluegrass from Kentucky or buffalo grass from the Great Plains. Bamboo is native to China.

➤ *Exotic:* A grass that is not native to the immediate region; for example, Missouri buffalo grass is exotic in California.

➤ *Annual grass:* A grass that sprouts from seed, matures, and produces new seed in one season before it dies.

➤ *Perennial grass:* A grass that lives indefinitely year after year.

➤ *Dormancy:* A period, usually in winter, during which the grass takes a rest and sometimes turns brown.

➤ *Stand:* The growing of wild grass in a given area.

Anatomical Terms

➤ *Rhizome:* An *underground* creeping stem by which a sod-type grass spreads.

➤ *Stolon:* An *above-ground* creeping stem by which sod-type turf grass spreads.

➤ *Seed head:* The stem or wand upon which the "flowers" and seeds are produced on grass plants.

➤ *Node:* the joints on a rhizome or stolon where either of these stems may produce shoots (above ground) or roots (underground).

Propagation Terms

➤ *Sexual reproduction:* Production of new plants through pollination and seed.

➤ *Asexual reproduction:* Growing grass from part of a plant.

➤ *Clone:* An identical offspring produced from a cell or group of cells of a mother plant.

➤ *Cutting:* A piece of stem from a plant forced to root and create a new plant identical to the original.

➤ *Sprig:* A piece of rhizome or stolon used to create a new plant.

➤ *Plug:* A cylindrical piece of sod about 1 inch in diameter that includes leaf, stem, roots, and some soil.

Know What You're Looking At

You probably think all grasses look alike, and frankly, they do bear such resemblance that you can't tell many wild ones apart until they bloom. Because turf grasses comprise about eight basic types, with all their many species and varieties, you would be able to identify these general classifications easily if you knew what to look for. You'd be surprised at just how different they are from one another. Fortunately, grasses are simple plants, and their visual anatomy will tell you a lot about how they grow.

Plants in general are best identified by their reproductive structures, such as flowers. But because lawns are mowed so often, these grasses never have a chance to flower, so we must look at another part of the plant for identification. Turf grasses are grown for the color and texture of their leaves, their chief distinguishing characteristics.

The grass leaf is also called a *blade*. A blade of grass carries on the process of photo-synthesis, which utilizes sunlight to manufacture food for the plant. Although you can't see this with the naked eye, each blade of grass is riddled with little holes that are the plant's version of your skin pores. These holes, technically called *stomata*, open and close like skin pores do when we perspire, to regulate the exchange of moisture and air. When it's really hot, the stomata close up to retain moisture in the plant. They also do this in dry wind, which can draw moisture out of the leaf at an alarming rate.

Leaf Blade Variations

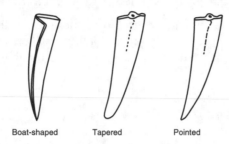

Boat-shaped   Tapered   Pointed

You are probably thinking that all grass blades look alike . . . well, think again. If you look closely, you'll see that they vary considerably from one species of grass to another. Grass species that originate in wet climates tend to be wide and succulent so that the greatest amount of leaf surface receives sunlight. In hot, arid climates, leaves evolved with a needlelike shape, or have rolled edges to reduce the amount of leaf surface exposed to the sun.

Consider these differences:

➤ Color—varies from green-gray to lime to emerald green

➤ Width—needlelike or up to $1/2$ inch wide

➤ Taper—narrowing toward the top of the blade

➤ Edges—may be smooth or serrated

➤ Surface—fuzzy, tacky, slippery, or smooth

➤ Tip—boat-shaped, rounded, or pointed

If you follow the grass blade down to the stem from which it originates, you will find a *sheath*. The point where the sheath connects to the stem is another body part called a *ligule*, which helps botanists distinguish between very similar grasses.

Rooting Around

Roots are the part of the plant that lives mostly underground. Roots take up moisture and nutrients from the soil. The vigor and depth of grass roots have much to do with the overall health of the grass, particularly when exposed to less than ideal circumstances.

Like leaf shape and size, the way a grass species roots tells us a lot about its origins too. Many grasses come from climate regions that experience very long, dry seasons that can be hot as well. These grasses survive because they have the ability to send out an extensive network of roots that reach very deep soil layers over a broad area. Moisture evaporates from the upper layers of soil first, but deeper down the moisture can remain trapped for many months at a time. During the dry season, the grasses access this deep moisture through their roots, which is enough to get them through until the rains come.

Turf grass breeders have taken a great interest in these naturally drought-adapted grasses. Whether you live in a dry region or not, aggressively rooting grasses mean that you need not water as much, and that the roots are better able to absorb lawn fertilizer for a healthier lawn.

Comparing Rooting Depth

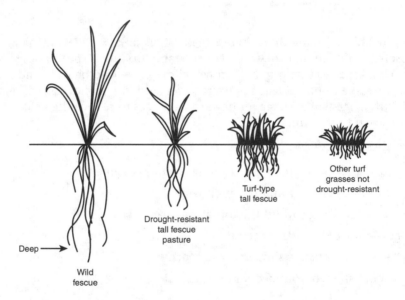

Grasses that descended from sod-forming species have a different rooting characteristic that makes them ideal turf grasses. This does not so much relate to depth as it does growth habit. These are the travelers of the family, which have unique structures that help them spread out. A single plant can travel quite a distance, rooting as it goes.

When a grass plant travels, it may do so by rhizomes, which are special types of roots that don't grow downwards, but sideways. The rhizome is an underground root that resembles a stem divided into segments. Segments are connected to one another by nodes or joints. A rhizome is able to produce true, downward-growing roots only at the bottom side of these nodes. On the top side of the node, the plant can produce shoots that poke up through the soil to produce what appears to be an entirely new plant next to the original. Actually, it's just an extension of the parent plant.

Traveling Grass by Rhizome

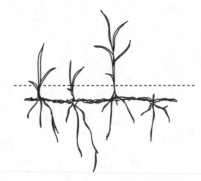

A grass plant also can travel by stolons, depending on the species. Stolons are the leap-frog stems, which, like rhizomes, are divided into segments by nodes. There will be leaves at each node, but if the node contacts soil, it is signaled to produce roots on the bottom side. Then a shoot also develops that produces a new plant.

Traveling Grass by Stolon

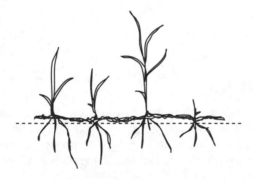

If you have a plant that's traveling by rhizome or stolon and has rooted at a node, you can sever it from the mother plant, and it will grow independently. Some grasses such as Bermuda can send out stolons up to 3 feet long or more before they decide to root. This has led these and similar aggressive grasses to be dubbed "runner" grasses because they grow so fast. It's not uncommon to see Bermuda run a stolon across a concrete curb and root on the other side to infest planters not designated for lawn.

This traveling tendency is important to know because it's a giant red warning flag that points out the bad boys of the grass world. Both rhizomes and stolons can be very tough and practically impossible to pull by hand unless you're really strong. Their speed can allow these plants to overwhelm a flower bed and weave themselves into groundcovers and shrubs before you know it. Once rhizomes and stolons have infested a bed, they can be a real nightmare.

Anatomy of a Grass Plant

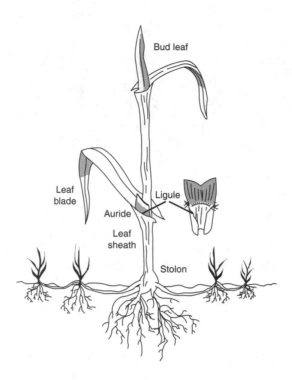

Bud leaf

Leaf blade

Ligule

Auride

Leaf sheath

Stolon

Sex and Sensimilia

When a lawn in the neighborhood starts to look like the owners have moved away, most folks say "that place has really gone to seed." The obvious sign that something is wrong is an unmowed lawn and a pile of rolled-up newspapers in the driveway. Without the intervention of a lawn mower, the grasses multiply without restraint.

All plants must flower to reproduce, but we can divide the whole into two groups. First are those that require bees or other animals and insects to carry pollen from one flower to the next. The shape and color of flowers, plus the production of nectar are designed by nature to attract these pollinators.

The second group of plants is pollinated by the wind, and these can be major offenders where allergy sufferers are concerned. Grasses are a major percentage of the wind-pollinated group, and they will reproduce at practically any time of year, except in the dead of winter.

The Grass Is Always Greener

Up to 90 percent of the weight of a grass plant is in its roots.

When grasses flower, they send up tall wands with structures on top that contain both male and female parts. The male part produces pollen, and the female part catches it; but many grasses are not self-fertile, which means that they must be pollinated by another plant to produce seed. The wands sit high so that the wind can catch and transport the pollen from one plant to another. Dry, windy weather is ideal for grass pollination to occur.

Seed Heads of Grasses

When we care for a turf grass lawn, we are practicing birth control. The plants never have a chance to develop a seed head because we cut it off all the time. Therefore, lawns are composed of *sensimilia*, or grass without seeds.

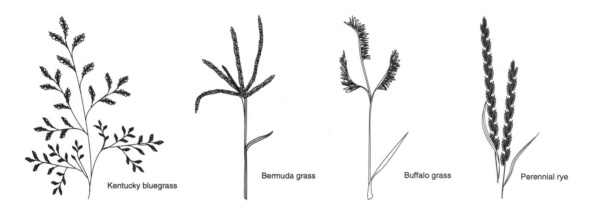

Kentucky bluegrass

Bermuda grass

Buffalo grass

Perennial rye

Here Today . . . Gone to Seed

The grass kingdom is divided into two groups that relate to the life span of the plant. If you know how the two groups differ, it helps you understand why lawn and other grasses in the garden behave the way they do.

The word *annus* is Latin for year and describes all plants known collectively as *annuals*. These plants germinate from seed, grow to maturity, and then flower and produce seed for the next year's population. This is a lot of work in a very short time.

Annuals take their signals from air temperature and day length. Warming in spring signals the seed that it's time to sprout. The long days of summer tell it that it's time to flower. Cooling days in autumn signal seed maturity, and frost kills annuals with the onset of winter. Annual grasses usually mature before the dog days of late summer and turn brown and shed seed well before the first frost. No matter how much you water them, after the seed matures, the plant dies and ends its life cycle.

Turf Talk

Plants grow in two ways: *vegetatively*, which means that they produce roots, stems, and leaves to enlarge their overall size; and *reproductively*, which is the production of flowers, fruits, and seeds. In the case of annual grasses, reproduce is about all they do! For lawns, we want to encourage vegetative growth to produce as many leaves as possible to keep them dense and evenly green.

You will see annual grasses growing along roadsides and in waste places where they can mature year after year, setting seed for ever larger colonies. They are often alongside annual wildflowers, which also do their job in a single season. Annual grasses are valuable for quick coverage of newly disturbed soils, such as construction sites and large-scale grading projects. The most commonly planted species is annual ryegrass because it germinates and produces roots more quickly than any other grass. You'll see this grass pop up later in this book as it relates to quick fixes for brown lawns and erosion control.

Perennial Parenthood

The vast majority of grasses used in lawns today are perennial, which means that each individual plant lives for many years. In the wild, a perennial grass will flower much like an annual, but the plant does not automatically die after producing seed. Instead it continues to grow vegetatively, increasing its overall size, which in turn supports a proportionately larger number of flowers the next year. The sod grasses that the pioneers encountered on the prairie could have been centuries old, because there was nothing that disturbed these perfectly adapted species.

Perennial turf grasses in your lawn may live for decades, perhaps most of your life. To keep them fat and happy, you must treat them gently, much like a growing child. They draw up nutrients from the soil at a startling rate, which results in depletion at an equal rate. That's why we must fertilize them so often. It's funny that some people wouldn't dream of harming their perennial garden flowers, but will turn their perennial lawn into a living driveway without a second thought.

Some new perennial turf grasses were developed to be prudish when it comes to reproduction. They do not readily produce flowers, which in turn produce little seed. Therefore, planting these grasses from seed isn't possible or may be expensive due to high demand and short supply. As a result, breeders have devised other ways to reproduce these grasses for lawns that bypass the need for seed.

These techniques are collectively called *vegetative propagation*, the terms of which are defined briefly at the beginning of this chapter. This method means that we grow new plants from cuttings taken from an existing plant. The cuttings are genetically identical to the parent plant to ensure that the lawn is the exact strain you have in mind.

The seed supplies of most of the warm season grasses such as Bermuda, centipede, buffalo, and St. Augustine are the most expensive, and supply is highly variable. It is standard for these grasses to be sold in forms called sprigs, plugs, or sod.

Earlier in this chapter, we talked about how grasses travel by stolons or rhizomes, and their method of rooting at intervals along these traveling stems. Sprigs are rhizomes or stolons encouraged by growers to produce roots and shoots at every node. After this occurs, the grower digs up the grass and cuts the nodes apart to produce a quantity of individual plants called *sprigs*. When you plant a lawn by sprigging, you simply replant the rooted nodes at a certain spacing or density, and this starts the new lawn.

In a lawn renovation process called *aerating*, a special machine punches holes in a lawn with special tines. Each tine is a tube about $3/8$ inch in diameter with the end sharpened to make it punch through the sod more cleanly. When the tine goes in, it fills up with a core, and when it comes out, the core of sod, attached soil, and root is called a *plug*. These plugs are up to 3 inches long. When you start a lawn with plugs, you simply plant them at regular intervals just like sprigs, and after the plugs are established, they spread out to cover the area.

Sod is the third way to produce a new lawn without seed. It's grown on sod farms. When mature, sod is dug up into long strips with root and soil attached and then transplanted to the new lawn site. Sod farms grow their grasses from seed, sprigs, or plugs depending on the type of grass. Sod is grown for practically every grass type whether or not the seed is in short supply. An "instant lawn" is attractive to everyone who can afford it because waiting until seed, sprigs, or plugs fill in can be time consuming. Perhaps most important of all, sod lawns virtually eliminate the need to pull weeds and look at a patchy lawn while it matures and fills in.

A Sprig, a Plug

Sprig   Plug

When Grass Sleeps

During the cold winter months, all grasses, both wild and high bred sleep out the gray days drawn back inside themselves. The frost kills back their blades, which turn brown and sometimes drop off entirely. They lie under a blanket of snow and rest out the frozen days and nights until the warmth of spring wakes them up again.

Some grasses, though, need no frost nor gray stormy days to sleep. With the slightest dip in the mercury to just 45 degrees, Bermuda grass promptly turns brown, and, at just 50 degrees, zoysia grass turns straw colored. These grasses are absolutely unresponsive until they are good and ready to grow again. This is a big problem in the warm winter areas where these types of grasses are popular because, without a frost, the rest of the landscape is green and even flowering much of the time. A brown lawn is totally incongruous.

Grasses with these sorts of pronounced periods of dormancy are treated with odd remedies to spruce them up for the still-verdant warm winter communities. Sometimes annual ryegrass is seeded over the top and sprouts in a week, covering up the brown until dormancy is broken.

Rather unorthodox yet widely practiced is the application of nontoxic green paint on the lawn; this does not harm the grass at all. Most lawn-care companies offer spray painting services. Remember this the next time you plan a garden party and the Bermuda grass is still sleeping off the winter.

Alternative Lawns

The manicured turf grass lawn is not for everyone. If you are a wildlife or organic gardening aficionado, you know that grasses need not always be mowed. The tall grass prairie and meadows are both examples of how nature views grass gangs. A natural lawn may be composed of grasses native to your region, or it may contain exotic grasses that are easy to grow. Either way, there must be enough natural rainfall to support this mini-ecosystem, or you need to provide irrigation.

This natural approach is so attractive because you don't grow just grasses but a huge variety of wildflowers too. Refer to the list of prairie wildflowers native to the American midwest that are highly compatible with grasslands. The flowers draw in bees and butterflies by the hundreds every day. Plus, you rarely have to mow, making these places both low maintenance and beautiful.

In many famous English gardens, you'll find lovely natural lawn meadows that also include fruit orchard trees. They allow the grasses to develop seed heads and the wildflowers to bloom as they would naturally. But you still need to get across these seas of grass, and to do so the gardeners actually mow paths through the meadow. The addition of mowed spaces for gathering or for walking is the most natural and loveliest application. In some gardens, gardeners place comfortable benches here and there to allow you to rest and observe all the wildlife activity.

Some people fail to realize that a meadow is a multi-dimensional ecosystem. You have all the animals that live in the soil, those that feed off the flowers, others that graze upon the succulent grasses, and a huge variety of birds that come to dine on the seeds and insects. Even at night, owls visit these places knowing that the rodents come out to feed.

Another approach to alternative lawns is the pasture. The difference between pasture and natural prairie-type lawns is that the pasture uses grasses and clovers that are both nutritious and palatable to livestock. The grasses are usually bunch types, which means they have a taller, rounded crown that gives the lawn a bumpy appearance. For some this is not a problem, and it makes a great surface under play structures for kids. Bunch grasses are springier and make a softer landing. However, they do present an uneven playing field, and you can trip and fall over a larger tuft if you're not careful.

Both natural meadow lawns and pasture can be mowed whenever and wherever you want. However, you must mow them with the blade at a higher setting because of taller crowns on the grass plants. If you mow them too short, you'll have an unattractive result and can so damage the plants that they will take much longer to recover.

Keep in mind that mowing very tall grass is rather brutal on lawn mowers, particularly when the grass is wet. The stalks that support seed heads tend to be more fibrous than the rest of the plant, so the mower will have to work harder to make it look good.

Taming the Wild Ones

Many grasses you won't read about in terms of traditional lawns, yet they are grown commercially all across America. These hard-working field grasses solve difficult problems, adapt to hostile soils, and are used extensively to reclaim land damaged by overgrazing, mining, and unscrupulous logging.

Each of the grasses in the following list has benefits and liabilities. The perennial bunch grasses take longer to become established for erosion control and are often combined with annuals, which take hold almost immediately the first season. They also make palatable livestock forage for alternative lawns grazed by a family horse, goat, or sheep.

They all provide vital protective cover for small animals and are perfect for growing around watering holes where the animals are most vulnerable. The annual seed production from these grasses is generous, supplementing the wild grass seed crop.

If you are planning a natural lawn, or live in a suburban or rural area where grasses are needed to serve specific purposes, some of the following grasses might fit the bill. Investigate them more fully with local officials of the USDA Resource Conservation Districts:

➤ Zorro Annual Fescue *Festuca megalura*

  Uses: Drought tolerant; erosion control; tolerates mowing

➤ Durar Hard Fescue *Festuca ovina duriuscula* Perennial bunch grass

  Uses: Erosion control; wildlife forage and cover

➤ Blando Brome *Bromus mollis* Annual

  Uses: Livestock forage; erosion control; wildlife forage and cover

➤ Barley *Hordeum vulgare* Annual

  Uses: Grain; pasture; erosion control; wildlife forage and cover

➤ "Sherman" Big Bluegrass *Poa ampla* Perennial bunch grass

  Uses: Permanent pasture; wildlife forage and cover

➤ Reed Canarygrass *Phalaris arundinacea* Perennial sod grass

  Uses: On land too wet for other grasses; erosion: livestock and wildlife fodder

➤ European Beachgrass *Ammophila arenaria* Perennial runner grass

  Uses: Salt tolerant and highly adapted to sand dunes, which makes an excellent erosion control plant for coast, desert, alkali soils, and persistent wind; water bird forage and cover

➤ Creeping Foxtail *Alpecurus arundinaceae* Perennial sod grass

  Uses: On land too wet for other grasses; pasture; wildlife forage and cover

➤ Western Wheatgrass *Agropyron smithii* Perennial sod grass

  Uses: Low land; wildlife forage and cover; erosion control

The Least You Need to Know

➤ Turf grasses go by their individual trade names.

➤ Nearly all turf grasses are perennials.

➤ Traveling grasses move by rhizomes and stolons.

➤ Natural lawns are composed of native and/or exotic grasses.

Chapter 3

Zoning Out on Turf Grass

In This Chapter

➤ The nuances of climate characteristics

➤ The relationship of turf grass to climate

➤ Turf grass zones of the United States

➤ What you can change and what you can't

➤ The qualities of a good turf grass

Grasses are living things that require special conditions to grow. Even more important is that grass has to grow well if it's to look decent in your yard. This all boils down to the fact that climate and environment are the most important things in a lawn's world, and if you don't get it right . . . you're finished before you get started.

Unchangeable Climate

You can change many things in the landscape such as soil, drainage, or shade, but you can't do a thing about the weather. The key to being a successful gardener, no matter what you grow, is to deeply understand the weather and climate patterns, and how they relate to plants.

There are really two types of climate to consider. One is regional climate, which is very general and defines average rainfall, frost dates, and temperatures averaged over many decades of recorded data. But as you probably know, the average doesn't always reflect anomalies—years when the rains fall heavier, the temperatures dip or soar, or snow falls at twice or three times the normal depth.

USDA Climate Zone Map

Remember this vagueness of climate because lines on a zone map do not always represent a true picture of the weather. There is always a danger of going strictly by a map because of the high degree of variability in climate—especially these days.

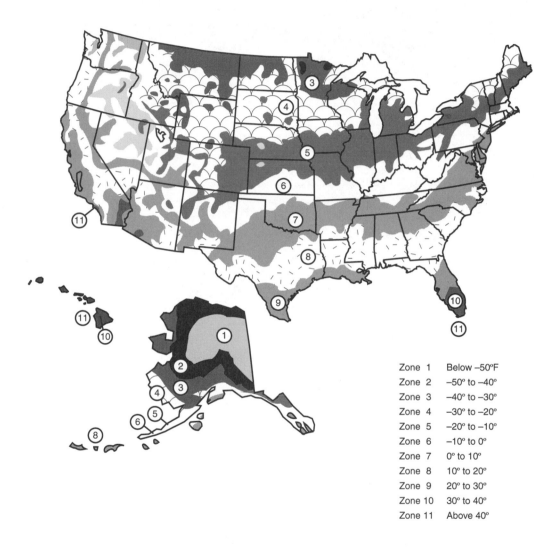

Zone 1	Below −50°F
Zone 2	−50° to −40°
Zone 3	−40° to −30°
Zone 4	−30° to −20°
Zone 5	−20° to −10°
Zone 6	−10° to 0°
Zone 7	0° to 10°
Zone 8	10° to 20°
Zone 9	20° to 30°
Zone 10	30° to 40°
Zone 11	Above 40°

Turf Tip

Farmers and experienced gardeners are always watching the nuances of weather. In farm towns, the old timers always begin their conversations with a few words about weather, because this is such an essential aspect of plant life. Good gardeners also become keen observers of weather because, when you notice how certain conditions influence plants, you know to expect the same thing to occur when the same weather conditions occur in the future.

When we look at the macro view of climate and how it influences turf grass lawns, there are four major factors to consider. These will individually or collectively impact the survival, performance, and variety of grass you choose to grow. People who have lived in the city or apartments all their lives rarely pay attention to these factors except for how they influence travel or outdoor activities. For home gardeners, climate becomes the major governing factor that tells you what you can do, when to do it, and how to do it.

Precipitation

Precipitation is the weatherman's term for water that falls from the heavens in all its forms. In warmer climates, it's rain; in colder climates, it's snow; and under worse conditions, it's hail.

When we consider precipitation, the key words are *when* and *how much*. Each region of the country experiences a different pattern of rainfall. When it rains frequently in summer, the need to irrigate a lawn is reduced considerably. Where there is a long summer drought, irrigation is absolutely essential to growing a lawn.

Snow is an equally important aspect of precipitation because grasses often are covered months at a time. This allows moisture to accumulate and restricts air movement, creating an environment for diseases such as snow mold. Small rodents can also be active beneath the snow, damaging grass by creating nests and tunnels.

Humidity

In humid climates, particularly those of the southern states, there exist a number of issues critical to turf grasses. These areas support much larger insect populations for much of the year, and in coastal areas such as Florida, there are new pests being introduced via shipping every year.

Humidity is related to rainfall. Where rainfall is heavy year round, perpetually moist climates create ideal conditions for a number of ugly turf grass diseases, which have a significant influence on what grass you grow. Soils are also impacted by rainfall-induced humidity, because the water filters down through the earth, carrying off specific nutrients that leave soils relatively infertile. Humidity also results in a change in soil pH, which must be treated in extreme cases. Only naturally aggressive turf grasses are grown in these humid areas because more well-behaved types can't withstand the weather.

Temperature

We live in a country of enormous geographic size, which includes states where winters rarely, if ever, freeze, and other states that experience extremes of 25 degrees below zero for weeks at a time. It's no wonder that so many types of turf grasses are sold in America.

Turf Talk

The term *frost hardy* relates to a plant's ability to withstand freezing temperatures and still stay alive. There are degrees of frost hardiness. Mild hardiness means a frost can kill the top growth and roots. Greater hardiness results in just the leaves and stems killed while roots remain alive underground. The term *frost tender* means the plant is highly vulnerable to any frost at all.

Where winters are exceptionally cold, one of the most vexing problems is frozen soil. The moisture inside the soil mass actually freezes as hard as a rock, and this frost line may extend a foot or more beneath the surface. Where grasses are hardy enough to survive in frozen soil, another factor is the source of damage.

You probably know from grammar school that water expands when it freezes. When soils freeze, the moisture expands and causes the surface to rise up. Sometimes you can see this in low spots where soils crack as they expand. In spring, the expanded soils contract during the day as sun melts the frozen soil. Then with nightfall, the temperature drops, and the soil freezes and expands again.

When this happens repeatedly, plant roots in these soils are literally torn apart by the heaving soils. When lawn soils heave, you can do certain things to reduce the damage potential. Gardeners often apply winter mulches, such as straw or leaves, to plants after they freeze in fall, not to protect the roots from freezing, but to reduce the amount of heaving that goes on in the spring.

Extremely high temperatures, like those experienced in the southwestern states, can exceed 110 degrees Fahrenheit. Bluegrass and other species that evolved in more moist climates have a hard time with dry heat. Also, grasses that lack the ability to root deeply will not be able to draw up moisture fast enough to meet the need.

Turf Tip

If you want to learn more about your local climate and growing season, consult the *Farmer's Almanac*, which is published each year. It details the date of the average last spring frost, first fall frost, and number of days in the growing season for most major cities in the United States. There's a lot of other useful information in there about weather, such as rainfalls and forecasts. It's definitely a worthy purchase for any homeowner.

Growing Season

The growing season is defined as the number of days between the average last frost of spring and the first frost of autumn. In Albany, New York, the growing season is 169 days long. In Phoenix, Arizona, it is a whopping 318 days. San Diego, California, has no frost at all, and the growing season is virtually year round.

Where growing seasons are very short, grasses with a dormant season aren't a problem. In San Diego, on the other hand, you need a grass that doesn't go dormant at all so that the lawn looks beautiful all year.

Micro-Management— Turf-Grass Style

Make a concerted effort to study and become familiar with your home's immediate micro-climate. It's easy if you know what to look for, and these factors help you know what plants want and how to provide it. More important, you will know what you can't give them. Sometimes you have to surrender to win.

The first and most important issue in a micro-climate is exposure. Every plant from turf grass to roses has a preferred exposure, and if you try to force it into less-than-ideal conditions, you'll struggle with the plant's health over its entire life span.

Turf Talk

The term *microclimate* is used to describe more subtle variations in environmental conditions from homesite to homesite. Each home and landscape has cold spots and warm ones based on many different factors. The best way to study your own microclimate is to sit outside and observe the climate in your yard. It's a tough job, but somebody's got to do it.

Your house has four general exposures:

➤ North side: This side of the house rarely receives any direct sunshine except around the summer solstice at midday. Often only ferns and other shade-loving plants will thrive there. It's hostile territory for lawns.

➤ South side: This side of the house gets sun for most of the day and is the most ideal exposure for lawns to receive even light. It also provides the most ideal solar exposure during the winter months.

➤ East side: The morning sun rises on this side, bathing plants in the gentle direct sunshine. This exposure dries up the dew very early in the day, which reduces fungus and other similar moisture-loving plant diseases.

➤ West side: This exposure bakes in the late afternoon sun of the summer months, but may be the warmest part of your garden in winter. Dew dries up last on this side of the house, which can be a problem in more humid, warm winter climates.

Trees can be as important as the house in terms of the ability to change exposures. A tree on the south side of the house can provide welcome shade for the building, but may cheat the lawn out of valuable sunshine. In your analysis of exposure as it relates to microclimate, don't forget to consider the shade of trees. Evergreens are the greatest offenders because they shade even in cold, clear weather and rarely can needled evergreens be thinned for dappled shade. Deciduous and broadleaf evergreen trees can be creatively thinned and pruned to reduce the density of the canopy, in turn allowing more light to the lawn areas within its influence.

Temperature and Topography

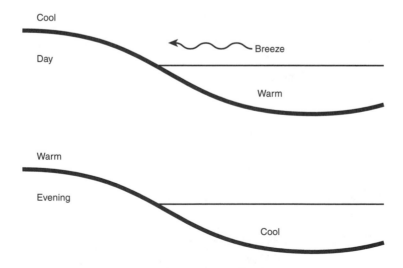

The Ups and Downs

Another factor that influences microclimate conditions is the lay of the land, also known as *topography*. You know that hot air rises, and cold air drops down to the lowest point. During the day, valleys and lowlands are sheltered from wind, and the air there heats up over the course of the day. As evening falls, cold air drops down to these low spots, and the warm air rises up to higher points. If you ride a bike or motorcycle through hills in the evening, you will notice that as you reach hill tops it gets warmer; then, when the road dips, you will hit a noticeable cold pocket.

This movement of air is important for determining how and where cold spots occur around your house. Even if you live on relatively flat ground, your homesite, relative to the surrounding topography, could put you in a colder or warmer spot depending on the air movement. You may have already noticed that one part of the yard will show white frost on a cold morning while other spots have no sign of frost at all.

Blowing in the Wind

Some parts of the country have difficulties with wind. This isn't so much the occasional breeze or March day, but persistent wind, often blowing in the same prevailing direction. On the prairies, pioneer women complained to their diaries that the ever-present wind would drive them crazy. Today homes in these areas are protected by *shelter belts*, which are beefed up windbreaks to deal with monster-sized winds. Coastal communities also suffer from persistent onshore winds. These are so constant that they contorted the cypress trees that made Carmel, California, famous and sculpted vegetation on the picturesque Maine coast.

Wind is damaging to plants because it draws moisture out of the leaves very quickly. Communities around deserts have difficulty growing soft, succulent-leaved plants because the hot winds desiccate them almost immediately. The plant simply can't draw up moisture fast enough to replace the rate of depletion. If you live in a notoriously windy climate, you'll have to compensate for moisture loss and mitigate the wind source. Simple solutions are to water more frequently, erect a wind fence, or plant a windbreak of trees or shrubs.

Turf Grass Climate Zone Map

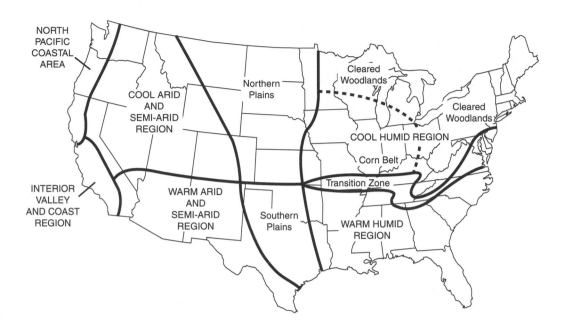

Turf Grass Zones

There's a difference between the climate zones on the USDA Climate Map and the turf grass zones. Turf grass zones were devised by the experts to roughly outline the parts of the country where weather impacts what kind of grass you can grow. Zones used to be far more critical a few decades ago when there were fewer grasses to choose from. Today's advanced turf grass breeding efforts have stretched the range of climatic tolerances of turf strains. Although there are many new advances, it's important to understand how experts view your region so that you will be better able to keep your lawn in tip-top shape.

The zones on the map have different climates, and for each climate there are certain designated grass groups you can grow. The industry lumps all the major types of grass into two groups: warm-season grasses and cool-season grasses. Some zones support only cool-season grasses, other zones support only warm-season grasses, and the more ambiguous zones may support both.

In general, the turf grass groups for cooler regions include bentgrass, bluegrass, fescue, and perennial rye. Warm-season grasses include the Bermuda grass clan, carpetgrass, centipede grass, St. Augustine grass, and a few other species.

Cool, Humid Region

This huge area extends east from Minnesota to Maine, covering the top half of the country. Winters can be bitterly cold and long, whereas summers are mild and humid. Grasses must be able to tolerate deep soil freezing, extreme low temperatures, and a deep covering of snow. Spring heaving is a problem. Periodic summer rains, the source of all the humidity, reduce the need for permanent sprinkler systems, but during dry spells, hand watering is essential. Cool-season grasses grow well here.

Warm, Humid Region

The warm, humid region is the southern counterpart to the cool, humid region to the north. It extends east from Louisiana to the Atlantic Coast and south to the Gulf Coast. This is the region most vulnerable to insect damage in lawns and moisture-related diseases common to turf. High water tables and perennially saturated soils allow only certain warm-season grasses to thrive, primarily those running grasses considered such invasive pests in more ideal climates. Most of the warm-season grasses have a pronounced period of dormancy so that, no matter how warm it is, the lawns in much of this area look bad even in the mild winter temperatures.

Transition Zone

Here is an example of an incredibly ambiguous turf grass zone. It's a narrow band that falls between the cool, humid region and the warm, humid region to the south. It runs from Virginia west to Kansas. The transition zone can bear qualities of both, which makes it a bit more dicey in terms of what you should or shouldn't grow. Therefore, you get to choose from both cool-season and warm-season grasses. But before you make an arbitrary choice, it's best to seek advice from the best local nursery you can find. These experts will tell you exactly what works and what doesn't for local lawns.

Plains Region

In general, the central "bread basket" of the nation is the region where the tall and short grass prairies once lived so successfully in the wild. Today these broad, flat plains still have the same climate and soils, except that now we replant them with more modified descendants of the wild ancestors.

It's a good idea to split this region in half, with the line running at about the middle of Missouri. The northern portion is much colder and the southern half warmer and more humid. Exactly where the split occurs is much like the transition zone described previously. In general, though, southern plains will better support warm-season grasses the closer they are to the Gulf Coast. Obviously, the farther north you go, the more likely the chance of successfully cultivating better-behaved cool-season grasses. Again, if you live near the regional dividing line, check with local experts.

Rainfall is fairly consistent during the summer in the plains region, but the farther west you go, the more arid it gets. When it comes to irrigation, it's a good idea to have an irrigation system to be prepared for inevitable dry spells because midwestern weather is notoriously fickle. You can go from dry, dead, and dusty to mud and flood with a single slow-moving thunderhead. Plus, if you have a busy lifestyle, an automatic system really comes in handy. When in doubt, check out what the neighbors with the best lawns are doing.

Arid and Semi-arid Regions

The wild west towns you saw on the movies with cattle drives and outlaws show you what it was like in this area before irrigation. This band of high desert and extremely arid plains extends from Canada to Mexico and west to the border of California. The range and desert areas can go a long time without rainfall, and in some areas, the only precipitation is in the form of snow. More and more people are living in these areas due to improvement in water supply.

The winters can be bitterly cold and dry, which is brutal on grasses. Soils freeze at the higher elevations of the Rockies and the deserts of Utah and the Great Basin. Conversely, these arid regions will bake to dry dust during the summer months with evening temperatures dropping radically. In general, these areas support cool-season grasses, particularly the deep-rooted fescues that will stand up to the dry weather. Frequent irrigation is recommended for lawns in most of these areas.

California Coast and Interior Valleys

California is indeed the land of sunshine, although there is a considerable difference in rainfall between the northern and southern halves of the state. However, in all cases, irrigation should be provided to lawns year round. Due to limited soil freezing, the standard in-ground sprinkler system is widely used.

Cool-season grasses are generally the norm in California; despite the heat, humidity levels are low, so they do far better than warm-season grasses. The emphasis is on the drought-resistant fescues. Growing population and dwindling water supplies make drought-resistant grasses and careful watering practices a must. On the south coast where salt air and humidity are unique in this state, the warm-season grass St. Augustine is common. The rest of the warm-season grasses are considered weeds in this region.

North Pacific Coastal Areas

This northern coastal region extends from the Canadian border south to California. The strong marine influence with cool fogs and salt air keeps conditions mild even during the dog days of August. Persistent breezes also keep temperatures too low for warm-season grasses, even in beach communities where it rarely freezes. Most cool-season grasses grow best here. Although summer rain is not uncommon, irrigation is necessary everywhere but on the immediate coast.

Conditions You Can Change

There are some climate-related things you can do to improve conditions in and around your existing lawn or where you propose to grow a new lawn. One common problem is that large old trees can make your yard so shady that your lawn starts to die out. You may either dispense with the lawn and replace it with paving or a shade-tolerant groundcover, or alter the tree to make the area more conducive to lawns.

Trees become problems when they become very large and bear a dense canopy that blocks out all sunlight. If the tree is a *conifer*, which is a needled evergreen, you're probably aware that it casts shade even in the winter when you'd much prefer at least some sun. These conifers also cause the soils beneath them to become hostile to most other plants due to an accumulation of acidic litter. Thinning a conifer is not common because it disrupts the natural beauty and symmetry so important to these species. Your options are limited to cutting off the lower branches, judicious thinning of dead or damaged branches throughout the tree, or removing it entirely.

Broadleaf canopy trees are different. Whether they are evergreen or deciduous doesn't really matter, because their open-headed form makes it easier and more attractive to thin out the branches in the canopy. When done well, this can greatly increase the overall grace and beauty of the tree. It also allows sunlight to reach the tree's interior and lower branches, rendering it more healthy in the long run. Plus, the lawn below will get a new lease on life and grow far better.

Thinning a Canopy: Before and After

Before

After

Turf Caveat

Thinning the canopies on old overgrown shade trees is a great way to increase sun without doing away with the beloved tree. A good certified arborist will be sure to do the job right. Be cautious about unscrupulous tree companies that prefer to "dead head" trees, which is a radical cutting back of the main branches into ugly, unnatural stumps. This not only looks awful; it also affects the health of the tree.

A Dead-headed Tree

You Can't Always Get What You Want . . . *But You Get What You Need*

Turf Caveat

Many chain store garden centers are staffed with people who know little about gardening. This is not the place to inquire about what variety of turf grass is best for you. Go instead to an established reputable nursery in your community and ask questions of the owner or their top expert. You don't want to gamble your entire lawn on a minimum wage cashier's opinion.

Each kind of turf grass out there today is on the market for a purpose. Problem-solving ability is of great importance, because certain climates pose so many challenges to grasses. But because lawns are important for beautifying home landscapes, aesthetic quality is equally as important.

Professional turf grass breeders are often faced with far more challenging problems than those afflicting home lawns. When the Million Man March descended on Washington, D.C., a few years ago, two million feet trampled the grass of the parks surrounding the monuments. How about the brutality of football stadium turf during damp weather, when the field turns into a sea of mud? What breeders developed to solve these enormous problems becomes a windfall for owners of home lawns.

It is important to know the qualities that professionals look for in a good turf grass. You and your lifestyle may also require many of these qualities, particularly if you have kids, dogs, bikes, and summer play pools set up on your lawn.

Traffic Tolerance

If you have kids and dogs, or just hang out a lot in the yard, then you know that grass takes a beating. How many days of slip-'n-slide will a turf grass take before it goes belly-up? Traffic tolerance relates to just how often you can walk on your lawn without killing it and also covers how quickly it comes back after damage.

Here's where we benefit from sports field turf science. Half the damage to grass on the football field is due to crushing the leaves and stems. The other half is the compaction of the soil to a concretelike mass. This affects root vigor and development. High traffic grasses such as bluegrass or tall fescue must be able both to repair themselves quickly and to root vigorously under less than ideal conditions.

Color

Did you know there are more shades of green than any other color in the spectrum? Greens can range from deep emerald to almost blue, and from lime green to char-treuse. Some of the more drought-tolerant grasses such as fescues tend to be lighter in color than bluegrasses. You may not have an opinion on this, but if you do, be sure to check the color of your future turf grass before you invest in an entire lawn.

Leaf Texture

If you study the bentgrass used for golf greens, you'll find that it is a very narrow, short leaf. Golf greens present such a crisp appearance that you'd have a difficult time telling a freshly mowed green surface from fine industrial carpeting of a similar color. This is because the grass they use exhibits a very fine texture.

Two kinds of fescues are used in lawns, and their differences are a good example of how textures differ. The tall fescues are the most coarse textured grass today. Their leaves can be up to $1/4$ inch wide, and, when mowed, the cut end is very stiff and visibly square. The fine fescues, on the other hand, have very thin, needlelike leaves that may average $1/16$ inch wide. When these are mowed, the result is similar to that of the golf green bentgrass. Both groups are fescues, but one is coarse, and one is fine textured.

Growth Habit

In Chapter 2, "Beginner's Botany," we looked at how grasses grow. Some produce dense bunches that are more upright in their posture. The more upright the growth habit, the more often a lawn requires mowing. Breeders have developed some interesting new varieties to reduce the frequency of mowing. These dwarfed grasses are just as beautiful and green as their predecessors, but growth rates are slowed considerably.

Runner grasses, on the other hand, grow quickly and spread horizontally before they develop more upright stems. Grasses such as Bermuda, buffalo, and carpetgrass have such an aggressive growth habit that once established they can ruin a landscape if they are allowed to grow into non-lawn areas. Their tenacious roots and fibrous stems make them difficult to pull by hand, and herbicides are often used to control them. Unless you are in need of a particularly rugged grass for poor soils or climate, avoid grasses with a running growth habit.

Density

Density is strictly defined as the number of plants per square foot of lawn. It also indicates how well the grass is able to cover the ground when planted in a lawn. Density relates to how many seeds, sprigs, or plugs you need to start a lawn so that it fills in within a reasonable amount of time. Over the long term, more dense grasses tend to recover from damage faster.

Disease and Insect Resistance

The vulnerability of plants to disease and pests has been problematic since the advent of agriculture many thousands of years ago. Plants are the natural host of many different organisms from snails to viruses. For the farmer, these problems may mean starvation. For lawnowners, pests and disease spell a patchy, ugly, and potentially dead lawn. Worse yet is the time and attention needed to fight the problems.

Turf Talk

The botanical term *symbiotic* is used to describe a relationship where two separate organisms live together without ill effects to either one. The term *endophyte* refers to the organism that lives inside another in a symbiotic relationship.

There are two ways to deal with this problem. First is the control approach, which focuses on techniques and materials that help us to reduce or eliminate a disease or pest afflicting the lawn. This means that the problem arises and damages the lawn before we can identify it and begin the eradication process.

The second and better path is to remove the damage potential ahead of time. If a grass were no longer tasteful to sod web worms for example, then we wouldn't need to find a control substance with which to eradicate them. Breeders seeking biological solutions are working on strains of grass that really are less tasteful to pests. They are also working on genetics to produce grasses that are naturally disease resistant.

For example, tomatoes have long been vulnerable to a disease called fusarium wilt. You couldn't grow tomatoes at all in many regions where the wilt is present in the soil. But in recent years, new strains of tomatoes have been developed that are naturally resistant to fusarium. Farmers can now grow tomatoes as a cash crop without having to resort to toxic chemicals for treating wilt.

Apply this scenario to turf grasses, and you can easily see why disease resistance is so important. If you live in the warm, humid regions, this is a vital issue when choosing a grass. Each year, there are new introductions, so consult a local expert to be sure that you explore the latest in disease-resistant turf before you make your final choice.

Any military strategist knows that a well-vaccinated healthy soldier will be able to withstand far worse battle conditions than one who is weakened by disease. Turf grass breeders have developed a sort of "vaccination" for lawn seed that introduces a fungal endophyte that will later live inside the grass plant. Many insects find certain endophytes distasteful and will not eat any plant that contains the fungus. Endophyte-treated seed is a new nontoxic means of reducing turf grass pests without an ounce of elbow grease or chemicals.

Drought Resistance

Even though a well-maintained lawn is not much of a water guzzler, the water supply and delivery systems in many parts of the country simply can't keep up with projected population growth. This is particularly true in the southwest, where very long, dry seasons are brutal on all landscaping. Supply-and-demand conditions always drive up prices, and although you may never have to ration water, when the bill comes each month, you'll wish you had.

Price and availability have fueled a big demand for more thrifty lawn grasses that still look great even under minimal watering. The fescues are among the most conservative, whereas bluegrass is the worst offender. New strains are increasing root depth, which adds to drought resistance and decreases leaf width to reduce the evaporative potential. If you irrigate your lawn or live in water-challenged regions, it's best to choose a drought-resistant turf grass.

Rate of Establishment

Let's face it, nobody wants to stare at bare ground any longer than is necessary for a newly planted lawn to fill in. The more time it takes for grasses to become established, the greater potential for weeds to take hold. In general, a mature, healthy lawn will crowd out weeds on its own, but in the meantime, it can be a nightmare. In general, perennial ryegrass and Bermuda grass vie for the position of fastest-growing grass. Bluegrass and tall fescue are average. Slowest of all are the fine fescues.

A new sod lawn eliminates the waiting period although it does take a few weeks for the roots to penetrate the soil. In this planting method, rate of establishment isn't an issue—it's instant. But if you're starting from seed, sprigs, or plugs, it's critical to both your sanity and the survivability of the lawn to plant at a time when it's more likely to get a fast, vigorous start.

Turf Talk

The term *thatch* describes an accumulation of dead roots and stems that builds up at the soil line. Thatch itself is not dangerous to grasses, but it becomes a barrier to water and fertilizer, sealing it off from the soil and roots. Diseases and pests also find thick thatch layers an ideal home and may be difficult to control until the thatch is removed.

Thatch Production

Some types of grass are more prone to develop thatch layers than others. It's most prevalent in the warm-season runner grasses such as Bermuda grass, St. Augustine, buffalo, centipede, carpetgrass, and zoysia. Thatch can also afflict bluegrass but far less often. One factor that contributes to thatch problems in cool-season lawns is failing to bag the clippings. Some mulching mowers can contribute to the problem, too, but this will be further discussed later.

Removing thatch from your lawn is a big maintenance chore, and if you have the choice, always lean toward a grass that does not have a thatch problem. To de-thatch the lawn, you'll probably have to rent a thatching machine, run it over the lawn, and then rake up all the shredded thatch and haul it away. Some people who have warm-season lawns do this at the onset of the dormant season and then, as part of the process, overseed with annual rye to green the lawn for the winter.

Shade Tolerance

Too much shade is the biggest problem facing many owners of older lawns. The trees grow bigger each year and cast more and more shade. All of a sudden, you realize that a lawn that was once in full sun is shaded for the afternoon, and the grass shows it with poor color, lanky growth, and thinning; and sometimes mosses seem to be more dominant there than turf.

If you have a shady homesite, you must choose a grass that will thrive under those conditions. Shade is devastating to some sun-loving grasses, and only a few are somewhat adapted to filtered shade. No grass will grow in complete shade, and although you may give these shade-tolerant grasses a try, there are no guarantees. For cool-season areas, look to *Poa trivialis* (rough-stalked bluegrass), or red fescue. The most shade-tolerant warm-season grasses are St. Augustine, centipede, and zoysia.

The Least You Need to Know

➤ Lawns are living things and *must* match the local climate.

➤ You can't change climate, but it does vary from year to year.

➤ Know how your home's immediate microclimate influences grass.

➤ The United States is broken down into special turf regions that define whether you grow cool–season or warm–season grasses.

➤ There are 10 ways turf grasses are evaluated.

➤ Beauty is not the only thing to look for in a turf grass.

Rating Top Turf Types

Grass feeds the ox: the ox nourishes man: man dies and goes to grass again; and so the tide of life, with everlasting repetition, in continuous circles, moves endlessly on and upward, and in more senses than one, all flesh is grass. But all flesh is not bluegrass. If it were, the devil's occupation would be gone.

—Senator John James Ingalls

Enchanted with the native bluegrass, the late Senator John James Ingalls (1873–1891) of the Kansas plains expressed his deep affinity for the luxuriant bluegrass of the midwest. He also summarized why we love lawns so much—they are fundamental, they are elemental, and they constitute the most vital link in the food and life chain of humanity. Perhaps most amusing, though, is that he clearly was biased and believed that bluegrass is the prince of the whole realm of grasses.

Beauty clearly is in the eye of the beholder, but it takes more than beauty to produce a successful lawn. It must look good, feel good, and withstand frequent haircuts and an occasional shave. In reality, there is no "best grass" because each genus, species, and variety was developed for different reasons. Sure they have their pros and cons, but all were at one time deemed suitable enough to experiment on in the field and laboratory.

This chapter is devoted to acquainting you with the heavy hitters of the residential lawn world. We aren't including all the grasses out there because many are specifically bred for high-maintenance purposes such as lawn bowling or putting greens. Some that were once popular have been entirely superseded by new strains of grass that are a vast improvement over the old-timers.

Turf Talk

Turf grasses are sold like a martini: mixed or blended. A seed *mix* is composed of more than one type of grass. A seed *blend* is composed of one type of grass, but includes many different strains of that same grass. Check the label on the seed box to find out whether it is a blend or mix.

Turf Caveat

Just because your dad or your neighbor has used a certain type of grass since the Stone Age doesn't mean that it's right for you. Scientific breeding of turf grasses is resulting in so many new strains each year that, by the time this book is published, there will be a whole new crop of better grasses to choose from. For example, old types of Kentucky bluegrass are vulnerable to a variety of fungal diseases, but new strains are far more resistant. Don't be afraid of the new grasses because they reduce the amount of time needed to maintain your lawn.

Would You Like Your Turf Grass Mixed or Blended?

Your lawn, or the place where you plan to grow a new lawn, may experience a variety of conditions. Parts of the lawn are shady, parts are shaded just some of the time, and other parts are always in full sun. Perhaps one portion of the lawn is brutally trod upon, whereas the rest experiences very little traffic at all. Under these varying circumstances, you would be hard pressed to find a single turf grass capable of meeting all these challenges.

The turf grass industry understands this all too well. Its solution is to produce grass seed or commercially grown sod with specially formulated mixtures of grass varieties. They are carefully chosen to combine turf grasses compatible enough to grow together well without undue competition. A typical mix will include two or more types, but often there are three. Each type will be dominant in its preferred exposure condition.

For example, a mix could be composed of bluegrass, fescue, and annual ryegrass. The bluegrass will thrive in the sunnier spots and shade out the fescue with its wide leaf blades. In the shady areas, the fescues grow thick and dense to become dominant. They may also be more successful where there is a lot of traffic, because bluegrass is less resilient. The ryegrass is there to sprout and cover very quickly to crowd out weeds while the slower bluegrass and fescues become established.

A seed blend is different from a mix. It's composed of a single type of grass such as perennial ryegrass. Dozens of perennial rye varieties are on the market, and experts choose just the right combinations to produce an ideal home lawn. However, unlike a mix, you don't get the degree of variation, because you are still working with just one type of grass.

A good analogy can be made by comparing mutual funds. A general mutual fund is composed of stocks from a wide variety of industries to protect the investor from failure in a specific sector of the economy. This is like a grass mix, which includes different kinds of grasses. A specialized mutual fund composed of stocks from companies in a specific sector, such as high tech or pharmaceuticals, is like a grass seed blend.

Grasses for Cool–Season Regions

The majority of grasses today are cool-season types, although the range of these grasses is expanding as new and more adaptable strains come on the market. The cool-season regions are divided into three main groups of grasses: bluegrass, perennial ryegrass, and the fescues.

Bentgrass was once among these, but it has fallen out of favor in recent years because other more low-maintenance alternatives have proved widely successful. Bentgrass is highly vulnerable to turf diseases, which is problematic for home lawns. Its chief feature is the ability to mow it so closely that it really does resemble industrial carpeting. Today, its use is limited to golf course greens where very close mowing and high density is mandatory.

These grasses will grow well in most states except in the very high heat and humidity conditions of the south and southeastern states.

Kentucky Bluegrass, *Poa pratensis*

Kentucky Bluegrass

Bluegrass is not blue; only its seed heads are, and we never see them in lawns. The blue tone of the grass can only be appreciated when grown as a field crop or in wild stands. Bluegrass is actually, as Ingalls so eloquently said, "most vividly and intensely green."

Bluegrass has long set the standard for what a perfect turf grass lawn should look like under ideal conditions. Its wide leaf blades are truly emerald, and, combined with a rapid spreading habit, these are the two most important qualities. Bluegrass is a cross between a bunch and sod grass, so it spreads well and is a vigorous grower overall.

Kentucky bluegrass prefers full sun exposure, although new varieties are a little more tolerant of limited shade. Bluegrass is not drought resistant and requires regular irrigation in most regions to maintain its rich color.

The species grows best in a cool, humid region, such as the north Pacific coast region. It also grows well in the transition zone, but grows only with irrigation in the northern plains, California coast, and interior valleys. The planting season for this grass is fall.

About 116 varieties of bluegrass are on the market today bred for use on golf courses, parks, home lawns, and sports fields. Because it is so popular a turf grass for humid regions, resistance to moisture-related turf grass diseases is paramount among breeders. Many of those in the following list bear resistance to specific diseases, and if you live where these afflictions are common, be sure you choose one that gives you a fighting chance. Here's how contemporary bluegrass varieties measure up in terms of disease resistance:

➤ Adelphi: Resistant to stripe smut, rusts, dollar spot, red thread, fusariums

➤ America: Resistant to stripe smut; moderately resistant to leaf spots, powdery mildew, fusarium blight, rust

➤ Eclipse: Resistant to stripe smut, rusts, fusarium blight, fusarium patch

➤ Flyking: Resistant to leaf spot, stripe smut, rusts, fusarium blight, fusarium patch

➤ Glade: Resistant to powdery mildew, rusts, smuts

➤ Merit: Resistant to leaf spot, stripe smut, rusts, dollar spot, red thread, fusarium blight

➤ Monopoly: Resistant to stripe smut, rusts, red thread, fusarium blight, fusarium patch

➤ Nassau: Resistant to leaf spot, stripe smut, rusts, red thread, dollar spot, fusarium blight, fusarium patch

- ➤ Nugget: Resistant to leaf spot, powdery mildew, leaf rust
- ➤ Ram 1: Resistant to stripe smut, powdery mildew, rusts, fusarium blight
- ➤ Rugby: Resistant to leaf spot, stripe smut, rusts, dollar spot, red thread, fusarium blight
- ➤ Sydsport: Resistant to leaf spot, stripe smut, powdery mildew, rusts, dollar spot, fusarium blight
- ➤ Touchdown: Resistant to leaf spot, stripe smut, powdery mildew, dollar spot, red thread, fusarium blight

Closely related to Kentucky bluegrass, *Poa trivialis*, known as rough bluegrass, has been of interest to breeders due to its adaptability in shade. There are a number of cultivars to look for: Cypress, Darkhorse, Laser, Laser II, Polder, Pro Am, Sabre II, Snowbird, Stardust, and Winterplay.

Perennial Rye, *Lolium perenne*

This grass is not related to the rye grain used for deli bread. Perennial rye is by far the fastest of all turf grasses to sprout from seed and develop into a plant, but it is not a particularly long-lived turf grass. More than 100 varieties are sold today commercially, bred specifically for disease resistance, because this is the Achilles heel of this grass in humid climates.

Perennial Rye

The major use for this grass is in turf seed mixes where it functions as a "nurse" crop to provide a quick lawn in the first year. It will die out entirely in the third or fourth year, but by that time the other more long-lived grasses will be well established and ready to take over. Look for mixes with a ratio of perennial rye combined with 15 to 40 percent bluegrass.

This rapid growth also makes it good for patching bald spots in existing lawns. It's a great shot-in-the-arm when used to overseed dormant grasses for a quick winter green-up. In the arid west, perennial ryegrass will require irrigation. You can plant this grass in spring, summer, or fall.

Turf Tip

Annual ryegrass is a nonconformist not to be confused with perennial rye turf grass. Annual rye is a one-season seed grass used for immediate coverage on disturbed ground. Its almost immediate germination anchors soil and acts as a nurse crop until other erosion control plants mature. It dies out in the second year compared to perennial rye, which declines in the third or fourth year.

A Fescue for All Seasons

Fescues are the most promising turf types to evolve in recent years because of their durability. As a whole, they are among our most drought- and traffic-tolerant turf grasses, and new cultivars are improving overall beauty.

Originally fescues weren't too popular because their needlelike leaves produced a rather unattractive texture, and the coloring tended to be far paler than bluegrass, the standard used for comparison. In recent years, the breeders have produced varieties that do stand up to some of the bluegrasses.

Fescue evolved from bunch grasses, which don't spread naturally. Their bunchy habit is also slow to repair when gouged. As a result, fescues are frequently combined with quick-to-heal perennial rye and some bluegrasses if used in high damage applications such as golf course tees.

The fescues are divided into two distinctly different categories: turf-type tall fescues of which there are about 100 cultivars, and fine fescues, which number about 75.

Turf-Type Tall Fescue

Turf-type tall fescues are by far the most widely used and adaptable because, although they are now shorter than their ancestors, they retain the same vigor and rooting depth. The plant was once a pasture or orchard grass valued by farmers for its deep root system that is roughly twice that of bluegrass. This rooting depth is the key to the tall fescues' renowned drought tolerance. Even though the plants require the same amount of moisture as other turf grasses, the roots allow them to draw it from deep soil layers when surface sources dry out.

Tall fescues are a bit more willing to survive traffic than the fine fescues because, as pasture grasses, they were forced to survive the constant trampling by hoofs. The weight of a human shoe is far less brutal than the PSI (pounds per square inch) of a hoof of a half-ton steer, making fescues in general the most traffic tolerant of all the turf grasses. They are also quite disease resistant and are among the first varieties offered with endophyte-treated seed.

Look for these top performers in turf-type tall fescues: Apache, Bonsai, Clemune, Falcon, Houndog, Rebel, Survivor, and Vegas.

51

Fine Fescue

Turf Caveat

So-called "miracle grasses" claim to need no water, withstand below-zero temperatures, and require mowing just once a year. Not only is this too good to be true, it could actually cause serious problems. Some grasses are extremely invasive. When they become established, the only way to eradicate them is by using herbicides. NEVER accept a miracle grass, because somebody's going to get stung big time.

Fine fescues are different from tall fescues and produce narrow, tough leaf blades. They are divided into three categories: red fescue, chewings fescue, and hard fescue. Of all these, the red fescues are the best for lawns because they are reliably long lived. However, these fescues are not good for warm, humid southern states because they are vulnerable to diseases prevalent there. New varieties are more resistant, which allows these fescues to be included in seed mixes, although southerners should not choose one with a high percentage of fine fescues.

Look for these top performers in fine fescues: Aurora, Beauty, Bighorn, Biljart, Estica, Reliant, Scaldis, ST-2, Valda, Victory, and Weekend.

Grasses for Warm-Season Regions

Warm-season grasses are not as popular as they once were. At one time, homeowners were willing to put up with invasiveness and unattractive dormancy to grow lawns in nearly tropical climates and in coastal salt air. Today, warm-season grasses are becoming less popular because new cool-season grass varieties are far more adaptable to these conditions than in the past. After all, who would prefer a bad-mannered grass that is brown half the year when you can enjoy all the beauty and benefits of cool-season strains.

Warm-season grasses are the great peccadilloes of the turf world. They are for the most part aggressive runner grasses that can quickly escape lawn boundaries and invade the garden. As if that isn't bad enough, some can have a long, ugly period of dormancy during which the plants turn brown and look dead.

Cool-season lawn aficionados consider these grasses weeds. If a warm-season grass creeps into the lawn and becomes established, its dormancy makes it stand out like a sore thumb during the cooler months. When temperatures warm up to bounce the grass out of dormancy, you may not be able to tell that more than one type of grass is growing there.

Warm-season turf grass managers are forced to overseed the lawns in the spring so that the beauty of the blooming garden is not spoiled by still dormant, ugly brown grass. Otherwise, they simply spray paint the dormant grass green.

Turf Talk

The term *overseeding* describes the process of sowing seed in an existing lawn. Overseeding may be done with the same kind of grass as the lawn, or an entirely new grass may be sown. Overseeding is often coupled with thatch removal and soil aeration, both of which are detailed in later chapters covering renovation of tired, battered lawns.

St. Augustine Grass

St. Augustine is one of the most frost tender of all the warm-season grasses.

It is very coarse textured, with wide leaf blades and bright green coloring. Rather well-behaved for a warm-season grass, it travels by surface stolons, which contribute to its tendency to quickly develop a dense thatch layer. If untreated, the thatch can dramatically raise the amount of irrigation this grass needs to survive.

The thatch makes an ideal haven for all kinds of pests and diseases that flourish in the moist environment. Plus, soil pests such as mole crickets and cinch bugs can be a real problem. Clearly, the need for frequent de-thatching is critical to the survival of St. Augustine lawns in most of the warm southeast. One characteristic of older neighborhoods where St. Augustine lawns are common is the level of the top of the turf is sometimes an inch or more above that of the surrounding pavement.

This grass is preferred along coastal areas and in Hawaii where its ability to tolerate fog, salt air, and year-round warm temperatures is ideal. St. Augustine lawns can suffer frost damage or death from exposure to temperatures below 25 degrees Fahrenheit. This grass is most often planted from plugs.

Look for these varieties of St. Augustine: Better Blue, Floratine, Seville, Floritam, Mercedes, Palmetto, and FX 10.

St. Augustine Grass

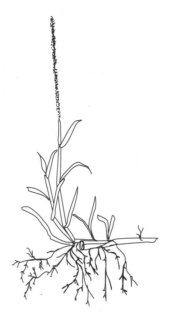

Bermuda Grass

Bermuda grass is king south of the Mason-Dixon line, although it can be found in lawns of southern New England and in the far west. This rugged grass grows well on poor soils and is more tolerant of heat, drought, and traffic than practically any other turf grass. However, to look its best, it does require a strict fertilization regime and should be mowed much shorter than other types of grasses.

Bermuda Grass

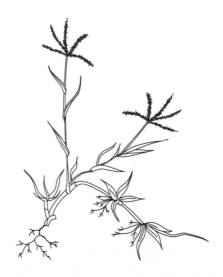

There are two types of Bermuda grass: Common Bermuda grows from seed, and hybrid Bermuda may only be grown from sprigs. Hybrid Bermuda was developed to reduce the seed production and thus provide better control of this extremely invasive runner grass.

All Bermuda grasses stop growing and turn brown when temperatures drop below 45 degrees Fahrenheit. The grass will not green up again until temperatures average 60 degrees or higher.

Yet another problem with hybrid Bermuda is that it takes a special beefed-up lawn mower to cut it properly. This is a much heavier machine than a common lawn mower, and much more expensive. It also may be too much to physically handle for some lawnowners.

Common Bermuda grass is sown from seed, but there is a great degree of variation in drought and heat resistance from plant to plant. Also, the even coloring is a crap-shoot because individual plants may prove less willing to respond to fertilization than others.

Currently, about 18 varieties of common Bermuda are on the market, with these being the most consistently available: Cheyenne, Delsol, Jackpot, Mirage, Primavera, Shanghai, Sonesta, and Sundevil II.

Hybrid Bermuda grass is sold only as sod or sprigs. They make a more reliable lawn for color and coverage. Look for sources of these varieties: Baby Bermuda, Santa Ana, Seashore, Tifdwarf, Tifgreen, Tifway, and Vanamount.

Zoysia, Centipede, and Bahia

These three constitute the remainder of the warm-season grasses. Each one is adapted to a small geographic area, although newer strains have extended their geographic limitations. Most often these grasses are used for acidic or sandy coastal soils with salt air that is hostile to other grass types.

They all share some real problems that may not be worth putting up with if you can grow a more well-behaved evergreen turf grass. All go dormant and brown for long periods, and lawnowners often overseed them with a temporary ryegrass crop in winter. They require special mowers to cut the highly fibrous stems.

Zoysia Grass

Zoysia is the most commonly planted and is available from seed, although starting a lawn from seed or sprigs is difficult because it takes a long time for this grass to fill in and mature. In some cases, this may be well more than two years. Once established, zoysia can be highly invasive. It suffers the most extended dormancy period of all the warm grasses, making it the first one to go dormant in fall and the last to green up in spring. It's also vulnerable to many pests and diseases. Forget picnics on the lawn or even walking barefoot on this one because its stiff needlelike leaves are like those of a scrub brush. Look for these varieties in zoysia seed, sod, or sprigs:

➤ El Toro: sod/sprig

➤ Emerald: sod/sprig

➤ JaMur: sod/sprig

➤ Links: sod

➤ Meyer: sod/sprig

➤ Omni: sod/sprig

➤ Sunrise: seed

➤ Traveler: seed

➤ Zen: seed

➤ Zen 100: seed

➤ Zoy-Boy: sod/sprig

Centipede grass is so shallow rooted it requires far more frequent watering, growth is abnormally slow, and as if that's not enough, it's prone to turning yellow if your soil is slightly alkaline. However, in Hawaii and other warm climates where soils are highly acidic, it is one of the few that grow well. There are no named varieties of centipede grass.

Bahia is so coarse that it is difficult to mow cleanly without exceptionally sharp blades. It's uniquely tolerant of drought and forgives more shade than any other grass but dies if exposed to temperatures below 20 degrees. It is quite tolerant of foot traffic. Look for these varieties of sod or sprigs: Argentine, Paraguay, Pensacola, Tifhi, and Wilmington.

Going Native . . . Naturally

The closely cropped, manicured turf grass lawn is a thing of the past in communities where water is scarce and expensive, and supply is unreliable. Water rationing during periodic drought has killed many a turf grass lawn, particularly in the desert southwest.

Turf grass lawns do not encourage wildlife nor are they sources of diversity in the home garden. For many lawnowners who are seeking a more integrated, organic lifestyle, the traditional lawn offers little, if any, benefits. The alternatives to turf-type grasses are those native to certain regions and others that have been the orchardist or stockman's preference.

To understand how they differ, simply imagine a meadow that grows up green and luxuriant in the spring and early summer. It is grazed by a herd of wild buffalo or cattle and lives from year to year surviving on natural rainfall. During the dry season or in cold winters, the grasses go dormant, but green up again once conditions are right. When established, most of these are able to crowd out broadleaf weeds, but this takes much longer than with grasses bred for rapid coverage.

There is an array of choices for alternative lawns that are highly drought tolerant and adapted for traffic of hoofed animals and small human feet as well. They retain the immune systems of wild species and are thus practically disease free. They are usually mowed much higher than a traditional lawn, sometimes at 3 to 5 inches compared to the average of 2 inches for traditional lawns. You will find some pure-strain lawns, such as buffalo grass, and other meadow or pasture mixes that combine a variety of agricultural and native species.

Buffalo Grass

This is a native grass that is attempting to edge out Bermuda grass in the west. It's a dominant species in the short-grass prairie of the midwest, so it's naturally wildlife adapted. It was not fully appreciated until recently when population growth in regions of low rainfall kicked off the hunt for drought-tolerant lawn substitutes.

Buffalo Grass

It is a great natural perennial sod grass but is slow to become established and may be reluctant to cover the soil evenly. Because of the way the seed is enclosed in little burrs on the plants, the cost of planting a buffalo grass lawn from seed can be hefty. You can also plant buffalo grass from sod or plugs, which is probably a better idea. Do be aware that the reason it can withstand midwestern winters is due to a prolonged dormant season. Only two named varieties of buffalo grass are available: Stampede and Prairie.

Turf Caveat

It's always best to buy pasture seed mixes from local sources. The feed stores and farm supply houses where these are sold will carry the most locally adapted types. If you buy from a national supplier, be sure to stipulate where you live and what is the best mix for your local conditions.

The Grass Is Always Greener

Ever wonder why grass is greener around clover weeds? Clovers are *legumes*, a group of plants that do some amazing things. Grasses rely on nitrogen in the soil as their main food source. Legumes take in nitrogen from the air through their leaves. It then travels through the plant body and exits into the soil through the roots, providing a high-calorie snack for the grass.

Pasture Grasses

Grasses planted for pasture are also ideal for wild or alternative home lawns. They are divided into two groups: irrigated pasture and dryland pasture. You can buy seed mixtures blended for varying conditions and uses, but in general they are fine for a more drought-tolerant or wildlife-friendly lawn.

Irrigated pasture mixes must be watered. They are composed of deep-rooted perennial grasses that take a while to mature. But once mature, they can draw upon water sources trapped in lower soil layers, which greatly reduces the amount of water they require each week. Pasture mixes are sometimes specially formulated for difficult conditions such as soils with high levels of boron or alkali.

You may also find alfalfa and other perennial clovers in irrigated pasture seed mixes because of their nutritive value to livestock. If you let the pasture grow long, or mow it very high, the clovers will bloom in pink and yellow flowers. This adds a secondary aesthetic value and makes it much more like a true meadow filled with wildflowers and wildlife.

Dryland pastures are designed to grow on natural rainfall just like the midwestern prairie. These are most often composed of annuals, both grasses and subclovers. As with annual plants in general, these must be reseeded each year for a new crop. Although the dryland pasture is not well suited to the alternative lawn, it is a great way to reduce soil erosion on a new homesite until you can plant a lawn or landscape.

The Least You Need to Know

➤ New strains of cool-season grasses make them more widely adaptable than ever before.

➤ Using a turf grass mix yields a lawn better able to tolerate a wide variety of conditions.

➤ Most warm-season grasses are highly invasive and are best reserved for the most difficult applications.

➤ A native or pasture grass lawn won't look manicured, uses little water, and supports a variety of wildlife.

Part 2
Civilized Grasses for Your Yard

This section is dedicated to getting a lawn started in your yard. Lawns aren't just something to look at, because we do many things on top of lawns, such as entertaining and playing sports. This makes a lawn more than just a pretty picture in your yard, it's actually an outdoor living space—an extension of what's inside your house. The easy-to-follow instructions in these chapters will help you think about your lawn so that, when it's planted and mature, it will serve all your personal needs.

It used to be simple when everyone planted his or her lawn from seed, but today there are a number of ways to go. Some give you a lawn in one day, others a month, and in some cases it takes up to a year for a solid, green lawn to fill in. Remember this as you plan so that you don't choose one of the Johnny-come-lately varieties if there's a faster choice available. After all, nobody wants to be doing lawn stuff when you can go to the beach or have a party on those warm summer afternoons.

Chapter 5

Turf Grass and the Landscape

In This Chapter

➤ How the lawn makes your house look good

➤ You, your lawn, and your lifestyle

➤ Making it big enough to use

➤ Don't overlook the ups and downs

➤ You have to have water

➤ Are you up for the all-organic lifestyle?

Nothing is more pleasant to the eye than green grass finely shorn.

—Sir Francis Bacon

Centuries ago, long before the advent of the lawn mower, Bacon knew people loved lawns composed of crisply cut turf grasses. They probably first got the idea from the pastures where sheep grazed the wild grasses down to a fine green carpet.

Today, we love them even more because they are much easier and more affordable to grow and maintain. Everyone can have a beautiful lawn to complement his or her home.

Lawns are located all around our homes. Front yards, back yards and, in larger lots, side yards too. The front is the eye to the world and makes the house look neatly landscaped and cared for. This is also where every little lawn care problem stands out like a sore thumb.

The Grass Is Always Greener

During the Middle Ages, special grounds known as a "flowery meade" combined wild grasses with flowers. This evolved into lawns planted with chamomile, a fragrant herb that grew better when "trod upon" and required no cutting. Bathing was uncommon, so the imparting of fragrance to trailing skirts was critical.

Turf Talk

Lawnowner is a term used in this book to collectively refer to anyone who cares for a lawn, whether you own the home or rent it.

In the backyard, the lawn is more functional because that's where family activities take place. These lawns really take a beating, especially where kids and pets are concerned. They require special care because there are so many ways that an active family abuses a lawn on a daily basis.

In the Eye of the Beholder

Grass is the shag carpet of the landscape, so think of it as you would carpet in your house. Carpeting makes your rooms look good and unifies the household with a single luxurious floor covering. Lawns unify the homesite and create a neutral field around which more interesting parts of the landscape are arranged.

Carpeting feels good against your feet and is made to be walked on. Likewise, lawns are great to walk on barefoot and make better access than walking through shrubbery or flower beds. Lawns figure in circulation of the homesite, but they should not be considered primary traffic sites.

Obviously, you wouldn't put carpet in the kitchen because there's too much traffic, and food stains will eventually mar its surface. In some homes, this will occur in less than an hour, depending on the number of kids around. The same reasoning applies outdoors as well. You don't want to put lawn where cars drip oil or where it is exposed to auto-care detergents. You also avoid lawn where you walk frequently, because it simply gets stomped into oblivion.

The Home Wrecker

A lawn that is the wrong size or shape is a home wrecker. It makes the house look bad, and it makes the adjacent landscape look worse.

The size of the lawn should be in scale with the size of your house. Think of lawn as a picture frame and your house as the picture. A small watercolor would be lost if surrounded by a monstrous gilded frame. Similarly, you wouldn't put a little house behind a huge football field of a lawn. The proportions just don't work.

The shape of the lawn also has a lot to do with character. You don't mix stripes and plaids when you dress, unless you're into the thrift-store grunge look. So don't mix a conflicting home style and lawn style. Formal architecture calls for a formal lawn, not a casual, free-form one.

Distinctive forms and shapes relate to architecture, and they also can enhance or play down negative qualities. The key is to understand the character of your house, or if it has no character, then to create a lawn that suits the style you like best. After all, paint and vines and all sorts of interesting architectural facade treatments can indeed add the character of choice to your home.

Turf Caveat

A giant lawn that is too ambitious for your lifestyle will tax your budget with the high cost of maintenance and eat up your free time. Be cautious about creating more lawn than you can handle.

Let's look at some of the most common home styles and the lawn forms that best complement them:

➤ American Country: Casual as the farmsteads they evolved from, these charming homes with picket fences, arbors, and lots of flowers call for a simple broad, rounded lawn.

American Country Lawn

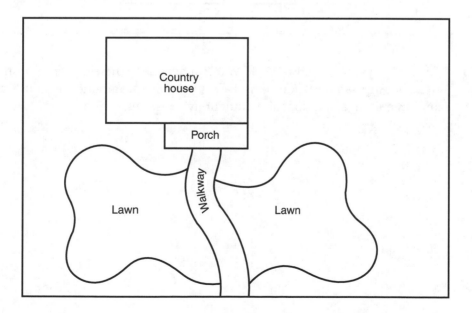

➤ Rustic Natural Wood: The wilds are the inspiration, so copy the soft, irregular undulations of a natural meadow or prairie.

➤ New England Cottage: Prim as a Puritan, these homes are laid out in neat, spare precision. Symmetry and rigid geometry are best.

➤ Victorian: Expansive lawns were laid out to contain special island plantings of extraordinary flowers. They were also for strolling, so graceful curves paralleled inviting pathways.

Southern Colonial Lawn

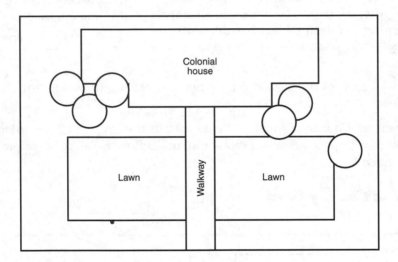

➤ Ranch: The favorite of post–World War II subdividers, these one-story wonders spread out in a rambling footprint. Lawns flow broadly around the house for a seamless marriage of indoor and outdoor living spaces.

Ranch House Lawn

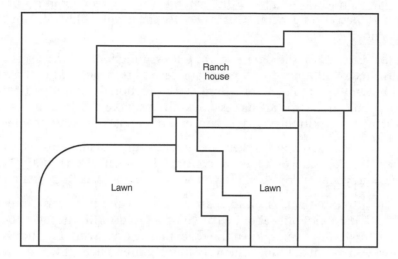

➤ Southern Colonial: A broad entry and white columns characterize the laid-back sophistication of plantation life. Formal lawns mirror the timeless classical architecture and symmetry so critical to these immense homes.

➤ Mediterranean: With large patios, the lawn may cut in and out in blocky segments that expand living space and respond to the Old World Moorish roots of this style.

➤ Townhouse: Whether it's Boston brick or Brooklyn brownstone, there is little space for lawns. The square and rectangular forms conserve precious useable space and provide a welcome relief from endless paving.

The Lawnowner Lifestyle

In any age of reason, it is the owner who finally decides the size of his garden and the purposes for which it shall be used. What do you want and need? Take a long and earnest look into your crystal ball.

—Thomas D. Church, the father of contemporary residential landscape design

The first and foremost rule of all spacial design, be it a landscape or a living room, is to be responsive to the needs of the immediate user. In lay terms, that means *you*. I always begin a project with a frank discussion with my client about his or her family, hobbies, and lifestyle in general. This is because the client will be the one living in the landscape, not me.

Good design is based on the phrase "form follows function." That means that the result must first of all function properly, and second be beautiful or attractive. If it's beautiful but not functional, it's a failure. If it's functional but not particularly beautiful, at least you can live with it successfully. Always place function over beauty, but strive to achieve both in the way you conceive of and lay out your new lawn.

To create your own new lawn and ensure that it is functional, you have to do some self-evaluation. No, you won't have to consult a shrink at $75 per hour. This is a self-help book, and you can do this all by yourself if you approach it systematically.

The easiest path to self-analysis is to answer the same questions I would pose to my clients. Think hard, not only about what you plan to do with the lawn today, but how it will work for you five years down the road, maybe even ten. The truth is that families are always in a state of flux, and even after children have grown up and moved out, there are weddings, parties, and eventually grandchildren to consider.

Go through these questions and note your answers on a piece of paper. You'll need it later when you start designing the lawn:

➤ Is the lawn to be a purely visual experience or an outdoor living space?

➤ If it is a front yard, will it double as play space too?

➤ Is the back lawn a play space for children? If you have more than two children, you can count on heavy traffic.

➤ If your kids are little, do they have a safe place to ride their tricycles or to skate?

➤ If your children are older, how long do you expect they will still use the lawn as adult play space?

➤ Do you plan on lawn games such as volleyball or badminton?

➤ Will the lawn be shared by a dog? How many dogs?

➤ Do you plan to erect a swing set or other play equipment on the lawn?

➤ Do you expect to use the lawn for outdoor dining? If so, how many tables would you expect to set up at any one time?

➤ Will you be barbecuing on the lawn?

How Big Is Big?

If, for example, your child wants to become an Olympic volleyball star, or even if you and your kids just like to play volleyball instead of hanging out at the mall, you might consider building a home court. Kids who can play and practice sports at home tend to congregate there.

Home sports from frisbee to horseshoes are most often played on lawns, although you don't always have an official court. And although nobody will be using it all winter if you live in the northern states, you still have to look at it all winter. The best approach is to design your lawn so that it is suitable to contain a court's perimeter in a way that makes it a good playing field.

Courts don't need lines or sand, just space, and preferably as level a ground as possible. To verify the size, you should know some basic dimensions of courts. Remember you don't have to shape the lawn itself like the court . . . the entire court simply has to *fit within the edges of the lawn.*

Turf Caveat

If you have a swimming pool, spa, or hot tub, be aware of how highly treated water interacts with the lawn. Water on grass in direct summer sunshine will burn the blades and cause ugly sun scald. Pool water running off onto the lawn may cause other problems. High mineral content in the water causes soils to experience mineral buildup and alteration of pH.

There should be some margin for error here. It's a good idea to allow at least 3 feet of lawn on all sides of a sports area to prevent injury from falls outside the playing court.

Be sure to orient the lawn sports court so that it is facing north-south if at all possible. This ensures that it's useable for most of the day no matter where the sun is. If you plan the court on an east-west axis, the sun will always be in one player's eyes. It's not only uncomfortable but also gives the other player an unfair advantage.

The Ups and Downs of Grading and Mounds

Some people are born mound builders and have problems with flat lawns. What they call mounds look more like giant Twinkies™ covered by green shag carpet. This is a highly unnatural act. If you want to see some well-done mounds, watch some golf tournaments on TV. Notice the sculpted bunkers that line the fairways of some of these top-notch courses, and you will see real grace, gentle form, and a model for your own creative grading. Then consider these basic rules to follow for successful mound grading.

Rule #1: Not Too Steep

Because lawns are composed of living plants, they must have water to grow well and look their best all year. Mounds that are too steep cause water to run off so fast that it never has a chance to penetrate the soil. No water in the dirt means no water gets to the roots. And no plant can live without water. If you start plants from seed, they never sprout, and if you lay sod, it will brown quickly. Then you're stuck with a Twinkie under a brown shag carpet.

When you shape mounds in the lawn, they should be soft and gradual. The *maximum* slope allowable for cultivation of a lawn is a 3:1 ratio. This means that for every vertical foot you go up, you need 3 horizontal feet. The IDEAL slope is 4:1 or 5:1, or even flatter.

Rule #2: Flat on Top

Water cannot penetrate a pointed-top mound any easier than it can penetrate overly steep sides. If no water enters the center of the mound, you will have a perennially dry spot inside. That will discourage the grasses from rooting deeply, which results in greater vulnerability in very hot or droughty weather.

Turf Talk

When a lawn mower blade cuts the grass too short, it *scalps* the lawn. All that are left are the stems and bare ground, which can take weeks to recover.

The lawn mower also has to go up and over the top of the mound. Ideally, it must cut the grass at a uniform height the whole way. A narrow mound with a pointed top means that you either scalp the top or get stuck at high center just like a four-wheel-drive pickup gets stuck on a sharp peak or ridge. If the mound cannot be mowed without scalping, it's worthless.

Allow enough flat or slightly rounded surface area on top of the mound. Use the size of your lawn mower as a guide. If your mower is about 2 feet in diameter, allow at least 3 feet on top. If you use a bigger mower, allow proportionately more area on top to avoid scalping. This also helps water hang around longer and penetrate into the center of the mound.

Slope Gradients

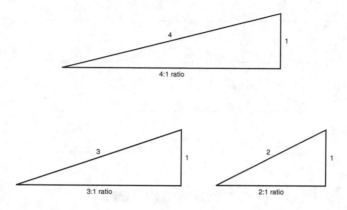

4:1 ratio

3:1 ratio

2:1 ratio

Mound Shapes

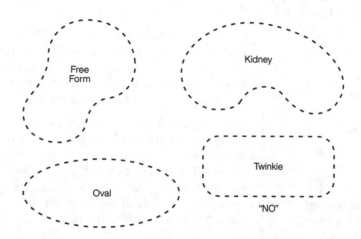

Free Form

Kidney

Oval

Twinkie

"NO"

Now that you know the rules, you'll understand how most folks fail by trying to make a big mound fit in a small space. When you study bunkers on the golf course, use people or carts to be sure you've got the scale right, because they look a lot smaller than they really are on the ground.

Let's look at how much space is required to create a mound 1 foot high. At a 4:1 slope ratio, you need 4 horizontal linear feet on the up side, 3 horizontal feet on top, and 4 more feet on the opposite down side. The total area needed to achieve that height is 11 horizontal feet. A 2-foot-tall mound requires 8 feet on the upside, 3 feet on top, and 8 more feet on the downside, which adds up to a whopping 19 feet!

1-Foot Mound

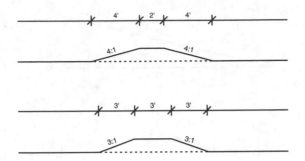

Irrigation Is Not Just for Farmers

Irrigation has a lot to do with how you design your lawn. (See Chapter 16, "The Basic Food Groups," for more on watering and sprinkler systems.) It's important that you know a few things up front even if you don't plan to have an underground sprinkler system for your lawn.

Turf Talk

Watering your lawn is called *irrigation*.

Radius is the distance from the sprinkler head itself to the limit of its coverage. *Diameter* is the overall width of the complete circle of coverage

Spray pattern is the shape of the area that the individual sprinkler is supposed to cover. These are expressed as a whole circle or percentages of a circle, such as $\frac{1}{2}$ or $\frac{1}{4}$.

Grass needs water above all to survive, roughly twice that of your flower beds. That's why sprinklers for lawns are always controlled separately from sprinklers for flower beds. It makes sense that the better you are able to water your lawn, the better it looks.

Also, the way lawns are watered is different from other parts of the landscape. You have to get every inch of the lawn equally wet if it's to bear an even green coloring. We call this *complete coverage*. No matter how you water, with a hose or a sprinkler system, the beauty of your lawn is dictated by how complete your water coverage is.

To ensure complete coverage, you must understand how sprinklers cover a lawn. This rules out any chance of you, the beginner, designing an impossible coverage situation that will doom your lawn to perpetual brown spots for the rest of its natural life.

Radii and Spray Patterns

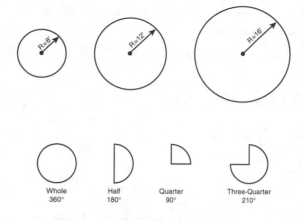

Distribution Patterns

Every sprinkler head, whether it fits on the end of the hose or pops up from underground, is manufactured to throw water on a specific area. Because most sprinklers go around in a circle, they each have a designated radius of coverage at a certain pressure. They also have a specific area of coverage. Some heads can be adjusted to virtually any angle of coverage, which is most common with pop-up impact sprinklers, fondly known as Rainbirds. These are most common on very large lawns.

In smaller spaces, the coverage gets more tricky. Common heads with smaller radii may require you to change the nozzle to alter the coverage, but in most cases these are still limited to whole, $1/2$, $1/4$, and occasionally $3/4$.

When turf grass lawns are designed, particularly in tighter spaces, you must always keep the sprinklers in mind. Lawns should not have corners less than 90 degrees, which fits a $1/4$ head. Corners from 180 degrees to 360 degrees can be equally difficult to water. Another problem occurs when the lawn is designed with little narrow fingers or strips. Few heads are designed to throw a radius fewer than about 5 feet, so anything more narrow than this is undesirable.

If you create these scenarios and then try to design your own sprinkler system, forget about it. Sprinkler designers respond to these oddball conditions by erring on the side of too many heads rather than too few. This relieves the designer from being taken to task over brown spots or *incomplete coverage*. It also jacks up the price of your system by requiring more pipe, heads, valves, wire, and perhaps an additional station on your automatic controller. Plus, you'll forever struggle with muddy, over-watered spots in the lawn, low-end drainage wallows, or over-spray that drowns nearby planters and stains paving.

Here are some easy guidelines for a sprinkler-sensitive design:

➤ Never create a corner at less than 90 degrees.

➤ Avoid tight curves less than the radii of the sprinkler head.

➤ Avoid narrow strips of lawn.

➤ Fill and grade out all low spots.

Examples of Sprinkler Coverage

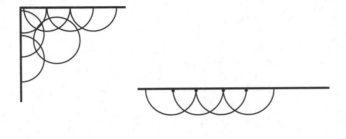

Do You Have What It Takes to Go Organic?

Political correctness has invaded the lawn world. There's a lot of pressure across the country to go organic. Strictly speaking, an organic lawn does not use any traditional granular lawn fertilizers, pest killers, herbicides, fungicides, and a few other materials. Keep in mind that all these products are approved by the EPA (Environmental Protection Agency) if used properly.

It's easy to say it, but, once you understand all the ramifications, it's much harder to go organic. Before falling victim to the politically correct spin, ask yourself these questions:

1. Do you want a perfect, emerald green lawn? The truth is that it's hard to get a lawn evenly green using steer manure or compost as the only nutrient source. These break down slowly and become available to the grass plants equally

slowly, so there's no quick green-up before having guests or a party. In fact, you may never see that rich color you so admire on TV golf courses. If you have a very large lawn, using manure or organic fertilizers is an enormous job that takes time, muscle, tools, and a ton of product.

2. Do you have a problem with invasive grasses in your yard? Bermuda and other extremely aggressive runner grasses are often present on new homesites as well as old ones. If these grasses are not removed, your new lawn will be a guaranteed disaster. If you've ever tried to pull runner grass by hand, you know they can be as tough as wire and then break into little pieces. Each piece is capable of growing into a new plant in just a couple of weeks. I have yet to see an organic solution to this vexing situation.

3a. Do you have enough money to buy tons of compost? The most important nutrient that makes turf grass green and beautiful is nitrogen. Composted, weed-seed-free steer manure on its best day contains barely 3 percent nitrogen. The most common granular lawn fertilizer averages about 20 percent nitrogen, with some up to 45 percent. To equal the nitrogen in a 15-pound bag of 20 per-cent nitrogen granular fertilizer that costs you about $10, you would need 100 pounds of pure steer manure that costs much more and that your neighbors like much less.

3b. Do you have a truck or trailer to haul organic fertilizers? To obtain enough steer manure to treat a 1,000-square-foot lawn would require you to buy dozens of bags of steer manure or a huge bulk load. If you don't have a truck or a trailer, you will be forced to make many trips in the car each and every time you fertilize your lawn. The follow up question here is: Do you have the spare time to make all those trips?

4. Do you have a strong back and lots of hand tools? When I was a private gardener, I often applied sand and other materials to lawns as part of the renovation process. This requires a wheelbarrow to move the material in close. Then, when I was young and strong, I had to heave shovelful after shovelful over the entire lawn surface. Finally, I had to rake it all down into the grass. If you choose the all-organic method, you need the tools, time, and a strong back to follow this same process every time you fertilize the lawn.

5. Do you live in the humid deep south? Let's face it, when aggressive insects such as fire ants or chiggers get in the lawn, it's no time to be hesitant. Young children have died from the bites of these common southern lawn pests. Ask yourself which is worse, fire ants at your barbecue or a well-controlled application of a tested and approved chemical pesticide? Similarly, when virus and fungal diseases invade the lawn during hot, humid weather, there is simply no organic alternative.

The Grass Is Always Greener

Fire ants originated in Argentina and were imported through Gulf Coast ports a century ago. They began to colonize California in 1998, and spreading throughout this state is expected to occur rapidly.

Turf Talk

The term *least toxic* describes a philosophical approach to problem solving in the garden. It means that you don't have to follow the hippie organic way, nor do you meet all problems with a barrage of chemicals. The approach suggests we use chemicals, in a limited way.

It's important for all of us to fully understand the impact of our actions on the environment. But it's equally important to be realistic. I want you to have the most beautiful, healthy, and personally satisfying lawn possible, and I would be remiss to suggest ideas that are neither feasible nor proven. That would cheat you out of your aims, and at the same time perpetuate false notions concerning lawn care.

Lawn Substitutes . . . No Can Do!

Approach groundcovers cautiously. Groundcovers take at least six months, maybe even years, to fill an area completely. Depending on climate and plant type, there's a chance they will never fully cover the soil. In the meantime, you have to weed and weed and weed. Plus, if you get an aggressive runner grass into a "lawn substitute," you're finished. There's just no real solution except to start over. The second time around, I guarantee you'll choose lawn. Don't believe anyone who says otherwise.

If you find parts of your landscape that should have lawn but, due to poor exposure, drainage, or other limitations, just can't support one, then you may, with my blessing, seek out alternatives detailed in Chapter 15, "Groundcovers Where Lawns Just Won't Do."

The Least You Need to Know

➤ The shape of your lawn should reflect your landscape and the house architecture.

➤ Your lawn should be large enough and oriented properly to accommodate sports or other family activities.

➤ Lawn grading should be soft and subtle to appear natural, to support a healthy lawn, and to avoid scalping when you mow.

➤ Before you decide on a wholly organic approach to lawn care, consider the time, expense, and logistics involved.

Chapter 6

No-Brainer Lawn Design

In This Chapter

➤ Learn how to measure the easy way

➤ How to draw a straight line

➤ Working at a known scale

➤ The basic dimensions you need to know

Designing a lawn isn't rocket science. It's actually a combination of first-grade drawing skills and elementary math, with a little imagination thrown into the mix. So unbutton that collar and roll up your sleeves, because you and your pencil have work to do.

Why do we go to all the trouble of drawing the lawn accurately? Because a drawing is your only means of estimating how big it will be, what it will look like, and how much it will cost to get it in the ground.

The most crucial step of the whole process is to record what's already there. This is critical when you are redesigning an existing yard. In fact, any architect will tell you that it is far more difficult to draw plans for a remodel job than a brand new building. This is because remodeling requires so much documentation of what's there to work within these limitations. Accuracy is of primary importance because an error at this stage can turn a simple job into a real problem.

Another reason that designing your lawn is so important is because sprinkler system design must be extremely accurate to ensure complete coverage. If you knew what it takes to design a system for an average home, you'd gain an entirely new appreciation of just what it takes to make it work. If you are planning an in-ground sprinkler system, you must have an accurate design so that the layout reflects what's really going on in the field. If there is a discrepancy between what's on the plan and what's actually out there in your yard, it will cost money, take a lot of time to fix, and cause a lot of frustration. This degree of accuracy applies whether you design the system yourself or hire an expert to do it.

When you go out to create a base map, you are really locating and documenting everything that will be included in your base map. It's also a process of learning by osmosis, because as you measure each element, you automatically become intimately aware of what's out there and how big it is. When you later draw it to spec, you gain a whole new understanding of sizes and spacial relationships. It's kind of like a psychiatric evaluation of the yard.

> ### Turf Talk
>
> A *base map* or *plot plan* is a drawing that shows everything that already exists on your site. These things can and will impact the design of a lawn or any other element in a proposed landscape. We will refer to the base map often in this chapter because it is the foundation of the design process.

> ### Turf Tip
>
> Do not use a yard stick or a dressmaker's tape to measure—you'd be surprised how many people try it. When measuring a yard, I prefer a 25- or 30-foot carpenter's tape measure for the shorter increments. If you have a large yard, you may want to use a second tape measure that is 50- to 100-feet long. Thin, floppy, wimpy tapes are more trouble than they're worth and difficult to use in tight spaces. If you measure in damp conditions with metal tapes, completely dry them and spray lightly with WD40 or household oil when you're finished to avoid rusting.

Step 1: Sketch Your Yard

Before you start, you will need the following items:

➤ Tape measure

➤ Soft pencil with eraser—do not use pen!

➤ Sheet of standard plain paper

If you plan to design a single lawn, either in the front or back yard, you'll need just one sheet of paper. If you want to design a second one, use another sheet of paper. Putting both front and back yard on a single sheet makes the sketch so small and detailed that you won't have enough space to write in the numbers legibly.

If you're lucky enough to be designing a lawn for a brand new house, the sketch will be a very simple proposition. There's probably just the fence or property line, the house, and perhaps a few utilities to consider. It's much more complicated if you live in an older home, because you must take into account preexisting conditions that might impact where and how you design a new lawn.

Park yourself in a chair where you can see the entire yard at once. If you're working on the back yard, lightly sketch the back walls of the house, and the garage if applicable, on your paper as proportionately accurate as you can. If it's just the front yard, do the same by defining the front walls.

You can assume that all corners are at 90 degrees. Any other diagonals on your house are probably at a 45-degree angle, which is standard for building trades. Even if the corners aren't shown on the sketch as 90 or 45 degrees, you'll know that, and it will be easy to make the proper adjustments on the final plan.

Next, sketch the approximate location of the property line around the house, showing the side, rear, and opposite side lines. DO NOT DRAW THE YARD TO SCALE! The house walls and perimeter property lines are the biggest, most important reference points on your plan. For the front yard, measure to the back of the sidewalk or curb, or edge of street pavement rather than property line.

With house and property lines shown, you now have enough reference points to roughly sketch in all the other elements that pertain to the plan. Here is a checklist of the most common things found in yards that should be included in your base plan:

➤ Property line and easements

➤ The house, garage, and attached structures

➤ Existing patios or decks

➤ Fences and walls

➤ Walks, paths, and stepping stones

➤ Shade structures, sheds, barns, and so on

Turf Caveat

You may already have plans of the house or a yard layout. These are not always accurate. Frequently, the original design was not built exactly to the dimensions on the plans. Always measure anyway and *verify* your measurements. This applies to assessor's parcel maps, health department plot plans, architect's drawings, or landscape plans by others. Don't start off with incorrect assumptions.

➤ Water features and swimming pools

➤ Flower beds and planting areas

➤ All trees to remain

➤ Septic system and leach lines

➤ Outside air conditioner or heating unit

➤ Drainage swales, pipes, or grates

➤ Plumbing: hose bibs, well, pump, and so on

Step 2: Measure the Dimensions for Your Sketch

Now that you've got a reasonably legible sketch of the area, you're ready to measure. If you follow my step-by-step instructions, you'll avoid all the frustration that always plagues a project that gets off on the wrong foot. My philosophy is do it right, do it once, and then enjoy the results.

How to Express Numbers

When you measure, express your dimensions on the paper in feet and inches. When expressing measurements less than 4 feet, however, they may be entirely in inches. For example, 1 foot 6 inches can also be expressed as 18 inches. This is useful because spaces less than 4 feet are usually rather tightly drawn on a sketch or plan, and using inches allows them to be expressed in smaller spaces.

Measuring the House

The house is the best reference point you can use on your plan because it is in a fixed location. It's wise to show more than just the walls. Designers prefer to know where the windows and doors are, too. These openings are critical to understanding what you see from the inside-out. Doorways show where foot traffic occurs, and you must design to these points of connection to ensure good circulation. We call these *controls*. It's also helpful if you want to go further and design other things between the lawn and the house, such as walkways or planting areas. You'll also need to know where windows are to avoid placing tall shrubs or trees in front of them or obscuring important views.

The easiest way to add doors and windows is first to measure and assign an overall dimension to every segment of wall. Then divide each wall so that there is a secondary segment for every window, door, and the pieces of wall that connect them. Measure again to provide a dimension for each of these segments. Because these may be in very small increments on your sketch, you can use a call-out line to connect your measurement number to the segment. It doesn't have to look neat, but it does have to be legible.

Sketch Plan with Measurements

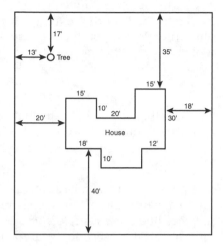

Measuring the Property Line

There is something to be said for nice square homesites in lot-and-block neighborhoods. Unfortunately, there are many oddball lots, which most often occur at the ends of cul-de-sacs or in hillside subdivisions where the lot shape is dictated by topography.

The best way to measure your property line accurately is to use the house for reference. If your lot is square or rectangular, and the house is placed square to the lot lines, your job will be easy. Just measure from the house wall to the property line at one point on each side of the house.

Measuring Oddball Lot Lines

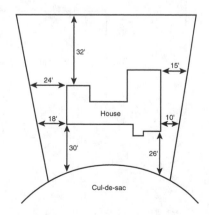

If you're living in an oddball lot, it's a bit more complicated, but don't be discouraged. You just need to take at least three measurements from each wall of the house instead of just one. It's simpler if you use the three-point system by taking dimension #1 at 1 foot in from the corner, dimension #2 at the center of the wall, and dimension #3 at 1 foot in from the opposite corner. When you connect the dots on your plan, you will have the exact alignment of your property line.

Measuring Curves

Fortunately, houses are usually rather square in shape, but other things such as planters, pools, and walkways are frequently curved or, in designer-speak, *curvalinear*. That means you have no corners for reference. So how do you measure curves? With a base line.

A *base line* is just a reference point. If you are measuring a curve, locate a base line off some known point that is conveniently close. One common way is to draw a line parallel to the house or property line for easier reference. Draw the line across the sketch, and then at regular intervals draw secondary lateral lines extending from the base line to the curve you're measuring. If it's a big curve, you can run laterals at 10-foot intervals. If it's a tighter curve, run your laterals at 2- or 4-foot intervals. Each lateral will be assigned a dimension; then, when you are drawing your scaled base map, you simply construct the laterals, take points, and connect the dots. Then erase the reference baseline.

Taking a Three-Point Measurement

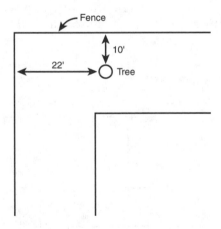

Measuring Curves

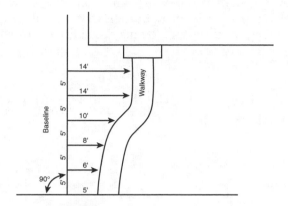

Measuring Other Stuff

After you have the house and property lines tied down, you may use them for references to other items. Start with the biggest items, such as the patio, for example, and then work your way down to the smallest ones. The checklist shown earlier in this chapter is arranged in this order for you to use as a guide.

By the time you sketch and measure everything in the yard, you'll probably have a dirty rumpled sketch that looks more like a toddler's scribbles than a field drawing. You may have discovered that the reason we don't use a pen on field drawings is that just one drop of water can smear the ink and ruin a whole day's work. But pencil is forgiving, and you've probably erased many times during the measuring process. Remember, you can always go back out and measure again if you forgot something or need further verification.

It doesn't matter if you've never drawn a straight line in your life. What does matter is that you draw softly and carry a big eraser.

Obviously, you have to scale down your yard to make it fit on a single sheet of paper. The exact size you use must be one that both fits on the sheet and can be measured accurately. In most cases, that scale is related to the inch.

The most common scale used on plans today is $^1/_8$ inch = 1 foot. If you were to measure a drawing at $^1/_8$ scale with a conventional ruler, you would have to divide each ruler inch by eight to find the actual number of feet on the plan. To get around all the calculations, you can use a special ruler that will allow you to measure directly off the plan. It's called an *architect's scale*. With the architect's $^1/_8$ scale, you can transfer real-time measurements directly onto the plan perfectly to scale.

Step 3: Gather Art Supplies

The truth is that everybody makes mistakes, and not all of us are artistically inclined. But that doesn't matter if you use the right tools that can turn anyone into a regular Picasso when it comes to yard design. You may be able to borrow some of the items listed, but others you'll have to buy.

You will need:

➤ One or two sheets of 24- × 36-inch vellum with $^1/_8$-inch grid

➤ Straight edge or ruler

➤ #2 pencil

➤ A big pink or white eraser

➤ Architect's scale

➤ French curve

➤ 45-degree triangle

Turf Caveat

When your mother told you "Never go shopping without a list," she was right. When you go to the drafting or art store, bring this list with you. Salespeople will try and talk you into buying all sorts of gadgets and tools you don't need. Stick to the list, and you'll have that much more money to spend on your garden.

Use the Right Paper

Drafters use a special kind of paper called *vellum*, which is sold at most drafting or art supply stores. The real beauty of vellum is that it is forgiving: you can erase markings on it over and over and still draw a clean line.

Another quality of vellum is that it has a pale blue grid on the sheets, which helps you draw straight lines without special equipment. If your plan is at $^1/_8$ scale, be sure to ask for vellum with an $^1/_8$-inch grid. Most lawn design projects fit on a 24- × 36-inch sheet, but if you have a very large or very small project, you may choose a proportionately sized sheet. I highly recommend that you buy two or three sheets just in case you spill coffee on your plan or the dog eats it.

Turf Tip

The cheapest way to make copies of vellum plans is with a blueprint machine, which relies on the transparency of this paper to reproduce well. A more expensive technology allows us to reproduce plans on opaque or transparent paper with photocopy machines. Both ways, though, require solid, dark lines because pale ones simply can't be seen by the machine. If the machine is turned up to make your weak lines bolder, you get all sorts of background just as with a regular copy machine. It's better to have a bold, smudged plan than a pale one that doesn't copy well.

All Pencils Are Not Created Equal

Remember when you were asked to use a number-two pencil to fill out computer-scanned test sheets in school? The number was important because it refers to the softness of the lead. Soft lead makes a bold line, and a softer eraser makes sure that you can erase repeatedly and make as many mistakes as you want. You may also use the drafter's F or HB pencils or leads. Using hard pencils means that you have to press down firmly to make a bold line, and trying to erase something etched into the paper is a challenge, even for vellum.

French Curve and 45-Degree Triangle

The French Curve

A French curve will be your most versatile drawing tool. This is a flat piece of clear plastic cut into a paisley shape with lots of curls and curves. It is designed to be used for sweeping, soft curves, which is exactly what we need for lawns. Buy a big one with a lot of complex edges for best results.

Getting Edges

Whenever you draw straight lines on your plan, you need a straight edge as a guide. Technically, a straight edge is just a flat ruler, which you may already have. If you need to draw a 45-degree line, you can try and use the vellum grid as your guideline, but this is tricky. It's best to buy a cheap 45-degree right triangle or snag your kid's geometry protractor to align them square to the page or grid, and *voilà*, you have an accurate diagonal. By the way, this is a great tool for drawing in bay windows.

Step 4: Transfer from the Sketch to a Plan

By now, you should have your field sketch, vellum, and art supplies laid out on the kitchen table. It's time to shake the cobwebs out of your brain and transfer the information. Again, it's not rocket science, so don't get nervous.

Begin by positioning your image on the paper. Allow a 2-inch margin of clear space around all the edges if possible, but if not, just make sure that the limits of the space fit. Then measure the overall dimensions of the area you are working with. For example, your backyard might be 75-feet deep by 42-feet wide. Use your scale and position the image on the paper within the margins. If it won't fit, get a bigger piece of paper.

The Plan with Property Lines and House

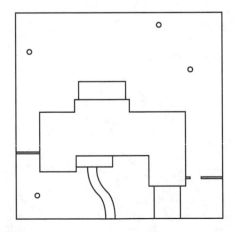

At this point, it's a good idea to draw in all your lines lightly; then when the plan is completed, go over it once again to darken them. If you start with dark lines and find you have a lot of erasures, it takes a lot longer and makes a big mess. Light lines erase easily.

Draw the limit lines on the paper, and then position the house where it should go by measuring in from the perimeters. If you're faced with an oddball lot, start with the house and then position the perimeter lines because otherwise you have no idea what the angles are. It takes a little work if you have a five- or six-sided lot, but keep trying until it's right and don't compromise, or you'll be very sorry later.

After the house is nailed down, add all the window and door openings to the house walls. You can use a double line for windows and a break in the line to indicate doors. Most doors are about 3-feet wide.

Using the property lines and house as your guide, begin to add in the other elements you've measured. Remember, all intersections are at 90 degrees, so most lines you draw will be parallel to the printed grids on the paper.

Graphic Standards

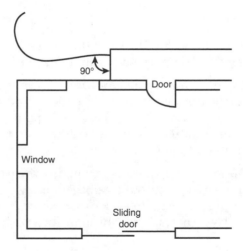

When you have transferred all the information from your field sketch to the plan, then you can darken them with hard lines. You can add a north arrow and write what scale it is in the corner. Print your last name and phone number in the lower right-hand corner in case it gets lost at the blueprint shop.

Step 5: Lay Out the Lawn

Congratulations! You have officially graduated from the first phase of the design process: gathering and documenting existing conditions. Now, we move on to the more creative aspect of the process.

Turf Tip

Blueprint machines do not "see" the color purple. Therefore designers use special purple "fade out" pencils to sketch ideas on their base plans, which saves a lot of erasing. You can buy one at the drafting store for less than a dollar, which is money well spent if you're dealing with a more complex landscape project.

Taking the Vitals

Vitals are the important relationships between the lawn and its surroundings. The most critical vital is the circulation or traffic patterns of your landscape.

One of the easiest ways to see how circulation works on your homesite is to watch kids and dogs. It is human (and canine) nature to take the most direct path between two points, which leads to the occurrence of specific traffic patterns in the back yard. If you don't pay attention to these patterns, they will continue anyway, wearing an unsightly path in your new lawn or through the flower beds.

Begin with doors to the house and gates. Sketch lightly the patterns you know of, such as the path from the back door to the garbage cans. Maybe it's from the door to the kid's play area, or across the yard to a back gate. Know them, use them, respond to them. Don't put the lawn there unless you allow for a path or stepping stones.

Edges

If you are designing a whole back yard with areas around the edges of the lawn for planting, you should know some basic dimensions. For example, how close to the fence should the edge of the lawn be?

In general, planting areas occur along fence lines because you can't get a mower or trimming machine close enough to make a neat edge. The same applies to the house walls, where we cover up ugly foundations, vents, and pipes with bushy plants. Allow a minimum of 3 feet for these planting areas, but you can make them larger if you so choose.

Arborescent Allowances

You measure the locations of all the trees because they have a big impact on the lawn. Here are some tree-related things to remember:

➤ Trees cast shade, and lawns aren't fond of it. Grass often will not grow within the drip line of a shady tree.

➤ Trees have surface roots that compete with the grass for water and fertilizer—and the tree always wins.

➤ Established tree-root systems make it impossible to trench for sprinklers within the drip line.

➤ Old trees with big roots at the surface of the soil make mowing the lawn difficult.

➤ You must always trim and edge around the base of every tree trunk in the lawn.

> **Turf Talk**
>
> The term *drip line* defines the outside edge of a tree canopy. Suppose that you were to draw a line on the ground that mirrors the edge of the canopy above it. What you do inside the drip line of a tree can have a big impact on the health of the tree, and the tree has great influence on what you place beneath it.

All these points add up to the fact that it is best to avoid existing trees when designing your new lawn. If you can skirt the drip line, it's even better. However, in some yards, this is unavoidable.

Active Versus Passive Lawn Space

Now that you've considered the most important constraints of trees and edges, you may proceed to defining the lawn itself. Consider the difference between passive and active lawn space.

If your lawn is primarily a passive space, one appreciated for its aesthetic value, then pay more attention to the shape, circulation, and relationship to outdoor living spaces.

Active spaces are for sports and play. You haven't lived until a volleyball comes in from out of the blue to shatter your wine glass. If you can manage it, keep these sports areas far from patios so that they won't bother passive users. However, because courts are best oriented north-south, you may not have an option.

If you're planning an active sports lawn for badminton or volleyball, you will need to be sure it is large enough to contain the limits of the court. This is important if some-one in the family is involved in school sports teams and needs a practice area that is similar to that of the official court.

There's a simple way to design for any specific, known item such as furniture, courts, or equipment. Make a little paper template that you can move around on the plan to experiment with orientation and placement. Simply draw to scale the limits of the court or anything else on a piece of paper using your $^1/_8$-inch architect's scale, and then cut it out. Move the pieces around, looking at them from various angles and in different combinations. When you find just the right arrangement, draw the limits on your plan. It's foolproof.

Of course, you don't *need* an official court, and most games can be played in much smaller spaces. Here are some basic dimensions:

➤ Volleyball: 30 × 60 feet

➤ Badminton: 20 × 44 feet

➤ Bocce ball: 12 × 60 feet

➤ Horseshoes: 6 × 50 feet

➤ Croquet: allow 1,800 square feet

How Your Final Plan Should Look

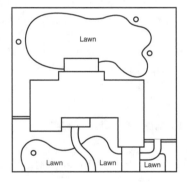

Fill in the Gaps

By now, you've worked through every possible control point for a home lawn— circulation, interface with adjacent planting areas, the courts, spacial needs, and many other factors. There will be gaps in between these control points, and when they are filled, you will find that the ultimate layout for your home lawn magically appears.

At this point, you can start to finesse it a bit if you're not happy with the layout. You can soften corners or make them more rigid. Also watch for what is called a "broken-back curve." This means that the smooth lines have a hiccup in them where they come together. You must redraw these so that all curves flow smoothly and transition with grace.

Broken-Back Curves

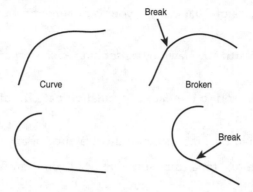

Before you're finished, be sure to go over your plan for sprinkler head accuracy. Above all, look for angles that are less than 90 degrees to avoid overspray.

Checking It in Real Time

As you proceed through your lawn design, you may feel disoriented doing it on paper, particularly if you are remodeling an older yard. The best way to get grounded again is to go out and see just how certain patterns feel to you in reality.

The easiest way to mark a potential lawn shape on the ground is to use kitchen flour the same way they make lines on turf sports fields. Flour is nontoxic and stands out against other colors. Another popular way is to use the garden hose, but this works only if you have a smaller lawn area.

The key to creating any design is to revise it again and again until you think it is just right. Whether you do this in the field and transfer it to the plan or vice versa, the more you refine it, the better it gets.

After you have a good plan showing exactly where the lawn will be, you may make an extra copy if you are planning to work with a sprinkler designer. He or she will also need a plan to work from.

The completed plan is ready for you to choose a grass type, decide how it will be planted, and decide what kind of edge material you will use. All this is covered in future chapters.

The Least You Need to Know

➤ Accurate measurements of what exists in your yard are critical to drawing a realistic plan.

➤ Anyone can draw an attractive lawn by performing each step of the process in its proper order.

➤ Lawn design must respond to the natural circulation patterns of your family and pets.

➤ The lawn design should take into account the presence of any trees in the lawn.

➤ Check your design in real time to be sure that what you drew will really look good on the ground.

Chapter 7

Ladies and Gentlemen . . . Buy Your Grasses

In This Chapter

➤ The different ways you can start a lawn

➤ Where and how to buy grasses

➤ Calculating area and quantities

➤ Understanding industry standards

Everything you know about shopping at the supermarket will apply when it comes to starting your new lawn. Although there are many generic products at the grocery store, sometimes you have to compromise quality to take advantage of the lower price.

An old saying goes: you can't afford to plant it right, but you can afford to plant it twice. This rings true with lawns because the planting process can be somewhat trying. If you follow certain guidelines, however, you will be able to enjoy your lawn sooner than you think.

Even though there's a rundown of lawn-grass types in previous chapters, remember that the local full-service nursery knows what everyone's growing in your neighborhood. They hear reports on what grasses are working and which ones fail to thrive. They want to keep you as a customer, so you can rely on their opinion. When in doubt about the choices, talk to the experts for foolproof advice.

Way to Go . . . and Why

There are two basic ways you can plant a lawn. Because your budget, climate, and lawn-grass type all play a role in the planting method, it's wise to understand the differences.

Seed, Sod, Sprigs, and Plugs

DNA, Sex, and Seed

Most grasses reproduce sexually, with genetic material contributed by two different parents. There is such a high degree of uniformity within the grass species, however, that genetic variations are often not visible to the naked eye. If you were to use the DNA matching process, you'd find that no two grasses are alike genetically, even though they may appear identical. Yet they are genetically stable enough to be sold and grown from seed. Most cool-season grasses are grown from seed.

On the other hand, when a plant breeder comes up with the one-in-a-million oddball he's been hoping for, there's not a lot of material to work with. And it's unlikely that his plant can sexually produce offspring with the very same set of characteristics anyway. He will use another kind of reproduction, a vegetative process of cloning, not from a single cell in the lab, but from a larger piece of the original, such as a root or stem cutting.

When you plant a lawn of that one-in-a-million variety, you are taking pieces of the original and transplanting them into your own soil. Most often this is the case with warm-season grasses that are either poor seed producers, too expensive to produce from seed, or altered to be relatively sterile in the lab.

Grasses propagated vegetatively are referenced in three ways:

➤ Sod is pregrown lawn taken from spot A and replanted in spot B.

➤ Sprigs are rooted cuttings of grass that are transplanted into a new lawn. When you plant sprigs, it's just like planting groundcover—you do it on a grid and evenly space them so that they can grow in.

➤ Plugs are cores taken out of turf containing leaf, stem, root, and soil—a virtual microcosm of your lawn's profile.

Sod and Sod Farms

When sod is commercially grown on sod farms, the grass is planted in a huge, perfectly level field. It's grown from seed, fertilized, and mowed just like any other home lawn. When growers decide it's ready, they send out a sod-cutting machine that peels up the grass by severing the roots off at about 1 inch below the soil line. The resulting product is a perfectly uniform strip about 4 feet long that varies in width depending on the type of grass.

The strips are rolled up neatly, stacked on a pallet, and shipped to your house. You then simply lay them out end to end and edge to edge, on a well-prepared bed of soft soil. Add sun and water, and you have a brand new perfect lawn that is ready to use in less than three weeks.

Layout of Sod, Sprigs, and Plugs

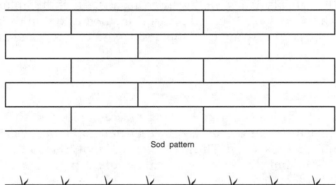

Sod pattern

Sprigs or plugs

Sprigs and Stolons

This is where it gets interesting . . . and sometimes downright weird. Turf grasses such as hybrid Bermuda, zoysia, and even buffalo grass are rarely grown from seed, and in many cases even the sod farms can't produce it at a reasonable price. Sure, Larry Big Bucks may use sod for his model homes, but it usually costs so much that it's way out of the ballpark for most homeowners.

Other methods were developed to bring the price down, but the labor skyrockets. So does the amount of waiting time until establishment, because each little grass plant must do a lot of traveling to meet with another one up to a foot away. During all that time, you must water and weed and water and weed and water and weed.

You can start a lawn this way by *spot sodding*, which is simply planting little brownie-sized cakes or big plugs of sod at regular intervals throughout the lawn. Because the grasses sold this way are usually fast runner types, the fill in is faster than you might think. You simply buy flats of grass, cut them into cubes, and plant out at the proper spacing.

Sprigging uses the same layout, but with small grass plants dug right out of the ground and immediately sold fresh in a bushel basket. These are *already rooted, but without soil,* which makes them perishable and time consuming to plant, but quite vigorous.

Still another variation is to plant *unrooted* stolons. These are taken from mature sod that has been ripped up and the pieces chopped to a certain size, with two to four nodes each. They are planted by simply inserting about half the stolon into the soil by hand or using a special tool. A second planting method is to simply distribute these pieces all over the lawn area and then topdress it with compost and pack it down with a roller.

Put a Plug in It

To understand what a *plug* is, imagine taking a piece of pipe and sticking it straight down about three inches into a turf lawn. When you pull it out again, there's a perfectly round hole in the ground. The grass, soil, and roots that once filled that hole are now jammed in the end of the pipe. Pull that out of the pipe in one piece, and you have a plug.

Lawns can be planted from plugs the same way you do spot sod and sprigs. You simply buy a bunch of fresh plugs, which are usually about 2 inches in diameter, and plant them the way you would any groundcover, by digging holes and inserting the plug at regular spacing around the lawn area.

A second kind of plug is a byproduct of the lawn renovation process. The aerating machine pulls plugs out of a lawn, but these plugs are much smaller, usually about the diameter of your thumb. Although this kind of plug isn't commonly sold, you can use them to start a new lawn or fill in bare spots on an old one. Because they are so small, you simply scatter them evenly over the lawn and then cover with a layer of compost like you do a newly sprigged lawn.

How and How Much to Plant

The kind of start that's best for your lawn depends on the grass type, your regional climate, price, and availability. If you're in doubt, chat with a local full-service nursery to find out what it recommends. Also be aware of price versus labor and time to complete coverage.

These basic guidelines show you how each grass type is most often planted. Some grasses are sold only from seed, others are available in sod, and still others are both. There may be some variation according to the exact variety you choose, so before buying anything, verify these amounts with your local nursery. Also double check the best season to plant, particularly if you're going with sprigs, because these may only be available at certain times of the year.

Common Bermuda Grass

➤ Seed at 2 or 3 pounds per 1,000 square feet

Hybrid Bermuda Grass

➤ How: Sod, sprigs, or plugs
➤ How much: Sprigs or plugs at 12-inch spacing

Kentucky Bluegrass

➤ How: Sod or seed
➤ How much: Seed at 1½ pounds per 1,000 square feet

Buffalo Grass

➤ How: Seed or plugs
➤ How much: Seed at 2 pounds per 1,000 square feet; plugs at 12-inch spacing

Centipede Grass

➤ How: Sod, sprigs, or seed
➤ How much: Sprigs at 9- to 12-inch spacing; seed at 1 to 2 pounds per 1,000 square feet

Fine Fescues

➤ Seed at 3 to 5 pounds per 1,000 square feet

Turf-Type Tall Fescues

➤ How: Sod or seed
➤ Seed at 6 to 10 pounds per 1,000 square feet

Perennial Ryegrass

➤ How: Sod or seed

➤ Seed at 4 to 5 pounds per 1,000 square feet

St. Augustine Grass

➤ How: Sod or plugs

➤ How much: Plugs at 12-inch spacing

Zoysia Grass

➤ Plugs at 6-inch spacing

If you are planting a seed mix or blend, then the pure seed distribution rates detailed previously won't apply. The packaging of the mix or blend carries a label that dictates its exact distribution rate. Determine this and then estimate how much seed you need.

How Big Is Your Lawn?

You probably noticed that the seed distribution rates for each type of lawn grass mentioned previously are calculated by area. It's common in landscaping of any kind when using bulk materials such as seed and soil conditioners to designate 1,000 square feet as the representative area quantity. It doesn't mean that your lawn needs to be divided into 1,000 square foot sections, only that this ratio is the designation with which you work.

Turf Tip

After you calculate the number of square feet in your lawn area, write it on the wall or someplace where you won't lose it. This is the magic number that you'll use to figure out how much seed, sod, plants, topdressing, soil amendments, and fertilizer you need. If you're not great at math, you can give the magic number to your nursery expert, and she will do the algebra to find out how much you need of each of these products and materials.

You probably remember enough geometry to get through this process, but a calculator helps if you're a somewhat slow mathematician.

The two formulas are:

➤ Rectangle or square: **A** (area) = **L** (length) × **W** (width)

➤ Circle: **A** (area) = **R** (radius) × **R** (radius) × 3.14 (Pi)

Measuring an Amoeba Lawn

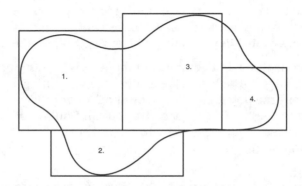

If your lawn shape resembles that of a rather drunken amoeba, then this formula suddenly doesn't look so simple. Break down the area into relatively rectangular zones that represent a balance of the area. Measure and calculate each one and then add up the total. When in doubt, overestimate to avoid a shortage, particularly if you are laying sod.

Turf Tip

Murphy's Law prevails; if you *can* run short on material, you *will*. The pros know this. Landscapers routinely add a contingency to their cost estimates. This allows for a little extra of everything to avoid a shortage, which can cost them a lot of time and money. If you run out, you must fight traffic to get to the store, stand in line, buy more stuff, and hope you can still finish the job that day. Always add 10 percent of your estimate to the total. It will save you time, money, gas, and a whole lot of Rolaids.

Consumer Consciousness

Nobody has money to burn, and a penny saved is a penny earned—or at least one you can spend on something else. You've probably been amazed at how the garden and landscaping marketplace has flourished in recent years. Ever greater areas are devoted to garden-related products and plants than was the case a decade ago when the neighborhood nursery was the only option. In fact, nurseries often can't compete on many fronts where volume buying and deep discounts have taken a big bite out of their marketplace.

The upside is that you have more choices and lower prices than ever before. It's also more complicated because you may be shopping to compare price, selection, and service, all of which are important. Because you will have a great deal of time, and, in most cases, a chunk of change invested in your lawn, it helps to get off on the right foot.

Saving money is one thing, but getting your money's worth is more important. The lowest price is not always the best value. Plants are living things and have to perform well to realize their true potential. When you shop for your lawn, which is 90 percent plants, you want the best seed, sod, or sprigs you can find. After you do all that work preparing to plant, it doesn't make sense to drop the ball when it comes to buying the plants themselves.

Pros and Cons of Nurseries, Home Improvement Stores, and Discount Chains

A full-service nursery is the top of the heap. You get good service, and it has access to a wide variety of products that are chosen by the owner who is skilled in horticulture. The nursery can also act as a supplier for sod or bulk materials you need for larger lawn products. It may even have special tools to lend you, such as a roller or sprig planter. You can develop a long-term personal relationship with your nursery to keep you on the right track, from design to maintenance.

Home improvement stores are great sources of all sorts of things from lawn seed to garden tractors and sprinkler parts. Their prices can be quite competitive, and the selection is ideal. But you won't get the personal service, and there's no guarantee that the staff is capable of answering your questions thoroughly. Some of these stores are geared to help you with your estimates, but they aren't as personal as the nursery. Here's where the convenience of buying everything for home improvement at one stop is more attractive than extra service.

Chain stores have also taken their piece of the pie, because their limited garden departments offer some of the very lowest prices of all. In some cases, profit margins are tiny. You're on your own here because staff is not well trained in horticulture, and their range of products sold is rather limited. This is where you might run into last year's leftover grass seed, or the cheapest compost in town. It's a mixed bag, but the convenience of picking up fertilizer while buying diapers is a big incentive.

Savvy Seed Shopping

Lawn seed, just like the seed of any other living thing, is alive. It doesn't look like it, however, and you wouldn't be able to tell a live seed from a dead one. This puts you at the mercy of any retailer who happens to carry the seed that you're looking for.

Just after harvest, grass seed is most viable, which means that the seed is so full of life it sprouts and grows immediately. With each month in storage, a little of that viability is diminished. This is why seed labels display a date that indicates the season in which it was harvested and packaged. Like food products, there must be a date on the bag or label that indicates for which season it was packaged. You wouldn't buy out-of-date food products, so be just as picky about your seed.

Lawn grass seed producers are required to label their products just like the FDA does food products. In grass seed, look for trade names, percentage of viability, weed content, and a few other details. You find some interesting facts on food labels, and the same holds true with seed. If there isn't a label, don't buy it.

Turf Caveat

Beware of buying lawn grass seed left over from last year's stock. If a retailer has seed left at the end of the fall planting season, he may store the seed and try to sell it the next spring. Always buy seed dated for the current year (it's on the label by law) to ensure your new lawn sprouts and fills in quickly.

1. Look for grass varieties listed by their trade name, not the generic one. For example, Kentucky bluegrass is generic—Flyking Kentucky bluegrass is a trade name.

2. You will find a germination reference that relates to the number of seeds that germinated in a test lot, with that test dated. In general, you can expect at least 75 percent with Kentucky bluegrasses, and 85 percent for perennial ryegrasses and tall and fine fescues. Anything lower is too low for you.

3. Don't buy someone else's weeds. If it contains any more than .5 percent weed seed (that's point-five percent not 5 percent), or any more than this under "other crop" designations, it's unacceptable.

4. All weeds are *persona non grata*, and if there is any number except zero behind the designation "Noxious weeds," it's also unacceptable. The red flags are annual bluegrass (*Poa annua*) or rough bentgrasses (*Poa trivialis*).

5. If you're ready to mix it up, say "no" to grass blends or mixes that contain any grasses designated as annuals. The major offenders are annual ryegrass and annual bluegrass.

Savvy Sod Shopping

Sod farms can be found in practically every state from coast to coast. These operations usually serve their immediate area because sod is extremely perishable and does not stand up to long-term shipping. Most folks order their sod through the local nursery, which oversees shipment and delivery, but if you want to buy directly from the supplier, you can save money if you know what you're doing.

Here are the pitfalls and power plays: Nurseries handle a lot of sod on a retail basis for their customers, which makes the nursery owner a repeat customer of the sod producer. If the nursery person is unsatisfied with the sod, he or she has the option of switching to another sod producer. Also, nursery people know exactly what to look for in sod quality. They can tell whether it's too old, too thin, or dried out. You'd be hard pressed to give it this kind of scrutiny. Should you order directly from the sod producer, you are a one-time sale, eliminating the incentive to ensure that you get top quality.

Whether you buy retail or from the sod producer, you should understand how sod is sold and what to look for when it arrives. Even though all sod may appear similar, it may actually be very different in quality and constitution.

➤ Know from whence you speak and exactly what grass variety you are buying. If it's a mix, be sure it conforms to the guidelines described previously concerning seed labels. The same applies to a blend. If it's a uniform grass, be sure you know not only the genus and species but also the variety.

➤ Is it government inspected? States set up their own guidelines for deeming sod certified or approved. This sod is guaranteed to be superior and grown from high-quality seed, sprigs, or stolons. It is inspected for purity to verify the absence of noxious weeds as well. Avoid sod designated "Nursery Turf Grass Sod" or "Field-Pasture Turf Grass Sod."

➤ A batch with thatch should be avoided. Older stands of Kentucky bluegrass, Bermuda grass, and zoysia can develop visible thatch. It will suffer the same afflictions of an established lawn with thatch, so why buy problems.

➤ Networks in your sod are actually fine plastic webbing laid out when the stand is first planted so that the grass grows into and around it. The net lends strength to the sod so that it won't fall apart when cut and rolled. This is really important if it gets a little dry because that's when the soil disintegrates. Clumping grasses such as fescue are most vulnerable to disintegration if not fully mature, compared to more-spreading runner grasses such as Bermuda.

➤ No skinny sod. The soil and root mass should be no less than about 1 inch thick. This does not include top growth or thatch. The thicker the sod, the better protected its roots will be and the quicker it will become established. Thicker sod has increased shipping and handling weight. Always stipulate rolled rather than folded sod, because it handles more easily and is less damaging to the grass.

➤ Know the time and day your sod was harvested because, like seed, it has a limited life span. The ideal time from harvest to delivery should be about eight hours; after this time, the plants gradually decline. Timing is even more critical in very hot or windy weather because both quickly dry out the freshly exposed roots and soil.

➤ Know the height of the mow at the sod farm. When you first mow the newly laid sod, do so slightly higher than at the farm because the grass needs more blade area to manufacture food, which speeds up repair and expansion of its severed roots.

Edge Options

No matter how you decide to plant your new lawn, it's how you treat the edges that counts. The way turf grasses grow encourages them to spread, and they don't know whether they are spreading to fill in the lawn or invade the adjacent flower bed. Neat edging is also a practical matter that keeps the lawn in its designated area. For warm-season grasses, this is a thousand times more important because of their preference for "running" across the garden.

A variety of edge options is available, varying in cost, aesthetics, and longevity. Always keep in mind that edging materials for any lawn take quite a beating from mowers, trimmers, foot traffic, and long-term exposure to the elements. This is a good example of why professional landscapers are reluctant to use any new product that hasn't been tested for a decade or more in all sorts of weather.

The Grass Is Always Greener

Pacific Sod, a west coast producer, has developed a revolutionary technology to grow hydroponic sod—sod without soil—which expands the areas where sod can be produced. It's done by laser and involves leveling the ground, covering it with plastic, and covering this with a special high fertility planting mix. Where conditions prohibit traditional sod farms, soilless sod is the wave of the future.

The old-time edge was no edge. Every gardener had a nice straight spade or a special blade tool that helped keep the edge of the lawn nice and clean, but it could take hours to do a thorough job on a new lawn. Obviously, everybody was screaming for a better barrier of some sort, and over the last few years the market has been flooded with options. Remember that edging materials can sometimes cost more than the lawn itself, so it's worthwhile to give this subject more careful thought.

These are the most common edging materials today with their pros and cons:

➤ *Redwood benderboard:* This traditional edging is about 3 inches wide and ¼ inch thick, and is milled in strips up to 20 feet long. It is nailed to wooden stakes that are then pounded into place all around the lawn. This has been the traditional material used for free-form lawns or those with curved edges. As with all wood, the benderboard's life span is shortened by decomposition, and as it breaks down it is prone to crack, splinter, and shatter.

Benderboard and Stake

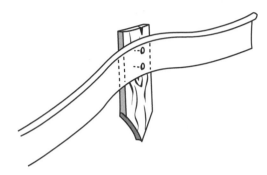

➤ *Combination redwood 2 × 6 and benderboard:* This is ideal for formal lawns with lots of straight lines. It allows you to use stiff boards for the straight edges and benderboard on the curves. Up to four benderboards can be laminated together to make the curves as thick and sturdy as the straights. Though this arrangement is less expensive and longer lasting than a single benderboard, it will decompose over time.

➤ *Precast concrete edging:* This rather new addition to the edging market is great looking. All you do is cut out a groove for their base and line them up nose to tail. The only problem is that you have less flexibility in the actual shape of your lawn because you have to work with preexisting units. If you use these, it may be better to design your lawn to their curves than to try to make them fit your design. For very large lawns, be prepared to have them delivered by truck, because most are just 2 feet in length.

➤ *Black plastic stripping:* New plastic products are edging into the mow strip market, but they do have their limitations. Above all, these products are thin and flexible, which makes them easy to set on curves, but they also tend to flop around. All plastic is vulnerable to extremes of heat and cold, and over time exposure will cause them to become increasingly brittle. Because the strips are attached with brackets, channel connections, or tubular fittings, these are the most vulnerable points. You can expect these to loosen and eventually come apart with continual battering by mowers, edgers, and string trimmers. Before you settle for these, compare prices with wood or concrete—they may be a lot more competitive than you think.

Plastic Edging

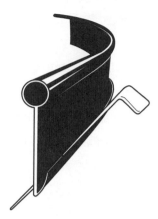

➤ *Metal:* Metal edging is not new, and any ferrous metals tend to rust so quickly that they were never really a viable option. Aluminum has proved to the most long lived and easiest to work with due to its light weight, but the cost is just too high for home use. These days, anything made out of aluminum is attractive to thieves if used in a public area where they have access, such as a front yard.

➤ *Oddball options:* Dozens of these are on the market in colors and tacky patterns and with a variety of strange anchoring systems. You'll only find them at home improvement and discount stores because a full-service nursery would not sell such an oddball product to its customers. It is best to avoid all of them unless you know for sure that the product works well in your climate, in your soils, and under continuous wear. Many are designed as bed dividers, and there's no way they could stand up to lawn edge conditions.

Concrete Mow Strips

Though quite expensive, the concrete mow strip is forever—well, in all but the most brutal climates. It is typically about 8 inches wide and is formed and poured by a contractor. The cost, surprisingly enough, is in the building of the wood forms, not in the concrete itself. Making forms, pouring concrete, and allowing for expansion joints are not a project for a novice, so beware of taking them on as a home improvement project.

Because you have to pay to have the forms built anyway, consider adding another 6 or 12 inches to the width, and the mow strip becomes a convenient walkway all around the lawn. It's perfect for the wheel of a wheelbarrow to get goodies to all the surrounding flower beds without munching the lawn. If you don't like the look of a white concrete edge, ask the contractor to tone it down with an earth-tone coloring agent. Olive green or soft brown looks much more natural than raw concrete.

The Least You Need to Know

➤ To buy garden supplies, choose a reliable place that balances service, selection, and price.

➤ Most cool-season grasses are planted from seed or sod.

➤ Warm-season grasses are often planted from sprigs or plugs.

➤ It's better to buy extra than to run short of anything.

➤ Choose an edging you can afford and that holds up for a long time.

Part 3

The Nuts and Bolts of Grass Roots Gardening

Growing a lawn is simple because you are gardening with a single type of plant—grass. Grass shares the same needs of other plants, namely, sunlight, soil, water, and oxygen. If you learn how to provide these for your lawn, you'll have a head start on learning to grow other plants as well. It's a lot like learning to read, which grants you access to all books, even if you're only interested in one kind.

You need an array of special items to grow and maintain your lawn. You can spend a ton of money on tools and fancy equipment designed to save you time and labor. Or, you can go with the minimum requirements and compensate with a bit more elbow grease. The key is to buy quality and take care of your tools and equipment so that the lawn never suffers the ravages of dull mower blades or irregular fertilizer applications. Your lawn will thank you by looking its best every day.

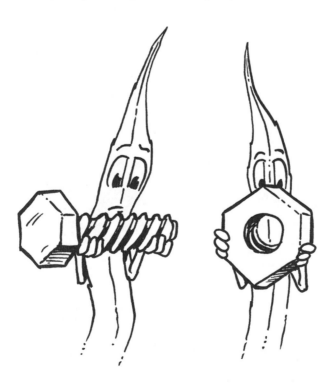

Chapter 8

HIT ME!

Dealing with Dirt

> **In This Chapter**
>
> ➤ How soil lives and breathes
>
> ➤ Soil is the most important part of the lawn
>
> ➤ Typical soil problems you can expect
>
> ➤ How you can change and improve soil

Soil is a chameleon that takes on so many forms it's hard to put into a defined box. It's a shape changer, varying according to weather and region and continent. It can be hard as concrete, frozen to ice, and baked into bricks. This same substance can be as soft as soup, thicken into quagmires, and even warmed into baths where health seekers spend hours soaking up its beneficial effects. When dry, it disintegrates into fine lung-coating dust, sandblasted by wind to peel even the most tenacious paint, and rises in giant clouds as dust storms are driven across the deserts. If you still think it's just dirt . . . think again.

Nearly every plant depends on soil in one way or another. Consider soil the living, breathing skin that covers the land mass of every continent except the arctic polar regions. It is one of the most fundamentally important things on earth.

Ask any good horticulturist what it takes to make a good garden, and he or she will immediately tell you that soil is the key. Yet, we have seen it devastated by ignorance and neglect, which results in erosion and most important, poor lawns. If you glean one thing out of this entire book, it should be a firm understanding of soil and its role in the garden. This knowledge will serve you in every aspect of gardening, from this lawn experience until death do you part.

It's What You Don't See That's Important

There's a whole lot going on in the average garden soil, but because the parties involved are so small, we assume that there's nothing there. The greatest revelation of beginner gardeners is the discovery that there is a whole Noah's Ark of micro-organisms in the mud. These little fellows are mostly decomposers, but some actually work with live plants to help them remain healthy and disease resistant.

A lot of chemistry is happening as well, which relates to how plants interact with soil while drawing up nutrients and water through their roots. Technically, it's called *cat-ion exchange*, which is not a feline expression but one vital to what goes on in this intimate relationship of animal to vegetable to mineral.

In horticulture, we look at three aspects of soil that bear on how well soil supports plant life. These properties determine how much water, air, and food get to the part of the plant that is underground. If this vital connection fails, so does the plant.

➤ *Soil structure* is its physical texture, such as whether it is fine or coarse.

➤ *Soil fertility* is how well it will feed a plant.

➤ *Soil pH*, which is a bit trickier, applies to whether it registers more acidic or alkaline (salty) on the scale.

One of the nuances of understanding and working with soils is the fact that we can improve and often change one or all of the above. These alterations can be as simple as adding fertilizer.

Soil Structure

We often see soil as a mass, but in fact it is a whole bunch of particles stuck together. Soil structure is determined by how big the BBs are relative to one another. The biggest particles are classified as sand, medium-sized particles are silt, and the smallest particles are clay. Most soils are a combination of sizes and are identified by the particle size that is most prevalent. It's rare to obtain pure sand, or pure clay, and either of these would be rather hostile to plants. Yet when we talk about soils, we most frequently use these same words to describe the predominant particle size.

Soil Particle Sizes

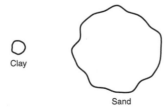

Clay

Sand

You don't have to be a genius to know what kind of soil you have. Obviously, if it sets like cement in the summertime, then it's probably mostly clay. Clay particles are so much smaller than either silt or sand that they're practically microscopic. In fact, they are so small that when molded and cooked in the fire they turn into waterproof pottery. If your lawn is on clay soil and it sits in summer sun hot enough to cook an egg on your car hood, then it's likely you'll end up with a lawn trying to grow on ceramic tile.

On the other hand, have you ever seen water pool on dry beach sand? Never. That's because sand particles are so large that the spaces between each one allow water to flow right through, just like washing rice in a colander. Growing lawns on pure sand demands that you water like a demon just to keep water in the root zone for about 20 seconds. Even worse is trying to get fertilizer to stay there.

Turf Talk

Technically, *organic matter* is anything of plant origin from bark to roots that happens to exist in the soil. Examples of this might be wood shavings or fresh leaves. Organic matter is not yet decomposed and is unavailable as plant nutrients. Once added to soil or a compost heap, it breaks down into *humus*, which is the richest, most desirable material to plants.

So, why do you need to know about structure at all? Because the remedying of structural problems drives the majority of the things we do to soils. For example, the remedy for hard, poorly drained clay soils is to force them to open up and allow the water and air, not to mention roots, to penetrate. The problem is they don't stay open very long after they get wet unless we shove stuff like compost in there.

The Back Yard Fertility Clinic

If everybody had perfect dirt, there would be no need for fertilizers.

Soils are fertile when they contain all sorts of nutrients needed to make plants grow. One reason why flood plain soils make such productive farmland is that flooding deposits a whole new layer of nutrients each time a river spills over its banks. In the meantime, plants grow there, consume a lot of these nutrients, and gradually deplete the nutrients. Like a diet, it's calories in, calories out.

So what do plants like to eat? The big three are nitrogen, phosphorous, and potassium. But a number of other lesser- or micronutrients and trace elements also contribute to plant growth. One reason that organic gardeners are such freaks about compost is because it's chock-full of all these things, whereas granular commercial fertilizers only contain the big three essential to lawns.

You might be surprised to find that the fertility of clay soils is a whole lot better than that of sandy soils. This is because all those little microorganisms mentioned earlier exist in larger quantities in average clays than they do in sand.

If you add a lot of humus to sandy soils, it remains a long time because there aren't many microorganisms to eat it. Add the same amount of humus to clay soils, and it vanishes like an all-you-can-eat seafood buffet. Clay soils literally eat up any organic matter you add to them, so you must do so often and in large quantities.

Peccadilloes of pH

You probably have heard of pH from shampoo ads on TV, but it applies to soils too. The only time you really have to worry about it with lawns is if you live in certain areas where soils are on extreme ends of the scale.

The pH scale ranges from 0 to 14, with 7 being the neutral or ideal level. From 7 to 0 the soil becomes increasingly more acidic. From 7 to 14 it becomes more alkaline. If you have soil that is too high or too low on the scale, it can actually reduce the amount of food plants can take out of that soil.

Problem soils with low pH tend to occur in specific climate regions or in spots under trees that shed leaves containing high amounts of acid. The major offenders are oak trees and the conifers, which are mostly needled evergreens. If you look closely, you'll see that very little grows well beneath their canopies except ferns, azaleas, camellias, and rhododendrons, which all love acidic conditions. The primary remedy for acidic soils is to add lime, which neutralizes the acid.

High pH soils are another matter. Salt in the form of alkali in the soil is a killer, and there's little you can do to get it out. If there's alkali in the water supply, it builds up in the soil every time you water. In most cases, the only solution is to choose a specialty grass that is more tolerant of salt. Buffalo grass, hybrid Bermuda, zoysia, and St. Augustine are all candidates, which is why they are far more prevalent in sea coast communities.

The Grass Is Always Greener

Here's the block party of macro and micro *florae* and *faunae* that live in the neighborhood called "your back yard soil":

earthworms	autotrophic bacteria	actinomycetes
arthropods	heterotrophic bacteria	algae
protozoa	symbiotic bacteria	viruses
nematodes	microrhizia	

Soil Horizon Sandwich

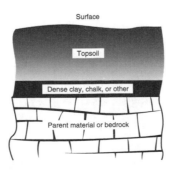

Surface

Topsoil

Dense clay, chalk, or other

Parent material or bedrock

Subdivision and Homesite Grading

If you were to watch a new subdivision being built, you would see a lot of heavy equipment moving around. Dozers, scrapers, and dump trucks are all part of creating the *building pad*, a flat place to build the house. These pads lie within the boundaries of the lots, which are connected with roads and storm drains so that the whole thing drains after it rains. If the subdivision is built on a hillside, the amount of earthwork required to make a building pad doubles or triples.

Turf Talk

The *soil horizon* is the sandwich of layers that makes up the soil beneath your feet. You see the horizon when roads cut through hillsides leaving a face exposed.

Cut-and-Fill Building Pad

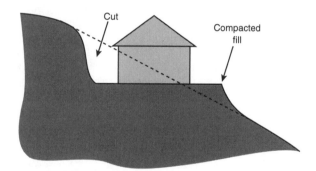

Pads on hillsides are called *cut-and-fill*. You cut a chunk out of the hillside and deposit it just below to build up a pad. In this process, you get a whole bunch of subsoil and sometimes parent material in the fill. On the cut side, you can be faced with pure parent material or even bedrock. Fill material is required to be compacted artificially to 95 percent to avoid landslides. This rate of compaction can be hostile to plant roots.

All this means that the original topsoil is history if it was scraped off to level the pad. Plus, a 50-ton grader literally packs the soil and subsoil into a concretelike mass, particularly if it is primarily composed of clays. This is far more common on newer homesites, so if you find strange color or densities of soils around your home, be prepared to do some improvement if you want grass to grow well there.

Turf Talk

Every soil horizon is different, but you should know the three most common layers: *Topsoil* is the surface soil that contains organic matter and is alive. *Subsoil* is lower down and is often infertile or very dense. *Parent material* or *bedrock* is the deepest layer and can be rock hard and completely restrict drainage.

113

Turf Tip

If you are planning to build a new home, don't leave your precious topsoil layer to be compacted and contaminated during the construction process. Before you begin, have the top few inches of soil scraped off and stockpiled out of the way. After the house is finished, you can have it spread out to make a perfect seed bed for your new lawn.

Subsoil Horizons

What you don't see can be deadly when it comes to growing plants and lawns. The soil horizon or cross-section described previously is an ideal, but frequently there are anomalies that change things. For example, some places simply have topsoil sitting right on top of bedrock.

When you add water, it collects just beneath the surface on top of the bedrock. Over water a little, and you drown the roots. This can be caused by weird, overly dense soils such as adobe, caliche, and a general condition known as hardpan. Break up hardpan with a tiller, and it will cement itself back together again.

Imported Soils

Whether you are building up the level of the lawn or just dealing with imported fill on a cut-and-fill homesite, the same risks apply. If the soil came from river bottoms, it's not uncommon to find it chock-full of roots and seeds of very aggressive weeds.

You can also import plant diseases caused by undesirable nematodes and fungi. Worse yet is that larvae of turf-eating bugs may be lying dormant, just waiting to hatch and go after your newly laid sod. The lesson here is to know where your topsoil comes from, especially if you know oak root fungus or Texas root rot are prevalent. In some areas, these diseases are so common that soils are fumigated.

Follow the Water

There is a big difference between how your homesite should be drained and how it really drains—or *doesn't* drain. Technically all lots are required to drain to the street. This means that water in the back yard must drain down the side yard to the curb and into the storm drain. It also means that water shed through your roof raingutter downspouts must also reach the curb.

Flat sites require the grading to be just right if this is to work as proposed on the subdivision drainage plans, but it's rare that it really does. Nobody is out there checking the contractor's grades, and they fudge it as much as they can. You can end up with a quagmire in the back yard, particularly if you live in a high-density neighborhood where the grading is tight. Be aware of this before you plan your lawn to ensure that the drainage is adequate.

If you are having problems, you may be able to grade the soil surface to drain by creating a swale or low spot that gently guides surface flow where you want it. For more challenging problems, there are three basic solutions:

1. You can install surface drains that tie into an underground pipe that extends from the back yard, under the sidewalk, and through the face of the curb. Obviously, you'll need to hire a professional for this.

2. You can install a French drain, which is simply a gravel packed perforated pipe that will draw water down through the soil to a lower level and then out to the curb.

3. Forget moving the water to the curb. Dig a deep hole, called a *sump*, pack it with gravel and let it gather the water. The water remains in the sump until it gradually drains away into the subsoil. This option is possible only where the underground water table is below the bottom of your sump.

Three Drainage Options

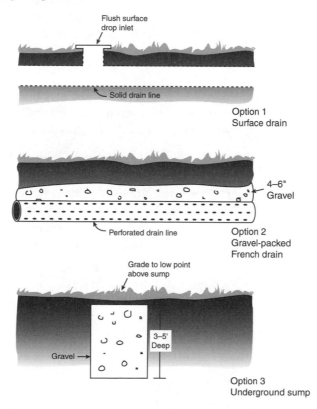

Flush surface drop inlet

Solid drain line

Option 1
Surface drain

4–6"
Gravel

Perforated drain line

Option 2
Gravel-packed
French drain

Grade to low point
above sump

3–5'
Deep

Gravel →

Option 3
Underground sump

How to Improve Soil for Lawns

When you add stuff to your soil or lawn to make it behave better, there are a number of ways to do it. The soil can be improved before you plant the lawn by tilling in fertilizer and amendments to as deep a level as you can manage. The more amendments you add, the better. This is a one-time opportunity because after the lawn is planted, you never have an equal second chance to improve soil that thoroughly again.

Lawn soils can be improved after planting, but to a far more limited extent. The most common way is called *topdressing*, which is like mulch for the lawn. This is simply the spreading of a thin layer of humus over the top of the lawn so that it filters down into the plants. There it decomposes gradually and nutrifies the soil and plants. You will read more about lawn renovation later in this book, but one step in that process involves punching holes a few inches deep all over the lawn. When you topdress immediately afterwards, the humus filters down into the holes to reach a deeper layer of soil more accessible to roots.

Turf Talk

A *fertilizer* is added to soil to make it more fertile in terms of nutrients. An *amendment* is added to soil to improve its structure. When a material, such as compost, acts as both a fertilizer and amendment, you get the best of both worlds.

You may already know something about your soil's structure by the way it behaves. If not, here are some basic guidelines on two extremes of soil behavior and what it means, and then a rundown of what it takes to fix it. All average soils are improved with compost, administered as often and as deeply as possible.

Challenging Clay

Clay soils are the most common, but they vary from mostly clay to just partly clay. The more clay in the soil, the more unique its behavior in terms of the interaction with water and plants. Here are some signs of soils with high clay content:

➤ It's really sticky when it gets wet. Tends to cling to your shoes and to the shovel, too. If you leave an impression in the surface, it stays there forever.

➤ The soil develops big cracks when it dries out. This is because clay soils can absorb an incredible amount of water. They suck up so much that their physical size actually expands just like water does when it freezes into ice. When that same soil dries out again, it contracts unevenly, and the difference in volume will result in the cracks.

➤ Water stands on top and won't soak in. Chalk this up to the fact that these soils can be so dense that they absorb water at a very slow rate. Water either pools on the surface or runs off. When a clay soil does finally become fully saturated, it seems to take forever to dry or for the water to drain away.

➤ The soil turns rock hard, and roots can't penetrate. This is the chief reason why clay soils can be so brutal on lawns. The ability to root deeply is important to turf grasses, but if the soil is extremely dense and compacted, roots simply can't get in.

The solution to improving heavy clay soils is to get them opened up by mixing in other materials or amendments. One old-style method was to use coarse construction sand because it will never decompose, and because its particles are so much larger than that of clay, they create irregularities in the soil that provide inroads for roots and water.

A second technique is to treat it with quantities of organic matter. The fresher and more woody the material, the longer it takes to break down and decompose, thus extending its effectiveness at opening up the soil. The redwood soil amendments are popular products for opening extra-heavy clay, such as adobe, because redwood is so resistant to decay. In some cases, you could put a ton of prime compost in clay soil, and it would be completely consumed by the following season. The reality is that affordability and availability are critical, so you should probably choose the most conveniently purchased product in your area.

Saving Sand

In regions where there is a lot of sand and some pockets of granular soils, such as in coastal or desert regions, the chief problem is getting water and nutrients to stay in the root zone. One benefit is that you can pull weeds out of these soils quickly and thoroughly. You can also grow great carrots.

Here are the characteristics of these soils:

➤ Water never pools on the surface. You could run the hose for five days straight, and every drop will disappear as soon as it hits the ground. There's also very little horizontal movement of water in the soil because it's never saturated enough to spread out.

➤ Plants dry out really quickly. This is due to the fact that the roots are never wet for very long. The big soil particles allow for a high rate of surface evaporation, leaving the top few inches forever at a loss, particularly in very hot or windy weather.

➤ Plants are always starving for nutrients. This is largely due to the lack of micro-organisms in these soils so that very little of the organic matter is ever converted to humus. Just as the water flashes through the root zone, the fertilizer goes through along with it. There is nothing to absorb the moisture and hold it long enough for plants to take it up.

The key to fixing sandy soils is to add humus, and lots of it. Fine humus, such as compost or ground peat, is absorbent, and each little piece acts like a miniature sponge. It sucks up the moisture and hangs onto it as tenaciously as it does fertilizer.

Turf Caveat

When adding woody soil amendments to heavy clay soils, be aware that the microorganisms that break down the wood require extra energy in the form of nitrogen, the most important nutrient to turf grasses. Microorganisms will rob the surrounding soil of nitrogen, and you may end up with a deficiency. Always add a boost of nitrogen fertilizer to offset any potential deficiency.

Popular Amendments

Even though you can work through soil structure problems yourself, it's always a good idea to consult a local experienced nursery person about any anomalies in local soils. If it's happening in your neighborhood, the experts know about it. Take the time, ask the right person, and listen carefully to his or her recommendations. It can make or break your lawn.

An array of soil amendments conveniently bagged up ahead of time is sold at home improvement stores, nurseries, and garden centers. Each different manufacturer produces its compostlike material under a separate trade name. These are often the best choice if you live in the city or are creating a small lawn. They also make some of the finest topdressings around. Shop prices because they vary considerably from store to store.

If you're planting a brand new lawn, especially one of any size, it might be a good idea to buy your material in bulk. You can have it delivered to your driveway and then use a wheelbarrow to distribute it. You will save a lot of money buying bulk, but it can be a bit more tricky in terms of timing. If you get hung up time wise, the material will sit there taking up space and staining your pavement indefinitely. Ask your local retail nursery or landscape supply for commercial sources of these bulk materials and time delivery carefully.

Like the peanut hulls in the following list, you may find agricultural byproducts in certain regions where specific crops are grown. For example, in California's central valley and along the Gulf Coast, rice farming has made rice hulls a perfect material for lawnowners to use as an amendment and are often added to bagged materials. They are small, easily worked into the soil, and resist decomposition due to their fibrous nature. If you're in a somewhat agricultural area, call around to processing plants and farm supply companies, because they know who is growing what and where to get the byproducts.

Likewise, in the forested parts of the Pacific Northwest you may find byproducts of sawmills, such as cedar or redwood soil amendments, both plentiful and more affordable than elsewhere. The following is a list of popular amendments:

➤ *Compost:* This all-purpose material is widely available and is perfect for both sand and clay. Some landfills operate ongoing composting programs on-site, where the organic refuse is collected and allowed to decompose into useful compost. Check here first before you pursue more costly options.

➤ *Manures:* You can buy composted and sterilized product in bags, which ensures that you don't buy weed seeds too. This makes excellent, if malodorous, nonburning topdressing material that's wholly organic. Steer, chicken, and other manures are all great organic sources, and often poultry manure is mixed with rice hulls or fine wood mulch for additional amendment benefits.

➤ *Nitrolized sawdust:* This is nothing more than wood shavings that have been treated to a dose of nitrogen fertilizer to avoid a loss of nutrients as soils break down the woody stuff. It's preferred by professional landscapers due to low price, consistent quality, light weight, and widespread availability. It doesn't smell, either.

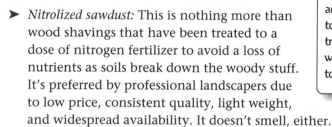

Turf Caveat

You would be surprised at the difference in weight between a cubic foot of dry compost and the same amount of wet compost. This applies to anything you haul in your car or truck, because buying materials in wet weather means you must be prepared to move nearly twice the weight.

➤ *Earthworm castings:* In short, this is worm "poop," a rich byproduct of earthworm farms. Castings are extremely high in nutrients and fine enough to improve both water retention and microorganism populations in sandy soils.

➤ *Gypsum*: This product is most often used in clay soils, and it can help neutralize alkaline pH, though only to a limited extent. It contributes to a chemical reaction that affects how nutrients are taken up in clay soils. This should not be considered organic matter or humus, but a specialized additive often recommended by experts in difficult soil communities.

➤ *Leaf mold:* This product comes from partially decomposed leaves, a material common to the floor of most hardwood forests. It's easy to make with your own fall leaves, but for lawn amendments, you'll need a lot more than you can make yourself. Landfill composting operations often have it in cities with a lot of large street trees.

➤ *Lime:* In the form of powder or granules, lime is the product of ground limestone and is important for raising the pH of acid soils. In areas of high acidity, you may have to add this product regularly to existing lawns, but there's more on this in the fertilizer chapter.

➤ *Oyster shell:* An alternative when limestone products aren't locally available. It does the same thing to soils as lime, but due to resistance to decomposition, finely ground shell can open up clay soils too.

➤ *Peanut hull meal:* This product is available in the peanut growing belt of the south, and ground hulls make a great slow-to-decompose amendment for heavy clay.

➤ *Milled peat:* Milled peat moss is more widely available in the northern states and has long been a favorite source of humus there. It is a good additive to lower pH levels of alkali soils. It can be expensive but is ideal for improving the water-holding potential of sand.

➤ *Other stuff:* A few other products have become popular among organic gardeners both as amendments and slow-release fertilizer. These are rather unorthodox in terms of lawn care, but in case you're organically inclined, here they are: alfalfa meal, castor pomace, cottonseed meal, soybean meal, seaweed, coffee grounds, cotton gin waste, winery pomace, and olive pomace.

The Least You Need to Know

➤ Garden soil texture is dictated by the predominant size of the soil particles.

➤ Clay soils can be the most fertile, whereas sandy soils can be the least fertile.

➤ If you live in a new subdivision, you may be working with really bad soil.

➤ You can improve most problems related to bad soil by adding the right kinds of amendments.

Chapter 9

Lawn Tools and Equipment

In This Chapter

➤ What lawn tools and equipment do

➤ Picking the right tool for the job

➤ Power: when and how to use it

➤ How to reduce power tool frustration

➤ When to buy tools and when to rent them

➤ New introductions and improvements in lawn equipment

You've probably heard the expression, "a carpenter is only as good as his tools." This really applies to lawns because inferior tools not only make the lawn look bad, but they also can double or triple the amount of work it takes to keep it looking bad. Also, using the wrong tool or a cheap one that breaks puts your safety in jeopardy not to mention that of innocent bystanders.

There are many innovations in the landscape care industry these days. New ideas, new products, and a whole bunch of gimmicky tools are filling home improvement store shelves, and unless you're a Bob Villa fan, it's all Greek. This chapter is designed to educate you on several levels regarding lawn tools and equipment.

First and foremost is separating what you need from what you think you need. Second is a rundown on how to protect your financial investment in tools of all kinds so that they function well for as long as possible. Third is protection from bodily injury, which is critical when it comes to tools with spinning blades. And finally, there's a list of tips on how to reduce and hopefully eliminate the frustration that faces everyone forced to bring gas-fired equipment to life after a long winter hiatus.

Divisions of Labor

One of the universal truths of humanity is that men like mechanical tools, preferably those with the biggest, most powerful engines. Offer a man a shovel or a mower, and he'll take the mower every time. This is the reason that on any given Saturday you'll see American homeowners carrying out the same division of labor: he mows; she pulls weeds and plants. It's also related to why so many Saturday mornings are spoiled by his temper tantrums when the power mower won't start up right away.

Everything you need to create or take care of your lawn can be divided into two categories: those driven by muscle power and those driven by higher powers such as electricity and gasoline. Lawn care involves far more power-driven tools than any other aspect of landscape maintenance, which is why men tend to take over the supervision of the lawn. This is so pervasive that lawn mowers themselves have been a big part of several popular sitcom shows on TV.

Before you ever consider purchasing any equipment, it's a good idea to understand some fundamental qualities about your lawn. These issues deal with how much tool you need relative to how you'll use it.

➤ Is your lawn small or large? Size relates to how much power you need in a mower.

➤ Is your lawn flat or sloping? Uneven surfaces influence whether riding equipment is possible.

➤ How long is your growing season? If you live in Bismarck, North Dakota, you'll be mowing for slightly more than two months each year. Compare that to Los Angeles, where it's a year-round activity.

➤ New lawn or old? Older lawns need more frequent renovation, and this requires some specialized tools, particularly if you are growing notorious thatch-producing grasses.

The Almighty Mower

Every lawnowner has got to have a mower. Cutting the grass is the most critical of all the turf care tasks. Just as there are many kinds of people, there are many kinds of mowers with all kinds of special features. If you already own a mower, go directly to mower maintenance later in this chapter. If you don't have a mower or are looking to buy a new one, keep reading.

When you review the following options in lawn mowers, keep the preceding questions in mind. In general, the larger the lawn, the larger the mower required to cut it well and do so in a reasonable amount of time. It stands to reason that a mower that cuts an 18-inch-wide swath will require more passes across the lawn than one with a 24-inch-wide blade. Also, a self-propelled mower will move faster and tackle hills better than a human-propelled one, and still leave you with some energy at the end of the day. There are six basic categories of mower to consider, each with its pros and cons.

Brand names can be important when you buy a mower because a well-established company will be there today and tomorrow to keep your investment repaired and running. Many cheap mowers today are not designed for long-term use, and repairs can be more expensive than the mower itself. Name brands may cost more up front, but you are assured that their products have been market-tested and will last as long as possible. Here are other benefits to name-brand lawn-care power equipment:

➤ Many outlets sell them, which makes price comparison shopping easier.

➤ If you buy the mower on credit, name brands are more widely accepted.

➤ A warranty covers all parts of the mower, and the time period can be extended beyond the average time periods.

➤ Replacement parts are readily available and compatible.

➤ Most repair shops are authorized for warranty service and repair.

➤ Mechanics have access to improved shop manuals, ongoing education, and factory assistance.

➤ You can buy a service contract that covers seasonal maintenance, which will ensure the maximum life span of the product.

Turf Talk

A *reel* mower depends on a scissorlike action of multiple blades mounted on a central gear-driven mechanism. This type is required for very close mowing and is standard on manual mowers. Reel mowers must be sharpened by a professional. A *rotary* mower has a long barlike blade mounted at the center and sharpened on the opposing ends. These blades are simple to sharpen at home.

Turf Talk

A *self-propelled* mower has the capability to push itself along, but you must walk behind and guide it every inch of the way. Self-propulsion is really desirable if you have a big lawn, you aren't very strong, or your lawn has hills and slopes. A *riding* mower is not only self-propelled but is also strong enough to carry you, too.

Manual Reel Mower

Until the 1960s, reel mowers were the major grass-cutting device for most residential lawnowners. They lost favor after gas-fired mowers became affordable but are reappearing on the scene. Because there's no small engine to start, you can rely on a manual mower to be ready for action at a moment's notice.

New designs and use of aluminum make them much more lightweight than before, which means that you don't need to be Mr. Universe to push one. They are primarily used for small city lawns on relatively flat surfaces. Some urban environments have or are enforcing bans on small gas engines to help curb air pollution, which is another factor driving manual-mower markets.

The disadvantage to these is that if you leave town or can't mow the lawn on schedule, it grows extra long and can be difficult to cut with this kind of mower. If the grass is too long and wet, the problems are compounded. Because the cutting blades involve a scissor action, it's easy to get sticks, cones, and similar small hard objects jammed in the mechanism. If you have overhanging trees that drop this kind of litter, you'll have to rake before you mow. These are the most affordable mowers today.

Manual Reel Mower

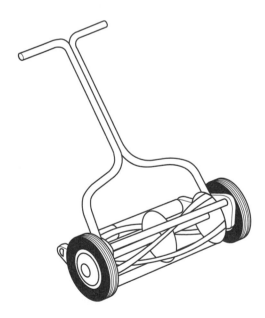

Turf Tip

Certain types of warm-season grasses such as hybrid Bermuda or zoysia are fibrous and tough, and only look their best when mowed very short. This is difficult to accomplish with a rotary mower. The most appropriate mower for these conditions is a power reel mower, which can be expensive and difficult to maneuver due to its weight. But these cut neatly with a scissor action the way putting greens are cut for that perfect carpetlike surface. If you allow the grass to grow overly long and try to cut it with a reel mower, you'll get an uneven result.

Electric Lawn Mower

These quiet mowers are rather new on the market relative to manual and gas-fired mowers. Electric mowers are nonpolluting, which makes them the only power-driven mower allowed in some cities with noise and pollution regulations. They cut like a rotary mower, but there is no engine, so you're relieved of the usual gasoline frustrations. No start rope to pull, no gas, oil, noise, or smoke. However, the electric mower is not nearly as powerful and is not self-propelled. You may have trouble in taller grass as well. As with all electric-powered tools, you should not mow in wet weather.

Turf Caveat

It is extremely dangerous to run any electric-powered garden tool in rain or very wet weather. There is a real threat of electrocution, particularly if you either accidentally cut the cord or if it is in poor condition.

Electric mowers are limited chiefly by the cord, which is always in the way when you turn or change directions. It's surprisingly easy to accidentally mow over the cord. These aren't realistic for large lawns or where there are no conveniently placed electric outlets. Electric mowers with the catcher located to the rear are much easier to use than those with it set on the side.

Power Rotary Mower

This is the most common kind of walk-behind lawn mower on the market today. It's gasoline driven with a single spinning blade, which you can remove and sharpen easily with a grinder or hand file. The catcher may be either on the rear or a side mount. Side-mount catchers can be difficult to maneuver on small lawns or tight spaces in and around trees. The size of the engine and optional features determine the sales price, which can range from cheap models at $150 to top-of-the-line models at $800 or more.

An average rotary mower has a 3- to 4-horsepower engine and a blade that cuts a swath just under 2 feet wide. These are surprisingly affordable and will do a fine job on the average lawn.

More powerful models include an array of features such as electric starter to eliminate the need to yank on a starter cord. They are also self-propelled and can offer a mulching feature, which eliminates the need for a catcher. Engine sizes to power all this range to more than 6 horsepower and prices can be hefty. Self-propelled mowers are equipped with all sorts of safety mechanisms, which increases the need for maintenance and repairs. They are also heavier.

Riding Lawn Mowers and Lawn Tractors

It always makes me smile when I see a big man riding around on a go-cart of a riding lawn mower. Maybe it's because the proportions are all wrong. Maybe it's because so much of the mower power is used to carry him around on Saturday morning that a fraction is left to actually do the mowing!

To avoid confusion, this is the difference between the riding lawn mowers and lawn tractors:

Riding lawn mowers do nothing but cut grass. Engines range from 8 to 10 horsepower, and the cutting swath maximum is 30 inches.

Lawn tractors or the slightly larger garden tractor have the capability to mow and pull attachments and trailers to accomplish other tasks. Engines range from 12 to 20 horsepower, and they cut swaths up to 50 inches. The multipurpose features make these a better buy overall if you have a large, diverse homesite.

Both these types of mowers are expensive, but if you can't manage a walk-behind, they are well worth the money. Turning radii of these mowers may not work well in tight spots, and often a second smaller mower is used for the details. Some of the weaker ones may have a hard time carrying you around and cutting tall grass in wet weather.

Consider these qualities when buying a riding mower:

➤ The mower cutting height should be easily adjusted.

➤ Be sure it is easy to check the oil and service the battery, plugs, and air filter without a lot of disassembly.

➤ The steering radius should be as tight as possible for maximum maneuverability.

➤ The mower should be easy to steer—this is important if you're not a very strong person.

➤ A wide wheel base reduces the tendency to tip and ensures you are as safe as possible on slopes.

➤ Big, fat tires distribute the weight of you and the mower over as many square inches as possible. This is critical when soils are wet so that ruts aren't produced.

➤ The seat should be comfortable and fit you personally. If you're extra tall or short, you may have to shop around for a mower that suits you.

➤ You should be able to easily reach all the controls without distorted movements or standing up.

More Horsepower

If you buy a car with a tiny engine, you might not even notice it with everyday city driving. But out on the highway when you need the power to pass another car quickly and safely, the extra horsepower comes in handy.

The same applies to a lawn mower. Everyday mowing activities aren't demanding, and an average engine keeps up just fine. But if you go on vacation, get sick, or the weather is abnormally bad, you are guaranteed to need more horsepower to do the job. Very tall grass is fibrous, and you can hear the mower strain to cut particularly dense stands. Slightly longer grass that's wet can clog the shoot of a rotary mower, and if there isn't enough power to force it out or into the catcher, you have to stop and clean it out frequently. It pays to buy a mower with extra power because it's a comfort to know it's always there when you need it.

Mulching Mowers

One of the newer features to come into the lawn-mower market is a rotary blade that cuts the grass into such fine pieces they go right back into the lawn as beneficial organic matter. These are always found in rotary-style mowers with two crossed blades that mince rather than chop the grass. This eliminates the need for a catcher, so you don't need to stop to dump the bag while using a mulching mower.

The disadvantage to mulching mowers is that, in theory, this return of the clippings is beneficial, but in reality it can contribute to increased thatch problems. If the grass grows faster than the accumulated clippings decompose, each time you mow you'll be adding to an ever-growing thatch layer. This in turn invites thatch-loving pests and disease, particularly in warm, humid climates. The second liability is that you have to mow frequently and stick to the schedule because long grass is too much for the mower to chop into mulch efficiently.

The Art of Lawn Mower Maintenance

If you can dazzle them with mechanical brilliance, throw it away. It's sad but true. These days, machines are becoming so complicated, it's growing more difficult for a back yard mechanic to fix them. It's obvious that a machine bristling with safety devices, energy conservation attachments, and anti-pollution devices is a far cry from the simple, ancestral one-cylinder engine.

Anatomy of a Gas Lawn Mower

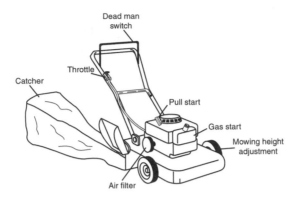

Even if you don't have the money to buy a top-of-the-line or a name-brand mower, you do have a chance to make it last much longer. During my golf course maintenance days, each time I mowed the putting greens, I returned the mower to the shop only after a thorough cleaning and inspection. If there was leftover grass, oil, or mud on the wheels or steering mechanism, I'd get a tongue-lashing from the head mechanic. He knew that, with a clean machine:

➤ If it doesn't start next time, it's easier to trace down the cause.

➤ If the engine or hydraulics had begun to leak, the seepage would be immediately noticeable. (These oils damage greens on contact!)

➤ Moisture could dry completely off all steel surfaces, thereby reducing the rust potential.

➤ Soil particles would not be left around the bearings to filter into the moving parts and degrade the mechanism.

➤ The reels and blades would be completely free to turn without resistance the next time out.

There are two types of maintenance for mowers, and in most cases these apply to any gas-fired power tool. First is the day-to-day maintenance, which is attended to before and after every time you use the machine. Second is the seasonal maintenance, which deals with an annual service and tasks related to winter storage.

The biggest hassle of using gasoline power tools is getting them started and running well enough to do the job. Every lawnowner who planned to get up early, mow the lawn, and then go do something really fun has found that the best laid plans often go awry. If the mower won't start and is all gunked up, you could spend all day fighting with it, and the next week at the chiropractor working out the kinks from yanking on the pull cord at least five dozen times.

Follow this checklist to keep your mower running smoothly:

➤ *Before use:* Check the gas. Be sure the tank is full. If in doubt, fill it now so that you don't run out while mowing.

➤ *Before use:* Check the oil level and fill if necessary before you start up the engine.

➤ *After use:* When the engine has cooled down, unhook the sparkplug wire from the plug. Tip up the mower and wash out all the grass stuck to the bottom of the housing, or in the reels. Then wash off the top of the housing and all adjacent surfaces.

➤ *Once a season:* Remove, inspect, and clean the air filter, or replace it if the air filter is disposable.

➤ *Once a season:* Drain the oil and refill it with fresh oil of the appropriate weight and viscosity for that tool.

➤ *Once a season:* Sharpen blades at least once a season or as needed.

➤ *Before storage:* Run the mower or tool out of gas completely so there is no fuel left in the carburetor or hoses.

Power Junkies

Lawn mowers and other lawn-maintenance equipment are powered in three ways. First are the electric tools that require a long extension cord. Second are four-stroke gasoline engines. Third are two-stroke engines that require a fuel mix. Understanding what makes mowers go allows you to operate them more safely and have fun doing so.

Passing Gas

Most lawn mowers are powered by four-stroke gasoline engines. You can buy regular automotive gas to use at home for your power equipment. In recent years, there have been a lot of changes in the gasoline supply. Most gas is now unleaded, and, depending on your state, it may contain other chemicals designed to reduce emissions. These are not good news for small engines, because the pollution-deterrent additives can turn to thick sludge much more quickly than regular gasoline. Older gas engines may not run nearly as well on unleaded gas either. For the least of all evils, choose name-brand gasoline and buy the highest octane supreme you can find. Above all, if your mower will be standing idle for a month or more, drain the gas tank and run it out of fuel, and always fuel your machines in the open air.

Turf Caveat

Whenever you tip over the mower, be aware that the gas can leak out of the tank through the cap. If the dip stick or cap is not tightly in place, you can have an oil leak, too. Avoid problems by checking the blade or underside of the mower before you fill the tank.

Two-Stroke Mixers

Two-stroke engines are most often found on string trimmers and leaf blowers. They run on a fuel of regular gasoline mixed with special two-stroke oil. Each engine will require a different ratio of gas to oil, so you must read the owner's manual and mix it exactly as instructed.

It's best to use a 1- or 2-gallon gas can and indicate with a marker or taped label that it is mix. This eliminates the chance of accidentally adding mix to a four-stroke engine, a deadly mistake. Pour the designated amount of oil in the can, then fill it up with gasoline and shake well. Give it another big shake to mix it up before you fill the gas tank of a tool, because these two fuels tend to separate during storage.

Turn on the Juice

Whereas gasoline explodes, an electric-powered mower or trimmer can fry you like a mini electric chair. Because fire and smoke are not a part of this picture, there is a tendency to become lax about the danger of electricity.

Most of these products come with a short connector plug cord just a few feet long. You have to plug in an outdoor extension cord, and this must reach an outlet. Each plug is a potential disconnection if you tug on the cord, so it's best to tie the cords together in a loose knot and then connect them. Do not plug your cord into the outlet until all the other connections are made first. If the extension cord is more than 100 feet long, be sure it is at least 14 gauge, which is thick enough to ensure the cord remains cool and that the maximum amount of power will reach the tool.

String Trimmer

When the string trimmer first hit the market, it revolutionized the lives of gardeners and lawnowners. Edges were the old-time dilemmas of garden makers because you had to use an edging machine or do it by hand with grass shears. If you lived in a rural area, the seasonal grasses in areas too rocky or uneven for mowers had to be laboriously cut.

String trimmers are now so widely used that they are available in many different price ranges and in both gas-fired and electric models. All are two-stroke engines and require mix. Electric models can be very affordable and are divided into two groups, those with a cord and those that run on a battery. Both electric types are fine for edging lawns but are not so good in the tall grass or weeds.

You can use a string trimmer for the edges of your lawn, but the end is not at a comfortable angle so it would not be able to do a sharp-edge job without scalping the grass. New models have reoriented the angle to make them much easier to use as lawn-edging devices, or the end may swivel so that they do dual duty most effectively. To make the strings cut bigger weeds better, you can now find string that is ribbed or serrated for improved cutting power.

String Trimmer

Specialty Lawn Tools

Not all tools used for lawns are power driven. A host of specialized hand tools make lawn planting and care much easier. The tool you use will be one suited to the size of your lawn and the type of turf grass you are cultivating. There are no gimmicky items here—they are the hard-core tools that you'd find stashed in the garage behind every beautiful lawn.

A *spreader* is nothing more than a device designed to distribute seed or fertilizer evenly over a large area. They all have a hopper and a means of distributing the material as gravity makes it fall out of the hopper. Most have adjustments to distribute more or less product. Some distribute more accurately than others, and they vary in terms of the type of material they will spread.

Spreaders

➤ *Drop spreader:* This, the most versatile, wheeled, push type, releases the material along the line of the axle in a precise swath that averages about 18 inches to 24 inches wide, but you can buy much wider models. This type is the most common for applying seed, granular fertilizer, and topdressing to small- and medium-sized residential lawns.

➤ *Whirlybird spreader:* This one can distribute seed or granular fertilizer up to 15 feet on either side and is not so accurate. It's sort of the scatter gun approach but is the best way to seed or fertilize large lawns in the shortest amount of time. As the granules fall, a whirling plastic paddle bats them into the outfield at all angles, but this doesn't work well with topdressing materials, which are too lumpy or heavy for the paddles.

➤ *Hand or belly spreader:* A hand-held spreader works beautifully for tiny spaces too small to make it worthwhile buying a drop spreader. It only holds about two cups of seed or granules and is inexpensive to buy. On the other end of the spectrum, the belly spreader is a canvas bag with a whirlybird mechanism at the bottom.

You actually wear it on a strap over the shoulder and across the chest. These are most commonly used to fertilize pastures and natural lawns with too irregular a surface for a wheeled spreader. They also work well for seeding the "rough" in wildflowers or native grasses.

Drop and Whirlybird Spreaders

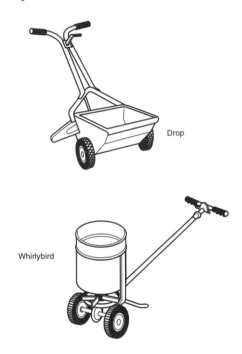

Drop

Whirlybird

Roller

A roller works on lawns like a steamroller does on roadbed construction. This is a large drum about 2 feet in diameter with a handle that allows you to pull it around. You can increase the weight of the roller by filling it with water. Some jobs need less weight than others. The roller serves a variety of functions for creating a new lawn or maintenance of an old one:

➤ Evens out the lawn after sowing seed.

➤ Compresses newly laid sod to force roots down into soil.

➤ Where soils heave in spring freeze-thaw conditions, the roller helps level it all out quickly and evenly.

Turf Tip

Most nurseries or sod retailers know their customers need a roller to install their new lawns. In many cases, it's a one-time need, and the cost of buying it is prohibitive. As a service, they may have a free loaner for you if you buy all your seed or sod from them. Another option is to rent one for the day. If your soils heave in spring to the extent that you must use a roller every year, then it may be cost effective and much more convenient to have one of your own.

Thatching Rake

Thatch removal can be an ongoing concern for grasses that tend to accumulate it. On a larger scale, it's recommended that power equipment be rented to thatch a lawn, but this isn't worth it for small lawns or specific spots where material accumulates.

Thatch removal can be done by hand with a special rake that allows you to cut and remove a good portion of the thatch. Be advised that this is a strenuous process in runner grasses with durable traveling stems but is far easier when used to remove accumulated clippings or other accumulations of organic matter. Keep in mind that you can also use an iron bow rake for this task if it's just soft organic matter.

Hand Shears and Battery Trimmers

In many cases, buying an edger or string trimmer is not feasible, yet lawns do require a clean-up around tree trunks and sprinkler heads from time to time. Small hand shears are the best tool, and the manual ones are now being replaced by battery-operated trimmers that are a snap to use.

Tool Time for Lawnowners

Chances are if you have a lawn or are creating one, you've got other planting areas as well. If you're new at the game, a visit to the home improvement store may be a mind-boggling experience when you're confronted with all the different types, sizes, and prices of gardening tools. Many of these are used in lawn creation, and a number of others are needed for not only maintaining the grass but also keeping the landscape beautiful. These are the most common lawn and landscape tools you may want to buy:

➤ *Iron bow rake:* This rigid rake is used for leveling seedbeds, raking up very heavy materials, and removing thatch or dead grass accumulations from the lawn.

➤ *Leaf rake:* This very lightweight rake has a fan-shaped end that's made of either aluminum, plastic, or bamboo. Use these for raking up leaves and thatch after de-thatching your lawn.

➤ *Flat shovel:* This doubles as a snow shovel in cold climates. In general, a flat shovel is used for scraping things off hard surfaces and works well for distributing topdressing materials on the lawn or into the hopper of a spreader.

➤ *Garden cart* or *wheelbarrow:* A garden cart has two wheels and is much larger than the one-wheel wheelbarrow. In small lots, it may be difficult to get a garden cart through the side yard gateway. Measure your smallest gate before choosing one for your lawn project.

Why Buy When You Can Rent

Some tools can be expensive to buy when they are used just once or infrequently. These are most often connected with planting a new lawn, or renovating an older one.

➤ *Rototiller:* Tillers are used to turn over the soil on new lawn areas. They also help mix in soil amendments and preplanting fertilizers before you seed or sod. They are pricey, and, unless you're tending a vegetable garden as well, which justifies the expense, simply rent one during the soil preparation phase of your planting project.

➤ *Verticutter:* This machine has a reel studded with sharp blades. It moves very quickly sliding the turf up and tearing it away from the ground. This is the primary de-thatching piece of equipment used by professionals, but you may rent one to quickly and thoroughly de-thatch the lawn. Despite all the ripping, it actually invigorates old thatch-ridden lawns.

➤ *Aerator:* This machine is designed to puncture overdense soil and remove plugs of sod and soil, leaving an open hole for water and fertilizer to reach the roots more quickly. This machine is a lawnowner's secret weapon in heavy clay soils that are slow to absorb water.

The Least You Need to Know

➤ Choose a mower that fits your lawn and yourself.

➤ Name brands hold up longer and are easier to fix.

➤ Maintenance is the key to equipment longevity.

➤ Spreaders and other tools are needed for lawn maintenance.

The Art of the Mow

It is probable that more damage is done to lawns and fine turf by improper mowing than any other practice.

—Howard Sprauge, 1976

Turf grass managers everywhere are faced with a high profile surface that is a tell-all when it has been rudely treated. Neglect mowing, and it shouts with shagginess. Under water, and it turns brown for all to see. Mow it too short, and the dirt shows through like a big hole in your sock. Turf grass is unforgiving, particularly if you're the greens-keeper at Wrigley Field or the White House. Millions will see even the slightest *faux pas.* Fortunately for you, only your relatives and neighbors will notice your mistakes.

Sprauge tells us that mowing can make a lawn look magnificent, but if done improperly, you could shoot yourself in the foot. Mowing the grass seems like such a mundane task, but there's no other single thing you can do that makes the yard look so good.

About Growth and Mowing

Imagine what would happen to a plant that was cut down to about 20 percent of its normal height during the growing season. Would it live through the assault? Chances are it would, but the vigor of the plant would be reduced because there are fewer leaves to carry on photosynthesis. The plant would lose much of its food-producing potential.

The rule of thumb is that the grass is never damaged by mowing too long, but mowing too short is a real physical assault. Overly short mowing eliminates all the leaves on the plant, forcing it to regrow meristematic tissue on what energy reserves it has.

Turf Talk

The term *meristem* applies to the center of the growing plant where cell reproduction is most active. Very close mowing can cut into this tissue, forcing a lot of healing of meristematic tissue before it will send out a new set of leaves.

Hot and Cold Exceptions

If you live in a hot, dry climate, when and how high you mow can also have a big effect on the grass. In general, it's better to mow slightly higher than the average to compensate for moisture loss.

It's never wise to cut your grass in direct midday sun—morning and evening are better. The same applies in dry winds because these can dry out the grass in minutes. The longer the grass blades, the better they are able to shade the soil and keep roots cooler. When you cut them off, not only is the soil more exposed, but they lose a lot of moisture through the cut tips. If you cut it overly short in this weather, the damage to the grass is even greater than before.

If you live in a very cold winter climate, you will have to mow differently at the end of the season. The more foliage left on the plants, the more frost-killed organic matter will be present under the snow. This becomes much like thatch, producing the ideal environment for disease that infects the spring lawn. This last mow of the season should be viewed as semi-scalped because it averages about 30 to 50 percent lower than the average mowing height.

Grass that is in shade or part shade has less exposure to sunlight, which drives photosynthesis. To compensate, the plant needs proportionately more leaf area to manufacture the same amount of food as a plant in the sun. The rule of thumb is to allow the grass to grow about an inch taller in shade than in the sun, but the exact differences are detailed in the following chart.

Mowing Heights in Inches

Grass	Average	Hot/Shade	End of Season
Bahia grass	2	3	1.5
Bermuda grass	.5	1	.5
Buffalo grass	1.5	2.5	1
Kentucky bluegrass	2.5	3	2
Annual ryegrass	2	2.5	2
Perennial ryegrass	1.5	2.5	1
Tall fescue	2.5	4	2
Fine fescue	1.5	2.5	1
St. Augustine grass	2	3	1.5
Zoysia grass	.5	1	.5

In general, these mowing heights reflect the growth habits of the grasses themselves. The very low, ground-hugging runner grasses such as Bermuda are mowed practically as low as the mower will go. That's why reel type mowers are preferred, because a rotary mower cannot cut accurately or cleanly at such short stature. They are mowed lower than the bunchy uprights, which bear higher root crowns that could be permanently damaged if mowed so low.

Turf Tip

A direct correlation exists between the height of the grass plant and the depth of the roots. If mowed too short, turf grass won't produce a healthy root system capable of supporting it under less than ideal conditions. Turf grass experts have arrived at the suggested mowing heights by determining the optimal balance of stem and root development.

You can make a simple gauge to know when and how high to mow your lawn. Use a clean wood stake that's about the length of a ruler. Based on the mowing heights of your grass as shown in the previous table, measure up from the blunt end to the height indicated in the "average" column. Draw a line across the stake there, and it will become your standard. Draw other lines above that if you adjust your lawn height for very hot weather or shaded parts of the lawn, where the grass should be slightly longer.

This is a great tool to use because it helps you know exactly how far above the standard your grass has grown, and it will also show you when it has reached the length where two mowings are needed to bring it down incrementally.

Grass Height Gauge

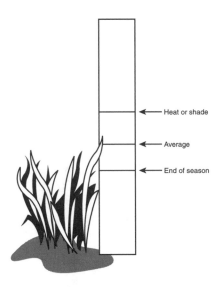

←— Heat or shade

←— Average

←— End of season

How to Adjust Mowing Height

From the mowing height table, it's clear that you'll have to change the setting on your lawn mower as the seasons change. The mowing height is measured from the soil surface to the bottom of the blade of a rotary mower, or to the cutter bar on a reel mower.

To set an accurate height, set the mower on a level paved surface, and then measure it to see how much adjustment you need. For a rotary mower, simply move the wheels up or down a notch. Most models have each wheel on a separate adjustment. For a reel mower, the height is changed by adjustments of the roller position, *not the cutter or reel blades*.

Turf Caveat

Don't become an accident statistic. If you want to check the cutting height or work on the blade assemblies of any gas-powered mower, don't just turn it off, *disconnect the spark plug wire too*. Small engines have been known to start up even while in the "off" position after their reel or blade has been turned.

> ### Turf Tip
>
> It's difficult to know what height a rotary mower is cutting because the housing obscures your view of the blade. For a clean look-see, remove the catcher and measure blade height through the discharge chute.

Clean-Cut Lawns

Mower blades, like knives in the kitchen, need to be sharpened periodically. Here are a few sources of dulled blades:

➤ Scalping the grass so that the blade contacts soil

➤ Running the mower up onto curbs or bed dividers

➤ Mowing in the rough where there are sticks and rocks

➤ Jamming an object in a reel mower

➤ Giving the blade a close encounter with a sprinkler head

You'll know the blades are dull when your grass exhibits any of these symptoms after you mow:

➤ The fresh cut grass has a white fuzziness to it. This is caused by the blade cutting the softer part of the plant but sliding along the edge of the more fibrous parts.

➤ Taller stems or thicker ones aren't cut at all and stick up after the mower passes over them.

➤ The ends of the grass are cut so roughly that moisture loss gives the lawn a brownish tint.

> ### Turf Talk
>
> Sometimes mowers are used to cut grass and weeds outside the confines of a traditional lawn. These areas are called the *rough* in golf course lingo, but this applies to many homesites as well.

Exactly how often your blade needs to be sharpened depends on the type of grass you have and how often you mow. In general, the warm-season grasses are more tough and fibrous, which increases to need to resharpen blades in those lawns.

Unless you're a real back yard mechanic, it is not a good idea to try to sharpen the blades of a reel mower because of the precision mechanism. The cutter bar must contact the cutting reel blades perfectly at a clean sharp edge. This is particularly important with a push-type reel mower, because if the blades are dull or out of alignment, the work load on your part doubles. You'll have to push that much harder if dull blades are to cut the grass at all. These blades can be easily and irreparably damaged in the hands of a novice, and they are dangerous to handle because they are honed to a very sharp edge. Take your reel mower to a lawn mower shop for sharpening; then you'll know it will be done well and will cut to its greatest potential.

Rotary Blade Sharpening

The best part about a rotary mower is that it's so easy to sharpen. Rotary blades spin at 130 miles per hour and use pure inertia to slice into the grass. They also hit objects at that speed, which not only dulls the blade, but also can nick and gouge it.

Turf Tip

If you have a large lawn and a rotary mower, you'd be surprised at just how cheap a new blade is. If you have two blades, you can sharpen one at your leisure while mowing with the other. That way you'll always have a fresh blade on hand to get the job done without unnecessary and frustrating wrenching before you start.

For sharpening, you'll need a flat bastard file. If you have a rotary power grinder, it can shorten the job and is really necessary for grinding down deep gouges. You'll need a vice, too. And when you're peeking under the housing of your rotary mower and are appalled at how much old grass has welded itself to the insider surface, you will understand how critical it is to keep it clean. While you're under there, why not scrape some of the junk off so that it will be nice and clean again? It makes the mower work better, and it keeps the blade mounting assembly in good order.

It's a simple process to sharpen a rotary blade:

➤ Disconnect the spark plug wire, and then tip the mower up or on its side to expose the blade. Be sure there's no gas or oil spilling out of the engine because it's not only a hazard, but it will stain your paving and kill your plants.

➤ Use a crescent wrench to remove the nut that holds the blade on. Do not use pliers or channel locks because these will damage the nut and make it impossible to tighten it again.

➤ Remove the blade and secure it in a vice with the beveled end up. Inspect it to see whether there are any deep gouges that might need a grinder. If you grind one end, you'll have to grind the other to match, even if it doesn't need it, because the blade must be balanced.

➤ Begin sharpening the blade by running the file in one direction parallel to the edge of the bevel. Count how many passes you make. When it's free of nicks and shows a clean bright edge, sharpen the other end using the same number of strokes. The aim is to sharpen both ends evenly. When you're finished, stick your finger or a pencil through the center hole and see whether it balances. If not, file a little more on the heavy end.

➤ Replace the blade on the mower so that the fins on the blade point down. Again, use a crescent wrench to tighten the nut securely. Remember, the only thing that separates a mower blade from a sling blade is that one little nut!

Turf Caveat

Nuts and bolts are made with hexagonal heads. The best tools for removing or adjusting them are an adjustable crescent wrench or box end wrench. Do not use pliers, channel locks, or pipe wrenches because these have ridges that gouge the metal so easily that the nut or bolt end becomes round. Do not use tools that have ridged teeth on the gripping parts.

Sharpen a Rotary Mower Blade

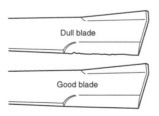

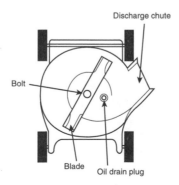

Bottom view of rotary mower

Safe Mowing

All mowers have sharp blades and are potentially dangerous. Power mowers are incredibly dangerous. Every year, hundreds of accidents are due to small engines and spinning blades. If you follow some basic guidelines, you won't become a statistic.

When all else fails, read the directions. This is the standard approach to new tools, yet most people end up having problems that are spelled out in detail in the owner's manual. Read your manual from cover to cover and be sure to heed its warnings and tips on safe operation.

It seems obvious, but you must not operate a power tool while under the influence of alcohol or drugs, both legal and illegal. How often have you enjoyed a beer before mowing or while you were on a mow break? Not a good idea.

Here are some other precautions to keep in mind:

➤ Do not remove any of the safety equipment that came with your power tool. It's there for a reason.

➤ Do not use a power machine that is damaged or defective.

➤ Wear shoes, not sandals, when mowing the lawn.

➤ Avoid dangling or overly loose clothing that can be caught in rotating mechanisms.

➤ Fill the mower gas tank before you start. If you must refill in the middle of the job, let the engine cool down first.

➤ Walk-behind mowers should be guided across the slope, not up and down. This prevents your foot from slipping under the housing where the blade is.

➤ Riding mowers and lawn tractors should be driven up and down the slope, not across it.

➤ If the mower is clogged or malfunctions, turn it off, disconnect the spark plug wire, and then clear the chute.

➤ Turn off the mower when crossing any surface other than lawns.

➤ Wear safety glasses and ear protection when operating an edger or string trimmer.

➤ Be aware of humans and pets around you when mowing, trimming, or using a blower because flying debris can blind them.

One of the least acknowledged lawn mower casualties is the trees that grow in lawns or around them. Whenever your mower bangs into a tree trunk, there is damage, and the younger the tree the greater the potential because the bark is so thin. There are also lawn trees from coast to coast that have been outright killed by careless use of string trimmers. A sapling can be ringed by the trimmer string in the blink of an eye, which is a fatal condition.

Tree Protectors

Be respectful of your trees because gouges accumulate and make the base of the trunk look bad. They provide an inroad for boarers and other serious tree pests. The wounds invite suckering, which are the nuisance shoots that crop up at ground level. To reduce the damage potential of young trees in your lawn, purchase a trunk protector, which slides over the young tree base, and even if you ding it with the mower or trimmer, it will come out unscathed. When the tree gets older, you can remove the trunk protectors after the bark has thickened enough to take a beating on a regular basis.

Pruning the Grass

Mowing truly is an art, and if you're not convinced, just turn on a baseball game. The fields are impeccably mowed, with perfectly straight stripes criss-crossing one another at such regular intervals the effect resembles a checkerboard of dark and light blocks.

If you tune into a golf tournament, you'll see an entirely different effect. Because fairways undulate around bunkers and sand traps, the mowing reflects this in stripes that wander in and out of the field of view. This is yet another precision job, but rather than being rigidly geometric, it is an artistic reflection of the grading.

If you look closely, you'll see that every blade of grass has two sides. Often one side is lighter in color than the other. It might be fuzzier too. When mowers pass over the grass their action turns all the leaf blades in the same direction. When a lawn is mowed in a back and forth pattern, going one way, the dark side of the leaf is up, and going the other way, the light side of the leaf is up.

One of the big differences between rotary and reel mowers is that the reel mower has a roller on it that resembles the platen in an old-fashioned typewriter. This roller bears on the grass as you pass over it, which forces the grass plants to grow flatter and spread out. It also does a better job than a rotary mower when it comes to turning the grass.

143

Fairway Mowing Pattern

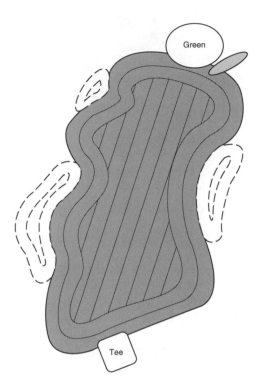

These examples show you that there's more to the art of the mow than just running the machine around the yard. On the golf course, the greens are mowed back and forth, but after that's done they run the mower around the edge to neaten it up at the end. This eliminates any turning marks made by the equipment. The same applies to fairways, which are mowed back and forth the long way, right up the middle. Then when nearing the side, the greenskeeper switches to a circular pattern that undulates around the mounded bunkers and sand traps.

Ways to Go, Ways to Mow

The shape of your lawn will suggest the most attractive patterns to work with. Natural shapes or those that curve gracefully can be mowed in a circular pattern. A city lawn that's square or rectangular is better mowed in stripes because this emphasizes the geometry.

No matter what pattern you choose, you'll need some alternates. Because grass is forced in a particular direction when you mow it, if you do it exactly the same way each time, eventually all the grass will lean. Have at least two mowing strategies, or mow in the opposite direction each time to ensure your grass always maintains good posture.

Optional Stripes

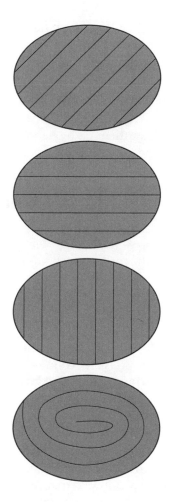

If you have a heavy mower and it's difficult to turn, then a circular pattern may be the best way to mow. Begin at the outside edge of the lawn and mow all in one direction until it's too narrow to continue at the center. Then switch to mowing back and forth.

If you are mowing without a catcher, mow in a circular pattern with the chute aimed at the yet unmowed grass. This will produce smaller clippings that won't clump up so badly.

If you are mowing very tall grass with a side mount catcher, it's best to mow in a circular direction so that the catcher is on the already mowed side. This reduces the amount of drag on the catcher.

Knowing how to mow also includes when to mow and when not to. Here are some helpful tips for success:

➤ Mow frequently. This is better for the mower and the grass. This also means fewer trips to dump the catcher.

➤ Don't cut more than a third of the overall height of the grass at any one time. If it's longer than that, don't try to cut it to the normal height. Mow it twice, bringing it down part way at the first mowing and then down to the normal height at the second mowing a few days or a week later.

➤ Avoid mowing when the lawn is wet. This spreads spores and disease around your lawn. The clippings will clog the chute, and these lumps will dry rock hard, so you'll have to clean them up by hand. Mower wheels also make ruts in muddy soil and will skid; you may lose your footing as well.

The Grass Is Always Greener

Did you know that $^1/_2$ acre of lawn will produce up to 6,000 pounds of clippings every year? It's estimated that around 30 percent of everything dumped in landfills is clippings and yard waste! This is particularly tragic when you consider the compost-making potential of just the leaves and grass clippings.

Thinking Green

Each time you mow the lawn, there are clippings. You have the choice of leaving them on the lawn or using the mower catcher to collect them for removal. If you think about grasses in nature, they die back at the end of the season and gradually decompose back into the soil in a natural process. Nobody removes their clippings.

Today turf grass experts are taking a second look at the process because of some unrelated problems. Landfills in cities are having a tough time dealing with the clippings discarded from thousands of lawn mowers. This taxes the garbage collecting systems and fails to take advantage of all this vital organic matter.

If you mow without the catcher, your mower will blow the clippings all over the lawn. This isn't a bad thing if you mow frequently, because the clippings will be nice and short. As suggested previously, mow so that the chute throws the clippings at the yet unmowed grass so each clipping is mowed twice.

Lawn clippings can be a great material for composting, although lawns with quantities of Bermuda may be risky. If bits of stem or roots of these aggressive runner grasses aren't completely killed in the composting process, you could introduce them to other parts of the garden with the compost. On the other hand, when legumes like clovers are in the lawn, they contain large quantities of nitrogen and make super compost.

Clippings when fresh are too moist for most compost heaps, and large concentrations of them slow the process. You can still use them though by making some minor alterations:

➤ Spread the clippings out on the ground to dry for a day or two, then add them to the compost pile little by little.

➤ Mix fresh clippings with leaves or other dry organic matter that will absorb some of the moisture.

➤ Add the clippings in thin layers between other types of material.

Turf Tip

If you have a good lawn mower that doesn't mulch, you can have it refitted to become a mulching mower for a fraction of the cost of buying a new one. Your local lawn mower repair shop can just change the blade and block the discharge chute and presto, you've got a mulching mower. Do be aware that after it's changed over, you should not attempt to use it to cut grass more than an inch taller than the suggested mowing height.

Seasonal Schedule for Mowing

You've probably noticed that your lawn grows faster during some seasons and slower during others. If you live in the northern states, it may just sit there for most of the year and then grow like crazy for a couple of months in high summer. Obviously, you have to change your frequency and the mowing height as the weather changes.

Because American lawns cover so many different climate zones, and there are such a variety of turf grasses, you will have to make some adjustments for your particular situation. But much of this relates to being a good observer of how your lawn is behaving.

Waking Up the Lawn—Spring

Lawns in cooler climates wake up gradually after their long winter sleep. They don't start growing until the temperature of the soil and the nights begin to rise. As spring progresses, the lawn can be encouraged to break its winter dormancy and start growing vigorously by mowing long before there is visible green growth.

When the lawn dries out enough to get the mower on it without quicksand conditions, even if it looks brown and dormant, mow it. At this point, set the mower so that it cuts off the top $1/2$ inch. Use the catcher or rake up the clippings. This early mowing gets rid of any shaggy dead growth so that the plants receive more direct sunlight on the meristem. This in turn stimulates more rapid recovery from the dormant state.

Dog Days—Summer

During these months, lawn growth will slow down in some regions and speed up in others. For regions with warm-season grasses, summer months find them growing vigorously, and they require proportionately more water and, depending on the species, more fertilizer. Mowing frequency steps up with these.

In cool-season grass regions, particularly in the northern states, summer rain or lack of it plays a big part. The periods of growth here are in spring and fall while, during midsummer, the lawns slow down. Either way, mowing slightly higher during the hot times is beneficial to both active warm-season grasses and temporarily slowed cool-season grasses.

Fall Down—Autumn

Cool-season grasses will experience a growth spurt as temperatures, particularly at night, drop. Gradually increasing rainfall stimulates the grasses but beware of allowing them to grow overly long at this time. It's important to actually mow lower at the end of autumn to remove as much of the plant as possible before winter sets in. Clippings and dead grass accumulations actually cause disease problems. Your last mowing of the year should be proportionately lower as designated by the "end of the season" column in the "Mowing Heights in Inches" table earlier in the chapter.

Warm-season grasses can be damaged by winter frost and by late fall are going dormant. If you live in a transition zone or where your grass is vulnerable to dips in temperature below 32 degrees, you'll want to mow a bit higher at the end of the season. This provides a better insulation for the roots so that if you do experience a killing frost, the plants will be as protected as possible.

Old Man Winter

Winter conditions in much of the country are severe enough for lawns to go completely dormant. Only in very warm climates do they remain green, or dormant grasses are overseeded with short-term grass for a temporary green-up.

You probably won't be mowing at all, which makes this season the best time to overhaul your power equipment. A season of mowing takes its toll on your mower, and if you put the mower in storage, this too should be done properly to increase the life span of the engine.

There are some things you should consider when protecting your dormant lawn, particularly if it snows a lot in your neighborhood:

➤ Rake up all leaves, clippings, and organic matter on the lawn before the first snow to limit the debris accumulation beneath it.

➤ Avoid using rock salt to de-ice surfaces adjacent to your lawn. Salt kills lawn grass, and, with the spring thaw, it will accumulate in the runoff.

➤ Avoid parking or walking on lawn areas when soils are frozen or when covered with snow. Mark your walkways and stick to them.

Winter Mower Care

By the end of the season, your mower and trimmer will have had a lot of use. If you just stick it in the garage for the winter as is, you are guaranteed to have a dead machine come spring. Before you put your equipment away for the winter, you have to give it some special attention.

Thoroughly clean the mower or trimmer, removing oil, clippings, and exhaust carbon. Drain the gas tank and run the engine completely out of gas. Loosen belts and pulleys.

If you're handy, use this downtime to inspect your mower. Remember that small engines, particularly those connected to rapidly spinning blades, suffer a number of problems related to the vibration. Use the following checklist:

➤ Properly tighten all nuts and bolts.

➤ Sand or brush off all signs of rust and paint with rust-resistant engine paint.

➤ Lubricate and oil all moving parts, especially reel mowers, which have more exposed gears and other precision parts.

➤ Replace belts and pulleys that are cracked or unevenly worn.

➤ Check the chain drive of self-propelled mowers for stretching, tension, wear, and broken sprockets.

➤ Check the electrical connections for broken or frayed wires and cracked solder joints.

➤ Look for sharp objects, punctures, and gouges in inflatable tires.

➤ Make sure that all safety mechanisms are in full operation.

➤ Replace rotary blade if badly worn or gouged.

➤ Change the engine oil.

➤ For electric tools, inspect the entire length of the cord for melted or gouged insulation and exposed wiring.

➤ On battery-operated equipment, inspect every cell in the battery and add water or special battery additives if low.

➤ For water-cooled mowers or tractors, drain the radiator or be sure you add anti-freeze.

Don't join all the other guys out there who run to the lawn mower repair shop in spring when the mower won't start. If you do, you'll have to stand in line while the lawn gets higher and higher!

Turf Caveat

The batteries used in riding mowers and lawn tractors are slightly smaller versions of those used in automobiles. They are extremely explosive, and you should never store them or work on them near an open flame. The fluid in the cells is highly corrosive to just about anything, so when doing maintenance on the battery, wear gloves and safety glasses.

To really free yourself from spring mower frustration, consider hauling your equipment to the repair shop in the dead of winter for a thorough tune up. This is a great idea if you've never overhauled your mower and it's aging rapidly. The mechanics are less busy and may take greater care than during the busy season.

This is essential for riding mowers because they have so many more parts that can suffer from lack of maintenance. Believe me, major repairs of these big rider mowers can be exorbitantly expensive, which really hurts if you find out that a little routine maintenance could have avoided the whole problem.

The Least You Need to Know

➤ Mow at the right height for your grass.

➤ Keep your blades razor sharp.

➤ Use a different pattern each time you mow.

➤ You can leave the clippings on the lawn.

Part 4
Creating a Green Carpet

There's more than one way to plant a lawn, and what's right for you depends on your budget, time limitations, local climate, and availability of the plants. Obviously, if no sod farms are nearby, you might not be able to plant from sod. The key is to try to make it as easy on yourself as possible, because the most labor-intensive period in a lawn's life is the time between sowing and complete coverage or fill-in. You don't want to become a slave to weekend weeding of a reluctant, sluggish new lawn.

Pay attention to some of the newer techniques in lawn making. Hydroseeding is great for large areas, but you'll have to hire someone to do it for you. Alternative lawns are ideal problem solvers for new yards that aren't yet landscaped because they can be sown and mature in just a few weeks. Then you can mow the lawn to keep the kids and dog from tracking mud all over the house. You should also be skeptical when people tell you to plant a groundcover instead of lawn, because there are some maintenance nightmares detailed in the following chapters that you really need to know before making a decision.

Chapter 11

Seeding a Turf Grass Lawn

In This Chapter

➤ Turf grasses from seed and how long they take to sprout

➤ Purging weeds from your lawn area

➤ Preparing to plant a lawn

➤ How to sow turf grass successfully

➤ Caring for your lawn after planting

If there is any living thing which might explain to us the mystery beyond this life, it should be seeds.

—Donald Culross Peattie, *The Sleep of the Seed,* 1939

Nothing else in nature holds the mystery and wonder of seeds. How can something barely visible to the eye produce plants of treelike proportions? Those seeds in your new grass lawn are equal in magnitude to the seeds of the Roman wheat that fueled centurions or the corn of the Aztec empire.

Now that you've got a good dose of worldly horticultural philosophy, let's get back to basics. Remember the classroom experiment in third grade when you grew beans in milk cartons filled with soil? What did you learn? First, a seed contains all the nutrition it needs to get started. Second, you have to water it to grow. Third, it needs dirt to take root. This is as simple as it seems, and the short version of what you'll do when you plant a lawn from seed.

Turf Talk

Sow means to put seed into the soil and cover it up. *Broadcasting* describes how you actually get the seed out there. For example, if you were to go out into a freshly plowed field and throw wheat seed around, you are sowing wheat and broadcasting by hand. *Germination* is technically the intake of water by a seed, resulting in the formation of new tissue.

A Black Thumb's Seed Primer

A tiny seed is jam-packed with energy, and the growth of that seed into a plant harnesses that energy to work for us. Each seed contains enough material for an entire plant, but it stays in reserve until the seed is exposed to just the right conditions. Seeds can stay on hold for a long time and are best stored in cool, dry, dark places like Egyptian pyramids. Some of the seeds found in these tombs were still able to sprout after five millennia in storage. But some seeds, such as poppies, won't live beyond a year no matter what you do.

Each species of plant has its own speed of germination. Parsley seed can take up to a month to germinate. Annual ryegrass in comparison seems to jump the gun in as little as five days. When you grow anything from seed, it is important to know how long it takes to germinate so that you know when to expect a plant to appear. If you don't have an anticipated germination date for your grasses, you won't know if they're late.

In Chapter 7, "Ladies and Gentlemen . . . Buy Your Grasses," the different types of turf grass were covered in detail. Some can be grown from seed, and some can't. Those that can't have to be planted a different way that's more expensive or time-consuming. Seeding is the cheapest, easiest way to get a lawn.

Each kind of lawn grass has a different time to germination. The weather and moisture levels can increase the time to germination. The minimum number of days in the following list are achieved under the most ideal conditions:

➤ Common Bermuda grass: 10 to 30 days

➤ Kentucky bluegrass: 14 to 28 days

➤ Buffalo grass: 14 to 21 days

➤ Centipede grass: 18 to 22 days

➤ Fine fescue: 10 to 21 days

➤ Tall fescue: 8 to 12 days

➤ Perennial ryegrass: 5 to 14 days

So, What's Ideal?

This section explains a few factors relating to sprouting conditions. Above all, the soil and air temperatures must be warm enough to suit the seed. The texture of soil must be loose and open but tilled and smoothed to a very fine consistency without big clods that deter seed from sprouting. The seed needs to be covered with very lightweight material that stays soft even when it's dry, so that the little shoots can come up through it with the least resistance. This whole mass must be evenly moist, but not super-saturated, because this makes the seed rot before it has a chance to sprout. If you accomplish all of the above, you're pretty much guaranteed an on-time show of green all across the lawn.

Timing Is Crucial

Knowing when to plant is as important as knowing how to plant. The first goal of timing is to sow at a time when grasses are naturally growing vigorously. Second, avoid peak high temperatures that will stress the new seedlings. Third, avoid the highest humidity levels, which are usually related to frequent rainfall.

The warm humidity and moisture factor is connected to a fungal disease known as *damping off*. It afflicts only new seedlings right at ground level. The symptom is that the new seedlings will flop over as the fungus invades them at the base.

The best way to avoid problems with damping off is to sow your lawn at the right time. In the vast majority of climates, early spring is recommended but before the onset of heat and summer rains. You can also plant at the tail end of summer and into autumn, since this is a drier, cooler period that is less vulnerable.

Unwanted Weeds

Before we go any further, one single factor is critical to any new lawn grown from seed—weeds. There are few places in this world where the soil is not already supporting plants. And there is no square inch of soil on this whole earth that doesn't contain at least a few weed seeds.

Seeds lie at various levels in the soil. Some sit on top, and others are deeper down. If they are too deep to sprout, the seeds just sit there waiting for a gopher to come along and push them up to the surface. Like those Egyptian seeds from the pyramids, these mini time bombs are waiting for you to till the soil, bringing them to the top to sprout.

The most important thing you can do is to purge your lawn area of weeds, weed seeds, and any plant parts that can start weeds in other ways. There are two methods of doing this, and both require a few weeks and a rototiller.

Turf Talk

The definition of a *weed* is simply "a plant out of place." One man's weed is another man's lawn. Bermuda grass is a horrible weed in California but is the main kind of turf grass in most southern states. What constitutes a weed in your new lawn should be any plant that didn't come in the seed package.

Turf Tip

Sedge weeds in your lawn are *personas non grata*. To identify them, refer to the end of Chapter 1. Consider them highly dangerous because they not only produce prodigious seed quantities; their roots have little pealike tubers that may survive even though the mother plant has been sprayed or tilled under. Before you till, dig out any clumps of sedge that you find in the proposed lawn area and be sure to get as large a root ball as possible. Bag them up and put them in the garbage can. Sedges can be a serious problem in low-lying wet lawns.

The deciding factor is: do you have runner grasses like Bermuda and a half-dozen other spreading species already established? If you till them, doing so just chops up the stems and roots into hundreds of new plants that quickly root and grow. The two methods of purging weeds listed in the following sections are similar, but one requires you to use an herbicide.

Purge Method #1: No Runner Grasses

The premise for this method is based on the fact that a seed can sprout and grow only once. When you till the proposed lawn area, all the seedlings and plants already growing there will be killed as they are turned under with the soil. But this in turn exposes a whole new crop of once-buried seeds to sprout when they reach the surface. After the first tilling, water the lawn area until the new crop has just turned the surface green. Then till these under as well. Because no new seeds are being deposited in the lawn area, after the second or third tilling, the majority of weed seeds are dead and gone. This isn't perfect, but it's the best you can do.

Purge Method #2: Runner Grass Assault

If you apply method #1 to a runner grass infested lawn, you will have a worse problem than you started with. For this method to work, you need to first have the grasses growing well, which means that you may have to wait until they break out of dormancy and turn green, and the more vigorously they are growing, the more effective the treatment.

Begin by applying a translocated herbicide (see the following section "Serial Weed Killers") to the entire area. Wait a couple of weeks for it all to die. Then till in the dead plants. Water the whole area thoroughly and let it grow again until the area turns green. Make a second application of the herbicide and wait for this stand to die. By this time, what can sprout will have done so, and your soil will be as free of these weed grasses as possible. If you have a particularly bad problem, feel free to repeat the till-spray cycle again for good measure. It can't hurt.

Turf Tip

If you intend to use Roundup or other types of herbicides to purge weeds from soil, you will need a sprayer to apply it. The best kind of sprayer is a small 1-gallon all-plastic pump sprayer because, although they look cheap, they don't suffer corrosion. Corrosion inside the applicator wand and the air seals can make the sprayer misbehave. It's a really good idea to mark your sprayer for herbicide only and keep it specifically for that purpose to avoid unfortunate mistakes. Do keep the sprayer, as well as all garden chemicals, out of the reach of children.

Pump Sprayer

Serial Weed Killers

It's not politically correct, and the organic gardening crowd is against it, but there are times when you can rely on chemistry to solve certain problems. Over the years, there have been some real abuses of herbicides, but if handled and applied properly, herbicides have a place in the weed purging process. And for lawnowners with very little spare time, a spray here and a spray there can make gardening much easier.

Turf Caveat

Herbicides such as Roundup are unforgiving if you spray them on the wrong plant. This is not a problem when you're spraying a future lawn site, except if the wind is blowing. Drift of sprayed material can kill plants in adjacent planters. To avoid any mistakes, never spray herbicide on a breezy day.

Not all herbicides work the same way. They can be divided into two categories: those that kill just the green or top part, and those that kill the plant right down to the roots. Top killers are not really suited to purging weeds in lawn areas because the roots are still viable, and the plants will grow back along with your new grass.

The second group is technically called *translocated* herbicides, such as Roundup, because the chemical is distributed throughout the entire plant. You won't see effects of your spraying for at least a week, and the entire process wraps up by the end of the second week. When you spray Roundup on your weeds, they must be green and growing, because it is through photosynthesis that the product is taken into the leaves. Then it travels through the plant, finally killing it.

This is important with runner grasses because a single plant may have spread out over a large area, putting down new roots as it was growing. Don't try to use Roundup on dormant grasses, because it is only effective on actively growing weeds. Some folks even water and fertilize their weeds to speed up the intake process, but that's not recommended.

Going to Seed

To plant your lawn, you will need to first take care of the weed problem. Then you must have seed and a covering material such as sterilized steer manure, fine compost, or peat, depending on what's available locally. Plan on covering the seed with a layer about 1/4 inch thick. Also have the seed on hand. Be sure to buy enough so that you won't run out.

Step 1: Soil Prep

If there's one thing you do right when creating your new lawn it's soil preparation. Bad soil can be fixed, but the biggest problem folks have is understanding just how much it takes to make a sizable change.

To really get a sense of what seed likes, imagine someone who grows flowers from seed professionally. He prepares just the right soil mix made out of fine, lightweight things such as peat and coarse sand. This is packed into trays, and the seed is carefully scattered over the top. More fine material is sprinkled over this to the exact depth for that particular seed. If the covering is just 1/8 inch thick, you get an idea of how exacting the process can be. Too thick, and the seed won't get through the covering. Too thin, and it receives too much light, which also causes failure.

Your lawn is a lot like this because grass seed is small, but fortunately it is among the fastest plant species on earth to germinate. But you must try to create a similar bed for your seeds as the professional grower, by working up your own soils with great care. The more attention you give the seed bed, the better your progeny of seeds will grow.

Chapter 8, "Dealing with Dirt," includes a rundown on some of the most common materials used to improve soils under lawns. Till as much as you can into the soil to a minimum depth of 4 inches, but 6 inches is ideal.

Turf Tip

If you plan on an underground sprinkler system, the time to install it is after soil prep and before finish grading. This is because after the pipes and heads are in the ground, you can't run a rototiller without risking a lot of damage. Finish the tilling and soil prep, and then roughly smooth the surface, and trench for pipes. After everything is in the ground and the trenches are filled, go on to Step 2: Finish Grading.

Step 2: Finish Grading

After tilling, you'll have a very uneven surface. Use an iron rake to gradually smooth it out as evenly as possible. This may take some time and a lot of elbow grease, but it's an important step. Rake off and discard any sticks and rocks or big hard dirt clods so that the remaining surface is soft and smooth and ready to make the perfect seed bed for your seed.

During finish grading, be sure to attend to these:

➤ Fill low spots to prevent mud holes in the lawn.

➤ Rake down high spots or bumps that will be dry and scalped.

➤ Dig out any rocks or boulders you encounter in the top 6 inches of soil—these limit rooting and get hot.

➤ Rake out all sticks and pieces of root that you encounter.

Special tools called *leveling rakes* are used by greenskeepers to smooth out sand traps on golf courses. These can be wood or aluminum, and the bar that has the teeth is up to 30 inches wide. Aluminum rakes are far more durable, particularly if you have hard or rocky soils. This makes easier work of finish grading, but it's probably not worth buying for one lawn project. If you have a very large lawn, however, give it a second thought or try borrowing one from a friend, nursery, or golf course. A thatching rake might make a more accessible alternative.

Iron Bow Rake and Leveling Rake

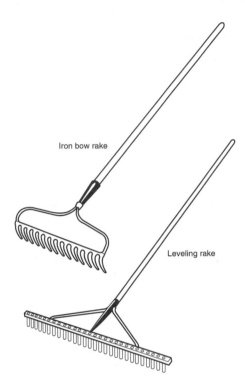

Iron bow rake

Leveling rake

During the finish grading process, you'll need to set the sprinkler heads to just the right height for your grass type. Refer to the grass mowing height chart in Chapter 10, "The Art of the Mow," for the proper level of various types of lawn grasses. Also note what the last mowing of the season height is because this is the control. Then cut that number in half so that there's no chance of ever hitting the head with the mower. For example, if the grass height is 2 inches, and you mow at the end of the season at $1^1/_2$ inches, then set the heads so that the top edge is about $^3/_4$ inch above the soil line.

Setting Heads

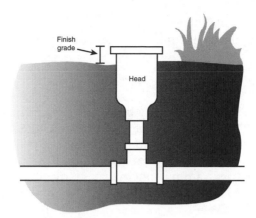

Now is the time to check sprinkler coverage. When the soil is newly graded, it shows clearly exactly how each sprinkler is performing. Turn on the system to check that all heads are covering their designated area and are properly adjusted.

Keep a watchful eye out for dry spots and fix them now. On the other hand, watch how the lawn surface dries out afterward. You will be able to see whether there are any depressions because these will still be visibly moist. Fill and grade out these as well. Even though it's a hassle, you'll find this last check and revision to the system far simpler to do right now, rather than farther down the road when the grass gets in your way.

Hydroseed Mania

Have you ever seen the crews out on the highway shooting strange colors on the newly graded slopes and edges? They aren't starting a new wave of art in public places—they're hydroseeding! The colored dye is used to show them where they've sprayed and how densely they've done it.

Hydroseed is the best way to plant large lawns from seed. Most sports fields and parks are now planted by hydroseeding because it produces a fine, even lawn for a fraction of the labor costs. The tank trucks used are filled with wood fibers, seed, dye, and water, called a *slurry*. It's mixed up evenly and then shot out of a hose under pressure to broadcast the seed complete with a nice lightweight covering of protective mulch.

This method of seeding can be used on a residential lawn, but only if it's large enough to make hydroseeding cost effective. Also, you can't really apply hydroseed to a small lawn anyway—it's like swatting a fly with a baseball bat.

If you decide to use a hydroseed contractor to plant your lawn, be sure you work with a reputable company that's been around a long time. One of the pitfalls of less-than-honest contractors is that they will cheat you to save money by:

➤ Using less seed than the recommended amount per 1,000 square feet

➤ Using a different variety than you asked for

➤ Failing to clean out their equipment so that you get more than you asked for

➤ Short-changing you on the mulch so that your seed is not adequately covered

Step 3: Broadcast Seeding

If you are planning to have the lawn hydroseeded, now is the time. There is no need for topdressing or seed cover because that is already included. The sprinkler heads should be set at their final height, and the entire surface perfectly graded for the contractor. By the way, if you have anything around the lawn such as cars, tools, toys, or other types of back-yard paraphernalia, remove it. If the hydroseeder's aim isn't great, or if the wind is blowing, there may be some unintentional spraying.

Turf Tip

The best all-around spreader for lawn planting and maintenance is the *drop spreader*. That's the one that distributes the material in the hopper along the axle. A series of teeth actually rotate as the wheels turn to move the material down and out as evenly as possible. If you have a small lawn, buy a smaller drop spreader for convenience. For a large lawn, look around for as wide a spreader as you can find because a small one means that you'll have to make many more passes to do every job from seeding to fertilizing.

Using a Spreader

To hand seed the lawn using a spreader, think about how you plan to attack the job in a most systematic way. Usually it is in stripes just like you mow. With a drop spreader, the process is simple because the wheel marks become convenient guides to remind you exactly how you made the last pass.

With a whirlybird spreader or a hand spreader, it's less obvious. You have to eyeball it by knowing approximately how far on each side of you the spreader throws the seed. Each pass must be calculated so that there is as little overlap as possible from one pass to the next. If you overlap, you'll have very dense stripes with twice the amount of grass seed than elsewhere.

A calibration adjustment on your spreader will indicate various distribution rates. You know from Chapter 7 how many pounds of seed you should apply per 1,000 square feet. Adjust your spreader accordingly, and then fill it on a paved surface so that you can check the spreading mechanism. If there is a problem or you change the rate of distribution, you can easily sweep up the seed and put it back in the hopper.

Plan to cover the lawn twice, first with a series of strips going in one direction, and then do the same in the opposite direction. This is the key to getting the most even distribution of grass on the lawn.

Step 4: Cover It Up

Grass seed must be covered evenly, and in a way that causes the least amount of damage to the seeds and seed bed surface. It's simple to insert the steer manure, compost, or peat into a drop spreader. Again, test the rate of distribution on a paved surface and then rake up the material and put it back into the hopper. Roll on this topdressing as evenly as possible, and you need not go in two directions as required with seed distribution.

A second option is the use of a peat spreader. It's like a roller, only the drum is perforated. You add the peat to the drum and, as you roll it out, the peat is distributed. Although these are commonly used for peat moss, they are useful for only one purpose, spreading peat. Unless you already have one, a drop spreader is more useful than a peat spreader.

Step 5: Roll with Caution

Never forget that the greatest enemy of lawns is soil compaction. If you have soil that tends to be claylike, roll with caution because, if you overdo it, there's no turning back. When you roll your newly seeded lawn, you are compacting it but only to a limited extent. The more water you add to the roller, the greater the compaction rate.

With seeded lawns, the roller need not have any water in it, or at most just a little because the weight can make it more difficult for the seed to root quickly. If you have sandy soils, the roller may be heavier to better smooth the surface, and sand does not suffer the ill effects of compaction, such as poor drainage or an overly dense soil mass.

Step 6: Make Rain

Your freshly planted lawn is now at its most vulnerable point. The major threats are related to water. Watering too little or too infrequently results in dryness that kills the seedlings. Too much water applied in the wrong way can also spell their demise. Like a newborn baby who needs attention around the clock, your newly planted lawn needs attention every day for the first few weeks. Your single most important goal is to keep the lawn area moist down to about 6 inches deep, and to be sure the top inch of the soil is even more moist, but not saturated. Never apply so much water that it pools anywhere on the lawn area.

How often you have to water to keep the lawn in that condition varies from place to place. The more damp and humid the climate, the less often you'll have to water to keep the seedbed damp. Also, if you have a sprinkler system, you'll be able to accomplish this much more easily than if you're using a garden hose. It is even simpler if your sprinklers can be put on a time clock that waters the lawn three times a day without your lifting a finger. No matter what method you use to water, keep a sharp eye out for dry spots that may need an extra sprinkling to get through the first week or two.

Turf Tip

It pays to be well prepared for spot watering because every lawn has its warm pockets. You'll need a nozzle that can be adjusted into a soft fan spray so that, when you need to moisten the area, you apply the water with the least amount of pressure. You don't want to risk washing out seed or knocking down the tender new shoots with the fire hose effect.

You would be surprised at how easily the seed can be washed out or the surface eroded by a little too much water. This is even more important if your lawn is sloped or on uneven terrain. The grass on the inclines will be far more vulnerable to wash out than the grass on level areas. The low points have their problems too because water may collect there, and when the rest of the lawn is ready for a shower, these areas may already be too saturated.

A Watering Primer

Chapter 17, "Water Right, Water Deep," offers much more on watering lawns, but for now it's important that you learn how to get your lawn off on the right foot. I wish I could tell you to water so many minutes each day, but like so much in horticulture, there aren't any hard and fast rules. It takes a computer like your brain to gather the information and then respond according to the data. This is not a no-brainer activity.

The real goal to watering properly is to apply water only as long as the lawn can absorb it. For heavy soils, the water absorption may be so slow that you need only water for a couple of minutes for the surface to become completely saturated. A sign of saturation is runoff or pooling water. In sandy soils, at the other extreme, you may have to water five to eight minutes with no saturation at all. This illustrates how the duration of time that you water is directly related to soil type.

Watering frequency relates more to evaporation than anything else. The higher the humidity levels, the slower the evaporation rate. If you were to take a 90-degree day, the lawn would dry out much faster if humidity was just 10 percent (Tucson) than if it was 95 percent (New Orleans). Remember that after you have seeded, but before the seeds sprout, you have a good idea of how often you need to turn on the sprinklers because of the soil color change as it dries. Use these first days as your barometer, set up a schedule that works, and stick to it.

The Virgin Mow

When you cut the top off of most plants, they will send more growth energy to the roots. It also forces the plant to grow more compactly and spread out, which explains why we pinch back houseplants to keep them bushy. The same thing applies to turf grasses, which, when newly sprouted from seed, have a natural tendency to grow upward. But turf grasses are chosen for their ability to *stool*, which means that they produce new shoots that grow outward. Early mowing encourages stooling to occur at a much greater rate, and we should support this the same way we do good posture in kids.

If you're working with a lawn seed mixture, the quick-to-germinate grasses such as perennial rye will sprout first. The slower grasses will still be in the germination stage and need sunlight. When you mow the grass, you will be heading back these early birds to create a better environment for the long termers.

Even though it seems like overkill, you should plan to mow your lawn for the first time when it's about 2 inches tall. This may be slightly higher or lower depending on the type of grass you are growing. When in doubt, err on the high side because seedlings can be badly damaged by too close a mow in their formative days.

For the first mow, be sure to treat your virgin grass with love. Don't mow when it's wet or muddy because there's no carpet of stems and roots to protect the soil from being rutted by your mower wheels. It's also kind to mow at a cool time of day. If you really care, do it just before you water, so the newly cut shoots will be bathed in moisture right away to lessen the shock.

First Feedings

If you used starter fertilizer when preparing the soil, your new lawn won't need a feeding right away. If you have notoriously poor soil though, you might want to feed a bit sooner, particularly if the new leaves are rather pale or yellow-green. If your grass needs a quick shot in the arm, it's advisable to consult your nursery for a quick diagnosis and recommended dietary supplement.

165

The Least You Need to Know

➤ Purge the soil of weeds before you plant a lawn.

➤ Improve the soil to a depth of 6 inches for best root development.

➤ Broadcast seed evenly over the entire lawn area.

➤ Be very attentive to how often and how long you water the young seedlings.

➤ Mowing encourages good posture in the maturing grass plants.

Chapter 12

Sodbusting a Turf Grass Lawn

In This Chapter

➤ Why sod is America's favorite way to plant a lawn

➤ Easy soil prep for sod

➤ Ordering and caring for your sod when it arrives

➤ How to lay a sod lawn in a weekend

➤ Watering and aftercare of your new sod lawn

Inside every one of us is a yearning for instant gratification that says six months is way too long to wait for a mature lawn to grow from seed. There's also a little voice inside our heads that hates to do yard work when we could be doing fun things instead. That six months is way too long to be surgically weeding and battling the kids, dogs, and birds that threaten the vulnerable young seedlings. You could solve the problem with Astroturf or, for a few pennies more, you can achieve overnight success by laying sod.

Sod has the unique capability to completely transform a yard or landscape in a single day. It's the ideal cover-up for bare ground, and it can be walked on almost from day one. This makes it a real problem-solver for anyone who needs a quick fix for the backyard. In fact, some folks will simply till in an old lawn and resod it for a garden party or wedding.

One of the greatest values of sod is its suitability to sloping ground. Getting seed to stick, germinate, and root on sloping ground can be difficult because water runs off so much faster there. Sodded slopes do not suffer soil erosion, and the lawn may be established instantly and evenly. For hillside lawns or on undulating terrain, sod is the best, and often the only, choice.

Here are the main reasons people prefer sodded lawns over those grown from seeds or sprigs:

➤ You get a perfect lawn from day one.

➤ The lawn will be more evenly grown in and uniformly green.

➤ You can fully use the lawn in two to three weeks.

➤ You can lay sod during almost any month of the year.

➤ There's no worry over soil erosion or runoff from bare ground.

➤ There is no need for weed control in most cases.

➤ Sod requires less water at the start.

As you read through this chapter, refer to Chapter 7, "Ladies and Gentlemen . . . Buy Your Grasses," for information on how sod is made and sold; Chapter 3, "Zoning Out on Turf Grass," for grasses that are best suited to your regional climate; and Chapter 9, "Lawn Tools and Equipment," for soil amendments.

The Grass Is Always Greener

Sod is among the few immediate erosion control plants. Reduction of runoff and its velocity is the aim of erosion control. Runoff carries away soil particles, known as *sediment*. A sod lawn is 15 times more effective in controlling runoff than seeded lawns and 10 times more effective than straw-covered soils. The velocity of runoff is 30 percent slower on sod than other soil coverings.

Getting Ready to Sod

Growing a lawn from sod is much like transplanting any other kind of plant. It is dug up at one place and replanted elsewhere. Because transplanting is always somewhat of a shock to a plant, it's best to do the project when temperatures are most neutral and grasses are actively growing. The more active the grass, the more rapidly it roots and anchors itself in the soil. Slow rooting means that the sod must be closely monitored for a longer period of time and won't look good until it finally does root deeply.

You can sod most of the year, but nobody in my neighborhood wants to be a slave to a new sod lawn any longer than is absolutely necessary. For best results, the time to sod in most climates is spring or fall. In summer, it's too hot, and that stresses the grass. In winter, it's too cold, and the sod is reluctant to grow. In places with exceptionally mild climates, sodding is done year round, but for most people, it's best to play it safe and save yourself a lot of work.

If you treat your sod gently and give it a good place to lie down, it will return the favor by growing quickly and vigorously. The most important thing you can do is to plan ahead because once the sod is in your hands, it has a limited life span until it's safely in the ground. The sod is most at risk while out of the ground in transit, and while waiting for you to lay it. Think of sod in rolls as you would a fish out of water—it won't last long.

Again with the Weeds

Even though you have fewer problems with weeds when you sod a lawn, they can still be a threat. Again, the biggest threat to sod is runner grasses, which are among the most tenacious weeds. Because most of these invaders exhibit a pronounced period of dormancy and turn brown for many months at a time, they can destroy the even green coloring of your lawn. This is particularly important in cool-season lawns where the grasses don't have a dormancy period.

Here's an example of how theory and reality don't always jibe. Theoretically, any lingering weeds under the sod will die from lack of light just as a mulch discourages weeds around other plants. But in truth, Bermuda grass in the soil under your new sod is slowed down by lack of light but retains enough life to travel around under the sod until it finds a seam. The seams between sod strips are less dense, and the stolons will always grow into areas of least resistance. If you don't do away with these weeds, or fail to rid the soil thoroughly enough, in a few months, the grasses will be showing up along the seams.

This is particularly important if you are replanting an old lawn by tilling the old grass under to lay new sod on top. If the runner grasses are already there, you should apply an herbicide first to at least put a dent in the number of living plants that survive the tilling. Keep in mind that these products require up to two weeks to be fully effective. For more information on purging weeds from your soil before laying sod, refer to the methods in Chapter 11, "Seeding a Turf Grass Lawn."

Soil Prep for Sod

A great thing about sod is that you don't have to improve and work the soil as thoroughly as you would for seeds. But when you lay sod you are transplanting, and although the new roots don't need a seed bed, they do appreciate a nice comfortable couch.

Till the entire lawn area thoroughly and as deeply as possible. Then spread your soil amendment, such as compost, sterilized steer manure, or peat. To be sure you get enough and at the same rate throughout the lawn, use a rake to spread a layer 2 to 3 inches deep over the entire surface. Then till it in all at once. This method ensures that the material is evenly distributed throughout the whole lawn and that it's incorporated into the soil to a sufficient depth.

You need not create such a fine seed bed for sod as you must for seeds. However, it's crucial that you remove all the rocks, sticks, roots, and dense dirt clods that you can. The rule of thumb for sod is to remove anything in the soil larger than 2 inches in diameter. If you live in a climate where there is soil heaving in spring, the freeze-thaw will gradually work hard objects such as rocks to the surface. These, depending on their size, can heat up in summer to burn the grass roots. Rocks can also seriously damage your mower or dull the blade. Dig up any low-lying rocks or boulders now while you can, because doing it later will leave your lawn with a big black eye.

A preplanting fertilizer is always beneficial to sod. The ideal nutrient ratio is 10-20-10, which is 10 percent nitrogen, 20 percent phosphorus, and 10 percent potassium. Phosphorus is crucial to root development, which is why it is present at roughly twice the amount of nitrogen and potassium. Addition of fertilizer now reduces the need for feeding later, which keeps you and your spreader off the new lawn.

Read the package label for the recommended application rate per 1,000 square feet to know how much fertilizer to buy. After all your tilling is complete, apply the fertilizer over the entire lawn area. Either till lightly again or use an iron bow rake to work it into the top few inches of soil. If you leave it on the surface, the fertilizer will burn the cut ends or the developing new roots on contact.

Turf Talk

Grade describes the elevation of the soil surface; *grading* describes the process of leveling and contouring a surface. The proper grade is relative to an unchanging control point—for example, a sidewalk. The finish grade of a lawn next to the sidewalk should be a little below the sidewalk. The top of the grass when freshly mowed should be at the same level as the top of the paving.

Making the Grade

The surface of the soil in lawns is always graded relative to the adjacent surfaces, such as sidewalks, slabs, or driveways. When you seed a lawn, the grade is much higher than it would be if you were to sod the lawn. Keep this in mind when adding soil amendments and topsoil to the lawn, because all of these will raise the finish grade.

If you know from the outset that your lawn is too high, the best way to work it down is to till once, and then rake off all the dirt clods and debris. This eliminates any loss of good soil in the process. For a more serious problem in shallow soils, you don't want to lower the grade by scraping off all the good topsoil. The best approach is to scrape off the topsoil, stockpile it nearby, and then reduce the elevation by removing the subsoil, which is more dense and less beneficial to plants. After that's accomplished, replace the topsoil.

Paving and Grades

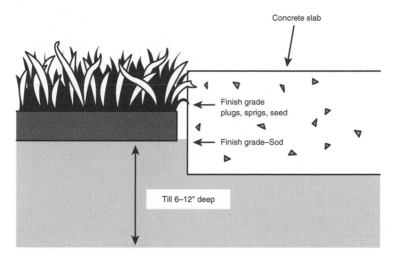

Concrete slab

Finish grade
plugs, sprigs, seed

Finish grade–Sod

Till 6–12" deep

There will be some rise in grade due to the fluffi-ness of the newly tilled soil. This will settle on its own over time after watering and foot traffic. A roller comes in handy for compressing fluffy soil. It also is a good way to work the grades around the edges of pavement to be sure that you've got the right relationships there. When you lay the sod at these critical points, you should not be able to see any roots or soil above the surface of the paving.

Finish grade is established by the thickness of the sod. Cool-season grasses tend to be thicker than warm-season grasses. Find out the overall thickness of your sod ahead of time to preset the grades. The dimension will include the height of the blades and the thickness of the soil/root mass. In general, these range from $1/2$ inch to 2 inches for the height of the grass blades, and from $5/8$ to 1 inch for the soil and roots.

Turf Caveat

Be cautious about using a roller if you have heavy clay soil, which is compacted easily when damp and newly tilled. Unless you really need it to smooth things out, you can achieve pretty good success with a rake and a little elbow grease. Save the rolling for after the sod is laid.

Sod Thickness Section

1.5"
to
2"

5/8"
to
1"

A smooth, uniform surface is important to the beauty and success of your new sod. It's also crucial to its health. Every dip or lump in the soil will be reflected in the sod, just like a golf ball or dinner plate under a new carpet. The sod may become too wet in the dips and rot, or it may dry out on the bumps that create air pockets. Air in this vital rooting zone can cause drying of roots, which immediately kills them and inhibits their penetration into the soil.

When you buy your soil amendments and fertilizer, purchase a few bags of really fine compost. Set these aside for later to cover vulnerable joints and exposed edges so that they don't dry out and turn brown. An ounce of edge protection saves a pound of sod patching any day of the week.

Turf Caveat

You are not required to accept your sod delivery if it's in bad shape. Be home the day it's delivered so that you can inspect it. The sod rolls should be neatly stacked and the soil edges damp. Sod should be green, healthy, and visibly fresh. If you're not home to reject a substandard load, exchanging it will be difficult.

Sod Pallets

Even though you can buy sod directly from sod farms, it's always better to work through your local nursery. Even though you pay a slight markup, if there are problems, the nursery owner will help you resolve them. Sod farms just aren't geared for the kind of personal service you get with retail nurseries.

When you order your sod, you will calculate the amount based on the size of your lawn in square feet. Just give that number to the nursery or sod retailer, and they will determine how much sod you need to buy. They will charge you by the square foot, so if you want to do some last-minute comparison shopping around town, use the square-foot price indicator.

You have to be organized enough at this point to know when you want the sod to be delivered. Sod is at its freshest when it is cut and delivered on the same day, or within a 24-hour time span. It's also a good idea to be there to accept the sod, or the delivery persons will simply place it in your driveway.

Sod is rolled up and stacked on wood pallets that are transported on big semitrailer rigs. A pallet usually contains about 500 square feet of sod, so you can figure out how many pallets to expect ahead of time. The driver also has a forklift that will offload the pallet and place it wherever you want. The pallet is heavy and impossible for you to move by hand, so be sure you get it placed right the first time.

If possible, position your pallet in the shade so that it remains fresh and cool for as long as possible. Choose locations close to your work area because this reduces the amount of carrying you need to do while laying the sod. If you have an exceptionally large lawn or a number of different smaller ones, ask the driver to place the pallets at points most convenient for each individual lawn. Do be aware that the pallets can only be placed where there is access to the forklift.

Sod's Limited Shelf Life

Strive to lay your sod immediately after delivery. The longer the sod is rolled up, particularly in warm weather, the greater the chance of rot or a half-dozen other unsavory problems. But life isn't always predictable, and if you are not able to do the job as soon as planned, then do your best to protect the sod until you can get out there. Each day that passes, the sod loses strength and the greater time it will take to become established.

If it will be a few days or up to a week, move the sod out of direct sunlight. Tighten any rolls that have loosened up because gaps expose roots to drying air. Wrap plastic around the sod rolls and poke holes in it to allow some oxygen exchange. You can also cover the pallet with a tarp to preserve moisture. This is critical if it's windy. If the sod appears to be drying out despite these protections, sprinkle it lightly with a hose to remoisten the exposed edges.

Turf Tip

After you lay your sod lawn, don't throw away any leftover rolls or sod pieces. They may be needed to patch brown spots or unexpected die-out in the new lawn. To preserve their viability, choose a shady, out-of-the-way place and use compost to make a nice bed at least 2 inches thick. Lay out the sod on the loose compost and water it well. The pieces will root into the soft compost instead of regular soil. If you need patching, you can simply peel up a piece and use it just like a patch for indoor carpeting.

Getting Laid

At this point, your new lawn area should be graded or rolled to a nice even surface. Unless it is already very damp, water the lawn generously, but not so much that it runs off or pools on the surface. If it's slow to absorb water, turn on the sprinklers a few times, but for a short duration each time. This will gradually move the dampness down deeper without causing surface problems. The soil should be evenly moist to a depth of 6 inches overall.

If you've ever pieced a quilt, worked a jigsaw puzzle, or laid carpet or bricks, you can lay sod in your sleep. The single most important thing to remember is to make the joints very tight. That means the joints on all four sides of each sod strip need to be butted up tightly against one another. Don't stretch or yank on the sod to tighten the joints, lay the sod closer and force the edges down. And never overlap the sod pieces, because the part on top always dies.

Sod Pattern

This is important because the edges are the most vulnerable parts of the sod piece. Sod is a real tattle-tale if you don't get it right. The edges of pieces laid too loosely will begin to turn color, probably brown or yellow, and then they will die, leaving the joint patterns fully visible. A well-laid sod lawn won't have much, if any, evidence of joints, because every inch of grass survived.

Here are the basic guidelines to follow:

➤ Before you begin, look at the location of the sod rolls and the configuration of the lawn. You don't want to "paint yourself into a corner" by choosing a starting point that forces you to walk across the new sod. Begin at the farthest distance and work your way back toward the sod pallet walking as much as possible on the soil.

➤ It's best to begin laying your sod along a straight line such as a driveway or sidewalk. This will help prevent curving of the sod pattern, because a small bend can become very pronounced as you work your way across the lawn.

➤ Stagger each row of sod so that the joints of one row are offset from those of the next. This helps distribute joints evenly across the lawn and increases stability when you walk on it.

➤ If you are sodding a slope, always lay the sod horizontally across the face, and staggering is even more important here. If it is an unusually steep slope, use wood pegs or U pins made out of wire coat hangers to stabilize each piece. Gravity and heavy watering can cause sod to sag under the combined weight.

➤ Use a sharp knife to cut the sod. Dull blades cause you to hack and tear. The knife should slide easily through the sod so that the cut roots heal cleanly. You'll have to cut the sod at the ends to make the last piece fit properly. Don't forget to save the pieces for patching.

Protecting Gaps and Edges

When you have finished laying out the sod, note where edges and joints are exposed. If you fail to cover and protect them, they will turn brown in just a few days. This is most often found around edges not bounded by benderboard or concrete mow strips. The exposed soil and roots need to be protected with a mound of compost a couple of inches deep. Pack the compost down tightly so that it doesn't wash away when you water. If you find any joints or odd connections that appear somewhat exposed, press the compost in the cavities so that the sod roots will grow into them quickly.

Edge Treatments

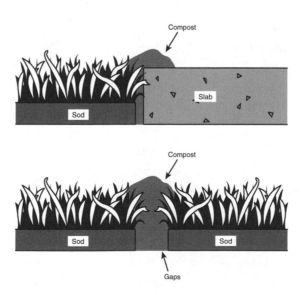

175

Roll Another One

You don't always need to roll the sod, but it looks better and makes a more even surface if you do. It also reduces the "squishiness" factor when it's walked on during the first couple of weeks. The roller pushes the sod roots down to make better contact with the soil and removes any air pockets between the bottom of the sod and the surface of the soil. Roll lightly, with no water or very little water in the roller to prevent crushing the grass or overcompacting the soil.

Aftercare for Sod Lawns

Having had all its roots chopped off, the sod won't be feeling too well. It will take a while to heal the wound, and because the roots are such a functional part of the grass plant, they have to get up and running as fast as possible.

The first days after you lay the new sod will be its most vulnerable time. Each severed root end is working hard to send out new hairs to immediately suck up water and nutrients, and these are followed by thicker, more tangible roots that are the real feeders. They need to grow as deeply as possible to the access as much soil as possible.

It won't kill your sod if you have to walk on it occasionally, but try to keep the kids and the family dog off. Walking on the sod crushes those fragile little hairs, which causes a temporary setback in root development.

The Water Regime

A water regime is simply a program for systematic watering rather than the "shoot from the hip" approach. Using rules and guidelines helps you water more effectively, avoid water waste, and get your sod off to a happy, healthy start. The overall goal is to keep the soil beneath the sod evenly moist but not super saturated for the first two weeks.

Water the lawn within 30 minutes of laying the last sod strip. Fully saturate the entire lawn on this first go-around. Ideally, it needs an inch of water, but because that's difficult to gauge, water until there is substantial runoff.

Plan to turn on the sprinklers at least twice a day, every day for the first week. Early morning watering is the most important because that's the time of day the grass is most actively growing. Sometimes during very hot or dry weather you may need to give it a sip during lunch, or in the heat of the afternoon, especially if it's looking wilted, bluish in color, or pale.

Keep a sharp eye out over the first three to five days for signs of discoloration in the grass. This will be the early warning sign that there is a spot problem with the sod, or that you aren't watering deeply enough.

Problems with incomplete coverage, or clogged, maladjusted, or misaligned sprinkler heads will show up now like a sore thumb. Yellow, brown, or unusually pale grass are signs of inadequate water. In very hot conditions, the radiant heat from paving can actually burn sod. You can protect vulnerable spots by hand watering with the garden hose until the sod is established. If discoloration persists, decide how best to make repairs.

If you're not sure whether you're giving the sod enough water during the first few days, peel up the edge of different pieces around the lawn to check the moisture content of the soil beneath. Stick a screw driver into the soil to verify how deeply the water has penetrated. Later on when you can't pull up the sod to check without damaging the new roots, stab the screwdriver down through the sod to see if you have the same resistance. The wetter it is, the easier it will be to insert the tool.

If you have planted young trees in the lawn, you need to be sure that their roots are receiving enough water. A young tree planted from its container has a limited rootball. The sprinklers may not be able to apply enough water to filter down and completely saturate the rootball. If temperatures are unusually warm and or dry, set the garden hose at the base of the trunk, turn it on to just a bare trickle, and leave it for a couple of hours or overnight. This ensures that the water is concentrated where it can wet the center of the rootball thoroughly.

Deep Water Trees

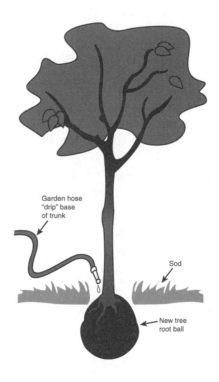

Garden hose "drip" base of trunk

Sod

New tree root ball

At the end of the first two-week period of intensive watering, you can begin to cut back. It's best to water in the early morning hours, about 4 to 6 A.M. because most people aren't out of bed and in the shower yet. This makes sure that the municipal water system is at peak pressure, which in turn ensures that your sprinkler system is also functioning at optimal flow and pressure rates.

Avoid watering often and for short periods. You want the sod roots to grow as deeply as possible because this has a big influence on the overall health and beauty of your lawn. To encourage deep watering, water less frequently but water longer. Be aware of just how long it takes for runoff to occur and time your watering accordingly.

First Feedings

Plan to fertilize your lawn four to six weeks after you laid the sod. If you fertilize too soon, your efforts may be wasted because grass that has few roots cannot draw up the nutrients. And the fertilizer may be a little strong on the healing root ends. If you added the preplanting fertilizer before you laid the sod, this will provide a good supply of nutrients early on.

Each type of grass requires a slightly different fertilizer regime, and for more on formulas and application rates refer to Chapter 16, "The Basic Food Groups."

A Clean Cut

You can expect to mow the lawn for the first time from 10 days to 2 weeks after it was laid. For best results, have the mower blade sharpened beforehand so that it cuts cleanly without any tearing or tugging. Mow when the lawn is on the dry side so that your weight and that of your mower are easier on the newly developing roots. Mow a little on the high side the first time out so that there's no risk of scalping, because without a fully mature root system, the plants can't heal top growth damage as quickly.

Problematic Projections

Fortunately, it's not common to have problems with new sod lawns, but problems sometimes do occur. One of my clients had a new sod lawn die out in enormous patches a couple of weeks after it was laid. After much frustration, he found out that the sod had been shipped with a disease, a rare kind of virus that proliferated in the new location. Needless to say, the old sod was ripped out, the lawn area treated for the virus, and new sod was laid, all at the expense of the contractor.

If this or anything similar happens to your lawn, you should know your rights as a consumer. The nursery industry has an obligation to guarantee all the plants it sells whether trees, flowers, or sod. This is because the death or signs of illness in a new plant is assumed to be a preexisting problem, unless some other planting or aftercare negligence can be identified. Your sod is equally guaranteed, and if it dies for no apparent reason, don't assume you are to blame.

If your new sod starts to act strangely, watch it closely and see if there's anything going on in the yard that might be a physical cause. Small discolorations due to dry spots or dog urine are to be expected, but if you see something growing worse by the day, or big patches of black, yellow, brown, or white grass, call your sod supplier immediately. The supplier should send someone out to diagnose the problem. If it proves to be a preexisting condition, the company is required to replace part or all of the sod.

The Least You Need to Know

➤ Prepare to lay sod by improving the soil, grade the surface smoothly, and time the sod delivery.

➤ Keep your sod moist and in the shade until you can get it laid.

➤ Sod requires two weeks of attentive care to get off on the right foot.

➤ Frequent and thorough watering is critical to both the survival and vigor of new sod.

Chapter 13

Planting a Lawn from Sprigs, Plugs, and Stolons

In This Chapter

➤ Which grasses are grown from sprigs, plugs, and stolons

➤ Ways to ensure your grass plants are most viable

➤ How to prepare the ground for planting

➤ Ways to set grids that help you plant on even spacings

➤ Weed control until the lawn fills in

In certain parts of America, only a few turf grasses will survive due to weather, insects, and some soil conditions. In the southern Gulf coast or Florida, for example, there aren't that many choices because only a few grasses can be expected to make a nice lawn. Most of these grasses are warm-season varieties that are more often planted vegetatively than any other way.

In this hostile territory, only the most vigorous warm-season grasses can be expected to thrive. They are described in detail in earlier chapters if you want a complete family history. Here is a review of some of their most important characteristics:

➤ They spread quickly by running stems.

➤ They turn brown in winter and go dormant for a few months.

➤ Tough blades and stems may require special lawn mowers.

➤ They tend to accumulate thatch more quickly than other grasses.

➤ They are almost always planted vegetatively.

Which Grasses Grow from Which

Sprigs, plugs, and stolons are all fundamentally the same thing—plantlets. They are pieces of one plant that are broken or torn off to be replanted elsewhere. Here's the short version of how they differ:

➤ Sprigs: Leaves, some stem, roots, but no soil

➤ Stolon: Stem with some leaves, but no roots

➤ Plugs: Leaves, stem, roots, and soil

Sprig, Plug, and Stolon

Sprig   Plug   Stolon

Exactly how you plant your warm-season grass lawn depends on what is being sold locally. In general, though, there are recommended forms for specific grasses. You also need to know the spacing because this tells you how far apart to put each one, which in turn tells you how many plantlets you need to fill a particular area. You can expect your lawn to fill in after a few weeks with Bermuda, but most grasses, except zoysia, average about two months.

The spacings recommended in this chapter are determined by the growers who weigh how much a lawn costs per square foot to plant against the number of weeks or months it takes to fill in the gaps. The optimal spacing balances both of these concerns, but if you're not a patient soul and have a problem with pulling weeds in the gaps until it fills in, then you can break the rules.

Obviously, if you plant sprigs 6 inches apart, the lawn will fill in twice as fast as if you plant them 12 inches apart. But at 6-inch spacings, you have to buy twice the number of sprigs, so you pay more to save on time. If you've got the cash, throw fiscal responsibility out the window and plant closer . . . Mom says it's okay.

All the following grasses are spaced at 12 inches on center. Hybrid Bermuda grass is sold as sprigs or plugs. Centipede grass is sold as sprigs. St. Augustine goes in with plugs, as does buffalo grass. Zoysia grass is the oddball planted from plugs spaced at 6 inches on center due to its slower growth rate. A zoysia lawn can take a whopping two years to reach complete coverage!

On-center Grid Spacing

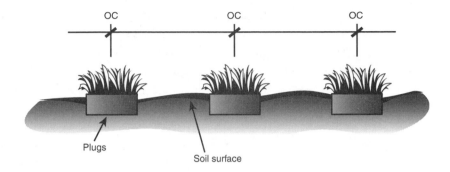

Spot Sodding

Spot sodding is a technique that takes advantage of the simplicity of commercial sod, but is much less expensive because you need only a small amount. Many of the warm-season grasses mentioned previously are sold as sod.

To spot sod a lawn, you simply cut a sod roll into pieces and plant them in lieu of sprigs or plugs. It's more work to do the cutting, but it saves you buying bushels of plugs or sprigs, which are more perishable than rolls of fresh sod.

Spot sodding uses pieces about 2 to 3 inches square. These are spaced about 6 inches apart, but some people use larger pieces and space them more widely. Either way, when you plant the pieces, you do so with the same accuracy as you would sprigs or plugs for even coverage, and then use a trowel to dig a hole for each piece.

Spot Sodding

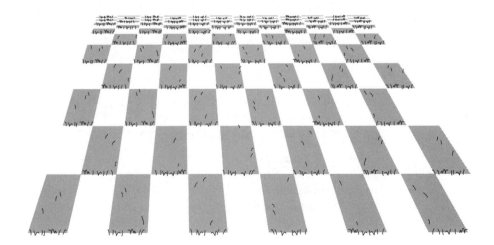

Vulnerable Purchases

When you buy sprigs, you buy plantlets that feel naked in public. Their roots, usually cloaked in moist soil, are bare and vulnerable. They are dug out of the fields, piled in bushel baskets, and sent to you. The more time that passes between the field and your soil, the weaker they become.

When you buy a bare root tree from the nursery at the end of winter, that tree is dormant, so, if the roots are exposed, it's less threatening; but lawns are planted during the growing season, and even though the roots are bare on your sprigs, the leaves are still actively breathing.

This process requires moisture, and after the leaves consume all that is stored in the stems, they will wilt. The only way to slow it down is to keep the sprigs in a cool, dark place where they have no light to stimulate photosynthesis. It must be moist there too so that the skin of the roots doesn't end up dry like a bad case of chapped lips.

When your sprig order arrives, be sure to check it over as carefully as you would salad lettuce, because you don't want to be a victim of bad nursery work. The sprigs should be moist and fresh, preferably newly dug. It's a good idea to get them home right away—don't go to the supermarket or shopping while they're in your car. Heat is their greatest enemy while in transit.

Once home, spray them with the hose and keep them out of sun and wind. Plan to get them into the ground immediately because even under the best circumstances, it is not a good thing to store this kind of material. Remember, the longer you delay, the more reluctant the plants will be to get started once in the ground.

Making Their Bed

Soil preparation for planting sprigs, plugs, stolons, or for spot sodding is the same as that for a seeded lawn. Because each of them will be planted, you must set the grade for a seeded lawn as well, unlike sod where you must accommodate the thickness of each strip. Refer to Chapter 8, "Dealing with Dirt," and Chapter 11, "Seeding a Turf Grass Lawn," for details on soil preparation, grading, and preplanting weed control.

Laying Out the Grid

Most of the plantlets are laid out at 12-inch spacings. Imagine your whole lawn as a giant checkerboard with the squares being 1 foot by 1 foot. That's a lot of squares! If the lawn is to grow evenly and fill in without any barren spots, you have to plant on a rigid grid.

The easiest way to achieve this is to use a string line with wooden stakes. It's best to use the yellow nylon carpenter's twine because, if you trip over kite string, it breaks, and you have to start all over again. If you don't have some wooden stakes on hand, buy a bundle when you get the twine. Be sure to use a hammer to pound in the stakes because, if you're wimpy about it, they will begin to lean under pressure.

String Grid

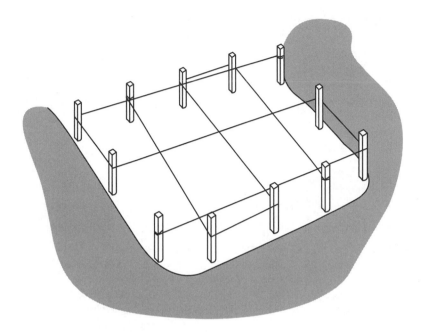

To section your lawn at 1-foot increments, begin on one edge and pound a stake every 12 inches. Go to the opposite edge and pound in as many corresponding stakes at the same intervals. Then tie your carpenter's twine to the first stake and cross the lawn to its partner and wrap it around this one so that there's reasonable tension. Step over to the next stake on your left or right, and tie the twine around this one too. Walk the twine back across the lawn to the corresponding stake and continue going back and forth.

You probably won't have enough twine and stakes to lay out the whole lawn at once. So make as many passes as you can, and then tie off the twine so that it stays tight. You can plant this portion of the lawn first, and then pull up all the stakes and lay out the next section.

If you were to plant on an actual checkerboard grid, you would have obvious rows of plantlets. To make a more natural appearance, you can plant on a *diagonal*. This means that you plant one row, and then plant the next one so that these plantlets are aligned with the spaces between those of the first row. Then the third row follows the exact pattern of the first row. By the way, this is the best way to plant groundcovers and masses of bedding plants for a better visual effect.

Square Spacing Versus Diagonal Spacing

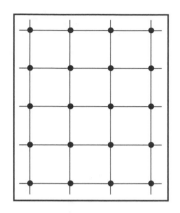 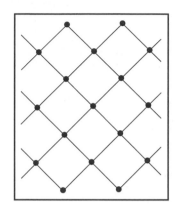

Planting Like a Square

The twine gives you a guideline to work from, but you'll need a spacing tool—a simple stick 12 inches long is ideal. When you plant, simply begin at the start of the first string line. Plant the first plantlet. Then measure with the stick 1 foot down to the center of the next plantlet. Continue all the way across the lawn. Then turn and do the same on the next string line, but alternate the plants so that you will produce diagonal spacing. Continue this way across the whole lawn.

To plant a sprig use a *dibble*, which is a long, narrow trowel, or a hand bulb-planting tool you'll find at practically any garden center or nursery. Feel free to use anything else you can get your hands on that digs the right size hole for you. There are special tools to speed up the process, designed to create a hole consistent with the size and diameter of a standardized plug. You simply punch the hole and then drop the plug right in and firm up the soil.

Planted Plug

Put your sprigs or plugs in a small bucket or basket that's easy to carry and refill it as you need to. Don't drag that bushel basket around with you; it slows things down.

When you plant a plug or a small square of sod, there will be soil attached. The roots in that soil mass can be very dense and the entire thing must be planted safely underground. If planted too high, the top edges will dry out and the roots inside will do so as well. This slows down the vigor of the grass, which in turn extends the time until the lawn fills in.

This is why it's critical that you dig a hole that is 1 inch wider and deeper than the root and soil mass. Set the plug in the hole so that the point at which the leaf blades and the soil meet is exactly level with the surrounding soil surface.

Then gently press the soil in around the root mass of each individual plant. The goal is to eliminate air pockets around the roots without squashing the roots and stems.

Turf Tip

Your soil is going to take a beating while you plant these little plants all over its surface. Deep footprints are not good for the finished lawn, so if you are big or exceptionally heavy, try to distribute your body weight over a larger area. One way to do this is to use a piece of plywood about 1 foot wide and 2 feet long. This shape fits between your string lines, and you can stand or kneel on it. Rather than 200 pounds on two size-11 feet, you spread it out over two much larger square feet!

Sticking Stolons

If you're planting stolons, which are pieces of runner grass stems that have no roots, the game plan is slightly different. Stolons are composed of a series of segments separated by nodes or joints. Roots will form wherever a node or joint touches the soil. When this occurs, stems and leaves grow on the joints that are exposed to sunlight. The trick is to keep the stolon green and alive long enough for it to produce roots of sufficient size to draw more moisture from the soil.

Planting method #1 requires you to insert one end of the stolon into damp soil so that at least one joint is underground. While in the soil, that part of the stolon won't dry out as quickly and buys time for rooting. This method requires you to use the string line and plant at the recommended intervals.

Planting Stolon on End

Planting method #2 eliminates the need to use string lines and goes much faster. It's is a lot like seeding a lawn and requires a spreader tool and a good supply of steer manure or peat as a topdressing. Anything you use to cover seed can work for this process.

Prepare the lawn surface just the same way as you would for seed. Then hand distribute the stolons evenly over the whole lawn surface. They will be lying down on the job rather than standing erect like in method #1. Wherever a stolon node contacts earth, that side will produce roots; on the opposite side, stems and leaves will develop later on.

Broadcast Planting of Stolons

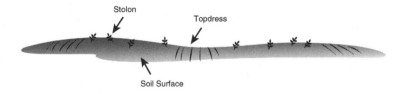

Stolon

Topdress

Soil Surface

Keep in mind, this is not an exact science, and you may want to buy extra stolons just in case you broadcast them too densely and run out at the end. The stolons must now be covered like seed with a thin layer of finely ground peat, compost, or manure using a drop spreader or perforated roller. This reduces the chance of their drying out before they have an opportunity to grow roots. If you use a drop spreader, it helps to roll the finished lawn with an empty water roller to lightly pack the covering down around the individual stolons.

Some people like to cover their sprigs with a special kind of roller that's perforated with evenly spaced holes about the size of a dime. This tool has a door where you shovel in fine compost, and, as you roll the sprigs, or stolons, and even spot sod, the material is evenly distributed over the entire area. This is a good tool to rent or borrow if you're planting this type of lawn but isn't really cost effective to buy.

Perforated Roller

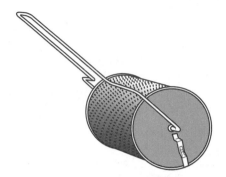

Cover-ups

No matter what kind of sprigs or plugs you use, there will be a lot of bare ground on that lawn between the new plantlets. This is the most vulnerable part of the project because the ground can dry out quickly in hot, dry, or windy weather. One of the main reasons these areas are covered with a mulch is to help keep the soil evenly moist on all sides of the plantlets as they suffer through culture shock.

Each plantlet needs to be lured out of its comfortable shell to start some adventurous growing into new uncharted territory. It takes bait, something grass plants like. Think about it: would you want to grow out into a dry, cracked, hostile soil? Probably not. You'd prefer to venture into cool, moist, soft ground where your developing roots won't have to fight for every centimeter of growth.

Coverage of all the exposed soil with compost or topdressing products designed for lawns shades the soil, helps retain even moisture, and eliminates sun-baked hardening. It also helps discourage weed growth from any seeds left in the soil, but won't stop it entirely. If you're in doubt about how much to use, just think like the plant . . . and be generous.

Sprinkle, Sprinkle Little Lawn

In some cases, lawns are planted while the soil is relatively dry to avoid problems with mud. It's most important in heavy clay soils or when clay layers are just inches below the surface. Clay soil is often called "plastic" because when it's wet, it can be shaped and will retain that shape to rock hardness after it dries out. This is best illustrated by ceramic pottery or bricks, both of which are made with wet clay and then super heated in a kiln to further the dried hardness. In saturated clay garden soil, footprints are forever.

Whether you began with a dry or damp soil bed for your new lawn, those little plant-lets, no matter what kind they are, need immediate watering. When you plant anything in the garden from trees to bedding flowers, you must water them well right after to collapse air pockets around the roots. If you don't water, the air pockets will dry and kill the roots in and around them. After planting plugs and sprigs, you need to water generously for the same reason.

If the soil connected to your plugs or spot sod dries out before or during planting, you need to be sure each one is thoroughly moistened. Sometimes a sprinkler system gets the surface wet, but the cores of the plugs are still on the dry side. If you see any of these turning bluish after planting, it's because the roots are too dry. Plan to hand water any that appear to be suffering so that they will recover and start growing more quickly.

With seeded lawns, you must water frequently over the first few weeks because the seedlings can dry out in a day and be irreparably damaged. With sprigs or plugs, this is not so crucial. What is most important is that you water deeply so that the soil is moist to the depth of the bottom of the plug hole.

If you water just on the surface, the roots an inch or so down will suffer from lack of moisture. This in turn forces growth energy into the remaining surface roots, which in the long run makes your mature lawn far less tolerant of drought. Deep rooting is crucial to the health and vigor of your lawn, and reduces watering frequency in the future.

Keep a sharp eye out for areas that are over dry, and if you have an in-ground sprinkler system, this is the time to make adjustments. You can sometimes adjust the sprinkler head or replace it with one that shoots farther. You can also add an extra head while the sprigs and plugs are still small.

Turf Tip

Grasses have a silent language that shows you when they want water. Be observant of these symptoms and be a good listener:

➤ Grass takes on a darker, almost blue-green hue when it can't draw enough moisture up from the roots.

➤ Grass blades roll up into tubes, which reduces their leaf surface and lowers water demand.

➤ When you walk on the lawn, your footprints remain behind because thirsty grass can't spring back the way it should.

Save Our Soil

One of the most vulnerable parts of your newly planted lawn is the bare soil, and you must be attentive to how you water if it is to stay put. Some soil types will be more vulnerable than others, so watch closely over the first few weeks. One of the best ways to preserve soil is to ensure that the protective mulch of compost stays in place.

Bare soil, particularly if it's on a slope of any kind, is an erosion disaster just waiting to happen. When it rains or you water, what isn't absorbed into the soil becomes runoff. When raindrops fall on the soil, they dislodge a few soil particles. The runoff then carries these particles away.

If the runoff is moving at a fast rate, it will scour even more soil particles from the surface. When there is uncontrolled, concentrated runoff, you get the most visible part of soil erosion, little gullies and depressions where the soil has been carried away.

The effects of soil erosion can be seen in two ways. The first one was just described, the scouring and removal of soil by fast-moving water. The second effect is that wherever the water slows down, the particles settle out in a sediment deposit.

Wicked Weeds

The single greatest challenge you face after planting from sprigs or plugs is weed control. With all that bare soil, weeds have a free-for-all, and any seed or rootlets present in the soil when you plant will indeed sprout under the tender-loving care you lavish on all those plantlets. With the worst-case-scenario grass type, zoysia, you can expect a battle that can last up to two years. With most of the others, plan to weed often for the next 60 days.

Weed seed can become airborne and come flying into your carefully prepared lawn. Even if you were diligent in the preplanting weed control, wind-borne seeds and those transported by birds are destined to arrive.

Some of these weeds will be easy to get rid of, whereas others, if not immediately slaughtered, will remain to infest your mature lawn. Remember, a mature lawn crowds out weeds because the grasses cover the ground so densely. But your new sprigged lawn may take quite a while to achieve that self-weeding capability.

Many people use herbicides to control weeds in the bare spots of their developing lawn. These over-the-counter products are easy to use, and you are assured that the spray will kill any weed permanently right down to its roots. This is particularly valuable in the first couple of weeks when any residual runner grasses make their appearance. A careful spray will kill them no matter how much root and under-ground stem is hidden beneath the surface. Once established, these grasses can ruin a new lawn.

191

The danger lies in the fact that the slightest breeze can carry the spray onto your plantlets. Remember, when planted a foot apart, there is no room for error and, with each week that passes, the bare soil gaps grow ever smaller. For this reason, many people use herbicides at first, but switch to hand weeding after a while when it's no longer safe to use them. See Chapter 11 for details on safe and effective herbicide use.

Manual weeding takes more time and energy, but it's much safer. You can use a hoe to scrape off more benign weeds without stooping or bending, and then rake them all up for removal. This is more realistic if you have a large lawn but do not want to use herbicide.

You get down and pull the weeds by hand, which is best done while the soil is nice and moist, because this allows the roots to slide out easily. If dry, the roots are more tenacious, forcing the plant to break off at the base of the stem and leaving the rest to grow again another day.

Pay careful attention to how you pull weeds such as wild morning glory (bindweed) and clovers, which have extensive underground root networks. Unless you get the bulk of the roots out, they will come back with a vengeance. Some people dig these out to get the whole thing, which makes a big mess. A careful spray when they first appear can completely stop these altogether.

Dandelions and others with a single, thick, fleshy taproot require you get the majority of that carrotlike root out of the ground. If it doesn't come out in one piece, you have to dig down to extract the rest of the root. If you find a large number of taproot weeds in your lawn, buy a simple root cutter, which can be inserted down beside the taproot to sever it at the bottom. Using a combination of root cutter and very moist soil really cuts down on the work to remove these unwanted plants.

Weed Root Types

Tap root

Fibrous roots

192

The Virgin Mow

With a seeded lawn, the first few times you mow are rough on the seedlings. But a sprig or plug lawn is far more forgiving. In fact, the weight of the mower passing over the plantlets actually encourages them to spread faster. Because these are newly transplanted plantlets, it's important that you allow them to become firmly established, which may require them to reach 5 inches tall before they will withstand mowing.

Do be careful not to mow the lawn too short at this time because scalping can cause the plants to be stressed. Most will stop growing temporarily until they heal.

While there is still bare soil visible, mow your lawn when it is on the dry side. If too moist, the mower wheels can make visible ruts in the soft ground. Follow these mowing tips during the first few months after planting:

➤ Mow grass when it is dry and at the proper height for that type of grass.

➤ Don't mow when exposed soils are wet to avoid ruts.

➤ Use caution the first few times you mow the lawn on slopes.

➤ Keep mower blades very sharp to prevent dislodging sprigs or plugs.

➤ Use the right kind of mower for your grass type; hybrid Bermuda requires a reel not a rotary mower.

➤ Be sure your broadcast stolon lawn is well anchored by roots before the first mowing.

Greedy Grasses

The turf grasses most often planted from sprigs or plugs are among the highest nitrogen users of all. They will require fertilizing after the second mowing, with a mild formula used half strength. While there is a lot of bare space, you can try a water-soluble fertilizer that you can spray on to concentrate it where the plants are and nowhere else.

Plan to fertilize warm-season grasses two to four weeks after they green up in spring. This makes sure that they are growing actively enough to gobble up a meal. Then feed every six to eight weeks until the onset of dormancy.

The Least You Need to Know

➤ Planting sprigs or plugs is a lot like planting flowers.

➤ Space plants 1 foot apart and plant on a grid.

➤ Lawns usually take about two months to fill in.

➤ Pay attention to how you water and weed the bare spots.

Chapter 14

Planting an Alternative Lawn

In This Chapter

➤ The beauty of natural lawns

➤ Natural grasslands as models

➤ Alternative lawns with other plants along with grasses

➤ Alternative lawns as havens for wildlife

It appears that the medieval lawn was not the pure grass sward that we strive to obtain today but more an imitation of a natural meadow containing flowers.

—Peter Hunt

We often assume that newer is better—that our modern conception is automatically better in every way than the ideas and practices of our ancestors. Yet, we in America have raised the concept of the lowly meadow with all its vibrant diversity to an homogenous monoculture that offers little but a flat green carpet.

Of all the legacies of the 1960s, the expanded view of horticulture has proven to be truly sustainable. A preference for natural living manifested itself in many ways. Quantities of plants appeared in homes and offices, making living spaces more soothing. A desire for organically grown vegetables made the home garden more than just a means of saving money at the grocery store. It even fostered an entire movement to gather and protect the varieties of food plants that would have otherwise disappeared in the wake of new, improved, mega-farming cultivars.

In terms of the home lawn, the legacy of this revolution has been interest in a more holistic suburban grassland. These follow models of native ecosystems of prairie and meadow that are naturally adapted to climate, rainfall, and soil conditions.

Turf Grass Counter Culture

You might call alternative lawns "hippie grasses" because they have long hair and sometimes look a bit unruly. But if you study an alternative lawn for any period of time, you will see butterflies and bees along with a variety of birds, all interacting with the grasses and flowers. This beauty draws us, but for many, this new concept is an essential problem solver for challenges faced by American homeowners.

Drought is a big problem in the west and other regions where population growth is exceeding the infrastructure's capability to deliver water. Water rationing during certain seasons may eliminate the traditional lawn, and although new turf grasses will survive with far less water, they don't look good when continually stressed. Native perennial bunch grasses are not only adapted to dry seasons, but they also need not be mowed so closely, so soil is shaded and retains its moisture more efficiently.

Traditional turf grass lawns must be mowed regularly to look their best. Alternative lawns are mowed only to renew the planting, which is also called a *stand*. Whether this is in the spring or the fall, just once a year is far more attractive to many homeowners than every weekend. Plus, there's less demand for fertilizer, so this task may be just once a year as well.

Natural grasslands have also proven to be ideal treatments for areas too steep for a regular lawn. The extensive rooting characteristics and surface coverage are vital for erosion control. In addition, these plants rush into ground where all turf grasses fear to tread.

Alternative lawns have always been a part of the rural homestead. It's difficult for people accustomed to a 50-by-75-foot back yard to understand how to treat 3- or 5-acre homesites. Traditionally, farmers planted pasture grasses around these homes, and wildflowers naturally worked their way into the stands. Today's high-tech communications let so many of us live in rural areas that more and more folks are faced with the dilemmas of how to cover acres rather than square feet of lawn.

Turf Talk

The term *native* when applied to plants means that the species originated in a particular place. For example, buffalo grass is native to South Dakota. It's also relative because buffalo grass is also native to North America. Plants are called *exotic* when they are not native to a given area. A grass native to North Carolina becomes an exotic when it appears in California.

Before You Go Native

There is indeed a stigma attached to alternative lawns. In some suburban communities, planting laws dictate that grasses are not to exceed 4 to 8 inches in height. This is particularly true in planned communities with rigid covenants, codes, or restrictions written to make sure that everyone's front yard looks exactly the same. If you violate the regulations, you can be fined for each day the problem is not rectified. Sometimes you can do whatever you want in the back yard as long as it's not visible from the street.

There's also a social stigma to consider. Let's face it, America is full of Hank Hills who believe that one's lawn is a reflection of one's self. Many people think that long grass is nothing more than an unmowed lawn, sign of negligent, low-class living. If you are in this scenario, be sure you are ready to deal with some disapproving stares as you enjoy the monarch butterflies feeding off your prairie coneflowers when walking out to get the morning paper.

The Green, Green Grass of Home

The term *alternative lawn* is generic. It simply means a grass area that isn't a traditional mowed, turf grass lawn. Yet, like all things generic, there are many brands or adaptations, each with its own origins, components, and purpose.

Native Grassland

This is the purist's alternative lawn. Native grasses are a specific group most often found in grassland plant communities such as meadows and prairies.

Meadows are usually associated with forests and will vary considerably from place to place. A meadow found at 6,000 feet in the Rocky Mountains will contain different native grasses than those found among the hardwood forests of Vermont.

Prairies tend to be wide open rangeland with few trees. These rich stands of perennial grasses combined with forbs produce very thick sod. Prairies can be wet or dry depending on the lay of the land, and different plants will inhabit each. Prairies also change as the season progresses, and in some months, the grasses will be dominant, while in other months, the forbs are more visible.

It is rare to find any intact native grasslands these days. Livestock have introduced exotic plants from around the globe, and, if the plant is well adapted to its new home, it becomes established and then multiplies rapidly.

> **Turf Talk**
>
> A *plant community* is a group of native plants that are often found together in a particular ecosystem. Buffalo grass, big bluestem grass, prairie coneflower, and wild sunflower are all part of the midwestern prairie plant community.

> **Turf Talk**
>
> You will see references to "grasses and forbs" in this chapter. A *forb* is a term for any nongrassy, herbaceous plant, which is usually a wildflower that grows in wild grasslands.

America's Favorite Native Grasses You Can Buy

➤ Buffalo grass, *Buchloe dactyloides*

➤ Meadow barley, *Hordeum brachyantherum*

➤ Big bluestem, *Andropogon gerardii*

➤ Little bluestem, *Andropogon scoparius*

➤ Switchgrass, *Panicum vrgatum*

➤ Blue grama, *Bouteloua gracilis*

➤ Indiangrass, *Sorghastrum nutans*

➤ Prairie sandreed, *Calamovilfa longifolia*

Pastures

Pastures encompass all sorts of grasslands that were first created to produce good forage for livestock. Early farmers found certain grasses to be fast growers that produced much more food for animals than other grasses. The farmer brought these grasses and their seed into his fields to upgrade their potential.

Pasture grasses can be native, but many are exotics. They generally produce big tufts and tall seed heads. Pasture grasses are frequently combined with legumes, which flower a lot like the wild forbs of native prairies. Legumes are members of the pea family, which produces some of the highest quality animal feed known. Alfalfa is a good example.

Pastures are usually irrigated, but where summer rainfall is sufficient, watering isn't necessary. Most western states require pasture irrigation because the perennial grasses cannot survive the long, hot summers on their own.

Ornamental Meadows

A number of ornamental grasses are used for coverage of large areas, and in most cases only one type of grass is used for the whole stand. With native and pasture grasslands, there is a variety of grasses combined. Fescues are among the most common species for ornamental meadows. These are not usually mowed and are always irrigated.

Mowing only occurs when the stand of grass becomes old and shows discoloration. Then you get to start over by mowing out the bad stuff and letting new luxuriant blades grow in their place. This is called *renewing the stand*. These meadows are often combined with trees and the most popular native perennials of American grasslands, such as Shasta daisy and prairie coneflower.

Now that you're totally confused about what was to be a simpler alternative to turf grass lawns, you're not alone. Many landscaping experts are overwhelmed at the options when you consider all our native grasses, exotic grasses, and ornamental grasses at once. They have put together blends of seeds that are compatible in their demands for water and care, so there's really nothing more confusing than picking the best one.

Meadow in a Can

No matter what kind of lawn you plan to grow, you must buy the plants. They can be had in a variety of different forms, but, for this kind of lawn, there are only two basic beginnings.

There's a big demand these days for native grasses by conservationists trying to re-create our presettlement grasslands on land that has been altered by human habitation. As you may know by now, plants like buffalo grass don't produce a lot of seed, which makes it prohibitively expensive to plant that way. Instead we plant little plugs of sod or sprigs to start a lawn.

Many of the best perennial native grasses are grown in special containers for revegetation purposes, which is economical for large projects. They may be sold in little test-tube-like containers, little 2-inch-square pots, or 4-inch pots, also called liners. When a meadow is planted from this kind of material, it's set out in much the same way described for sprigs and plugs in Chapter 13, "Planting a Lawn from Sprigs, Plugs, and Stolons."

Perennial ornamental grasses are grown in containers as well, but there isn't a demand for such quantities as the natives. These will have larger container size, usually 1 gallon. Occasionally, you can find them in 4-inch pots, particularly fountain grass, *Pennisetum setaceum*, the most widely planted of all ornamental grasses.

The benefit of starting your alternative lawn from live plants is that you know it's viable from the start, whereas seeds aren't always cooperative because they need special conditions to germinate. The biggest challenge, though, is finding the grasses to buy. This is a specialized type of plant that many retail nurseries don't carry.

Other annual grasses, quick-to-germinate perennials, and wildflowers are sold in seed form. Unless you really know your plants, it's a good idea to buy a prepared mixture. One popular version is called Meadow in a Can, which is just exactly what you get with these mixtures. Seed mixes can be composed of just about any combination of native or exotic grasses and forbs.

This is an ideal example of a seed mixture that combines both perennial grasses with wildflowers:

Wild Meadow Mix
➤ Blanketflower
➤ Crimson clover
➤ Purple coneflower

199

➤ Rocket larkspur

➤ Scarlet flax

➤ Durar hard fescue

➤ Sheep fescue

Seedy Options

Seed is the most widely available means of starting an alternative lawn. There are a number of places you can go to find out what's available locally. Because there are so many climates in the United States, you must choose a mixture that is well adapted to local conditions. Because the bulk of this kind of planting is perennial grasses, they must be able to survive through the extremes of winter and summer to become fully mature. Perennial grasses can take three years to reach their full size and beauty, with some taking even longer if planted from seed.

There are a few retail outlets to go to. A full-service retail nursery is the place to start. This is not a home-improvement store chain but a real nursery. Ask the owner about the seed mixtures available for the local climate. This may be the only way to get seed mixes that are predominately native grasses because they aren't commonly stocked. The nursery will have a brochure or availability list and will probably have to order the seed for you.

The second source is a farm supply or agricultural seed source. If you're in a farming region, this kind of operation is common, but the closer to the city you get, the less chance of finding one. These companies are geared for irrigated or dryland pasture seeds. Dryland pasture seed mixes are used by farmers who want to upgrade their natural rangeland to make it more nutritious for livestock. Irrigated pasture is usually a combination of perennial bunch grasses and low-growing clovers that offer lots of flowers.

Because the most beautiful plantings also contain wildflowers, you may want to have a little bit more control. There are some excellent sellers of wildflower seed in bulk that you can mix into your grass seed. They tend to group wildflowers according to region, so you know the plants are regionally adapted.

Here are some examples of wildflower mixes you can choose from to add to grass seed for a blooming meadow:

➤ California Coastal Range Wildflowers

➤ Midwestern U.S.

➤ Rocky Mountain

➤ Northeastern U.S.

➤ Pacific Northwest

➤ Southwest Desert

➤ Southeastern U.S.

➤ Texas Gulf Coast

Here are some examples of pasture mixes formulated for different purposes:

Livestock Mix—Irrigated Pasture

➤ 25% Tall fescue

➤ 20% Tetraploid perennial ryegrass

➤ 20% Orchardgrass

➤ 15% Tetraploid annual ryegrass

➤ 3% Ladino clover

➤ 6% Strawberry clover

➤ 6% Birdsfoot trefoil clover

➤ 5% Red Clover

Forage Blend—Dryland Pasture

➤ 35% White oats

➤ 30% Red oats

➤ 10% Beardless barley

➤ 10% Awnless wheat

➤ 15% Vetch (legume)

California Native Grass Mix—Dryland

Equal parts:

➤ California brome grass

➤ Blue wildrye

➤ California barley

How Much to Buy and When the Time Is Right

Wherever you buy your seed, the grower always includes a recommended seeding rate per acre or per 1,000 square feet. You'll need a rough idea of how large an area you have in order to order enough seed. You'll find measuring instructions in Chapter 7, "Ladies and Gentlemen . . . Buy Your Grasses."

Turf Tip

For larger pieces of property where you're seeding more than an acre, there are 43,560 square feet in an acre.

If you will be irrigating your alternative lawn, you can plant it anytime you can plant a traditional turf grass lawn. It does help to plant in spring because this is when seeds germinate in natural meadows and prairies. As long as the soil can be worked and you can move around on it without creating a muddy quagmire, it's acceptable to plant.

If you are growing a seasonal meadow without irrigation, you should understand the natural weather cycles and growth patterns of grasses in your area. In the far west, rains may diminish relatively early in the spring, so planting must be done in mid to late winter because that's when the wild grasses get started. If you try and sow later in the season, there won't be enough moisture to sustain the crop.

In humid regions where there is plentiful rain in early summer, the natural planting time is spring, and if you try to sow at other times, the grass may be too cold or the days too short to sustain the young seedlings.

Conditions to Consider

You have to have sun to grow a turf grass lawn, and you need it to grow an alternative lawn as well. The difference is that a natural lawn can tolerate more shade because you aren't after that perfect monoculture of evenly green turf. Slight variations in color and growth habit in alternative lawns go unnoticed most of the time.

Here are the environmental conditions to consider:

➤ The area should receive six hours or more of sunshine each day during the growing season. This is especially important for prairie perennial native grasses.

➤ You can grow an alternative lawn on relatively steep slopes, but they should be facing south or west for best results. In nature, the east- and north-facing slopes are usually covered with trees.

➤ Most alternative lawns can be grown on almost every soil, but if it is very wet, you may be forced to use special blends of grasses accustomed to wetland conditions.

Turf Tip

You need not be limited to growing plants from seed. Some natural lawns contain native shrubs or perennials that don't grow easily from seed. To achieve this diversity, plant the shrubs and perennials from container stock in the places where you want them to grow. You may want to make a water well around each one to water them more deeply than the seed-grown plants at first. Then smooth the soil and plant the seed around them. Professionals hydroseed on top of these plants, and then wash the mulch off with a jet from the garden hose when they're through.

Revegetation Containers

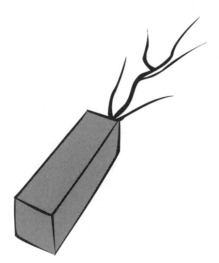

Cross Section—Container Plants and Overseed

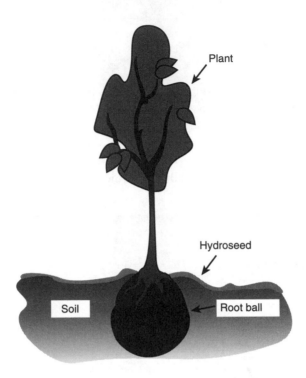

The final consideration is the size of your lawn. The way it is planted relates to its size and the lay of the land. Small sites are easy because you throw the seed out by hand and rake it in. For slightly larger areas that are relatively flat, use a lawn-seed spreader.

If the ground is uneven or steep, a belly spreader is the best broadcasting device. This handy little canvas-and-wood tool hangs across your chest and holds about a gallon and a half of seed. As you walk, you crank the paddle wheel and it flings the seed out about 10 feet to the front and side of you.

Belly Spreader

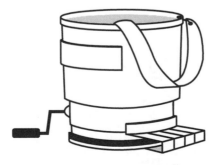

If you can afford it, you can plant moderate to large plots by hydroseed, which is a combination of seed and ground fiber shot out under pressure from a tank truck. This is a two-in-one method that broadcasts and covers the seed at the same time. You find more about the hydroseeding process in Chapter 11, "Seeding a Turf Grass Lawn." Hydroseeding costs a bit more but saves you the labor and materials, plus the job ends up more evenly covered, and germination rates are higher.

One special benefit of hydroseeding applies to natural lawns planted on moderate to severe slopes. You can add an organic glue called a *tackifier* to the hydroseed slurry mix. This adhesive actually glues the seed and mulch to the soil so that when you water or if it rains, the seed won't wash off the steep parts. There's no way to seed a difficult slope by hand that compares to the success rate of hydroseeding with tackifier.

For giant areas where a tractor implement is required, consider a drill seeder, which plants the seed in a neat grid over many acres. You can only use a drill seeder on relatively rock-free soils that are level enough for a farm tractor to negotiate.

Turf Tip

If you live out in the country and have a tractor, put your tax dollars to work! Government resource conservation district offices across America have drill seeders that they lend out to farmers to aid in large-scale erosion control and revegetation projects. Plant a prairie on your land in just a few hours. Look for these offices under the United States Department of Agriculture listings for your county.

Planting a Natural Lawn or Pasture from Seed

Natural lawns and pastures are planted in much the same way as regular turf grass, but the seed bed doesn't have to be quite so perfect. It's important to purge the soil of weeds before you start because, if aggressive grasses already exist, they may overwhelm the new ones rather quickly.

It's a good idea to try to remove any larger rocks because even though natural lawns aren't mowed like turf grass, you will have to renew the stand by removing the chaff. This may be done every year to keep it looking good and growing vigorously. If rocks are hidden in the grass, you can severely damage a mower, and they're not good for the tiller either.

Plowing the Back 40

For suburban homes where a large area is dedicated to pasture or meadow, you will need to till the ground before planting. There's less emphasis on seed beds and fine grading because these areas are naturally rough. However, you will find greater germination rates if you add steer manure, compost, or peat to the soil during the tilling. After all, it will be your only opportunity to get under there, so you might as well do all you can.

Adding organic matter of any kind is good for all soils, particularly heavy clays. On expansive suburban or rural sites, it can take a huge amount of material to make a difference. For these sites, it's common to add an organic-based, concentrated fertilizer such as dehydrated sewage sludge, or to use granular pasture fertilizers from the farm supply. You find more information on soil improvement and organic matter in Chapter 8, "Dealing with Dirt." Granular fertilizers are detailed in Chapter 16, "The Basic Food Groups."

Turf Talk

In nature, grass grows vegetatively until summer; then the plants send up seed heads. These stiff stems, called *chaff,* remain even after the seeds are released; by winter, they turn golden brown. In nature, fires and grazing keep the chaff to a minimum, but we use mowing to produce the same benefits. Mowing helps the plants recover in the spring and produce luxuriant new growth.

Use a rototiller to work up all the soil because no matter how tenacious the plant, seed has a tough time on rock-hard earth.

For larger rural properties, it's best to call out the big guns: a tractor disk or rotovator. A tractor disk looks like a bunch of round, steel dinner plates arranged on a series of axels all hooked together. The disk is towed behind a tractor, and the movement turns the disks that plow up the soil. Disking does not produce a very finely tilled soil, but it is quick and more suitable if you have big boulders underneath the surface because it just rolls over the tops of them.

A rotovator is a rototiller that's made to be used by a tractor. It requires a power connection to the tractor engine to turn the tines. You can expect the rotovator to till large areas as well as a rototiller does a small space. For large estate-sized lawns, hiring an experienced rotovator service rather than attempting it yourself may be quicker, safer, and more efficient.

Plant the Plants

Before you seed, plant your container-grown plants. These can be trees or shrubs and even perennials and grasses. Dig the proper hole and allow for a watering basin if they need special irrigation to get started the first few years. It's a good idea to add some wood chips or mulch around the base of the trees and shrubs so there's clear space between the base of the trunk and the meadow grass. Often the grass is too competitive and gobbles up water and fertilizer so that the container plants get an abnormally slow start.

If you are planting native grasses or ornamental grasses from containers, be sure to spot them in at an appropriate spacing like sprigs or plugs. This avoids barren spots where weeds can thrive.

A Sowing Bee

Whether you sow a 100 square feet or a 100 acres, the seed is broadcast at the same rate. It's a simple process on smaller lawns, but if you're doing an acre or more, it's difficult to tell. The best way to do it without doing any extensive math is to simply divide the seed and the site into a number of equal portions.

Fill up the spreader with the first portion and set the distribution rate as fine as it will go—that means as little comes out as possible. If you go over the designated area and there's a little left over, you can open up the hopper for a more generous flow. Then go over the area faster to broadcast the remaining seed as evenly as possible. Use the first area to experiment so that you know exactly how it will go for the rest.

Turf Tip

When you sow very small seed, or the seeding rate is very low, it's difficult to distribute it evenly over large areas. Professional contractors sowing wildflower seed mixes, which are some of the smallest of all seeds, mix the seed with sand. They distribute the seed with the sand, and it flows through their spreaders more constantly and covers the site evenly.

Drag Racing

After the seed is broadcast, you must cover it up for good germination. For a small site, you may simply rake and smooth the surface of the lawn area, and the seed will settle into the nooks and crannies of soil. If you have a lawn roller or borrow one, roll it lightly over this surface for a smoother appearance.

For big sites, farmers have covered their pasture seed by "dragging it in." In the old days, they would take a log and attach it with ropes to their plow horse, and the horse would drag the log behind to cover and firm the seed in place. They also used an old, milled timber beam studded with nails pulled behind a horse or tractor. Today the all-time favorite is a piece of chain-link fencing dragged behind mules or a tractor.

Water or Rain

Pastures or natural lawns with irrigation should be watered immediately after seeding. The soil should be kept evenly moist for the first few weeks so that there is maximum germination. Some wildflowers require this period of moisture in their natural environment during spring or summer rains. You must re-create this same condition. If you have container plants in there too, be sure that you give them extra water.

Dryland pastures are usually seeded at a time that takes advantage of the start of the rainy season. But sometimes nature does not cooperate, and you need to provide supplemental water in an extreme drought.

Turf Caveat

When you grow a natural lawn that includes forbs, wildflowers, clovers, and other plants besides grass, be attentive to lawn fertilizer labels. Some of these products have herbicide in them that kills certain grasses, or that kills any plant other than grass. A mistake with this kind of herbicide-enhanced product can wipe out all your flowers permanently in one application!

What to Expect

It can take a while for perennial grasses to become established. A mature plant will produce a dense, spongy mound out of which the leaves and seed heads grow. This mass makes these grasses drought tolerant, and under drought conditions, they simply go dormant until the rains come. They are also so strong that it takes a serious effort to kill them, and most weeds will disappear as the clumps grow together. As a natural lawn evolves, some plants will be obvious whereas others won't take off until the second or third year.

Farmers fertilize their pastures to keep the forage levels high, and your natural lawn will grow faster and look greener with regular fertilization. If you are growing an organic lawn to encourage wildlife diversity, stick with products such as fish emulsion and manure tea (manure soaked in water, and then the water poured on the plants). Otherwise, any lawn fertilizer that does not contain herbicides is suitable.

The Least You Need to Know

➤ Native grasses are species that originated in the United States.

➤ Alternative lawns are really just prairies and meadows on a small scale.

➤ You can buy special seed mixes adapted to your climate that contain grasses and flowers that grow together naturally.

➤ Natural lawns need to be mowed at least once a year to remove unattractive chaff and renew the stand.

Chapter 15

Groundcovers Where Lawns Just Won't Do

> ### In This Chapter
>
> ➤ Solving problems with groundcovers
>
> ➤ Ways groundcovers are grouped according to habit
>
> ➤ How to choose and buy groundcovers
>
> ➤ How to plant and care for groundcovers

Groundcovers do just that—they cover the ground. This illustrates just how generic the term really is. It more accurately describes a practice of planting anything close enough together and in sufficient quantity to cover an area of ground with foliage.

A hundred common garden petunias planted close together over a large area make this flower a groundcover. Plant a vine with nothing to climb on and it will creep across the ground; in the process it becomes a groundcover, too. Choose a dwarf shrub, buy a truckload of them, plant them close together and *voilà*—they, too, become groundcovers.

When we look for a substitute for lawns in areas not suited to turf grasses, we seek plants that adapt themselves to covering the ground. Our choices might be those that most closely mimic the lawn effect. We also could go in the opposite direction and look for bold, colorful flowering plants that are low growing. It all depends on your personal preferences and conditions in your yard.

Here are some examples of preferences both in terms of beauty and practicality:

➤ Groundcovers produce a colorful flower display.

➤ Groundcovers absorb glare with a dark, rich, green foliage.

➤ Groundcovers offer us brilliant fall color.

➤ Groundcovers are well adapted to rugged slopes.

➤ Groundcovers will grow where it's too shady for lawn.

Groundcovers Now and Then

The idea of groundcovers is rather new in the grand scheme of landscape gardening. They really came into their own in the 1950s in California and other warm-climate states because they were viewed for their low-maintenance qualities.

The 1950s were a time when growing lawns was more time and labor intensive than it is today. Sprinker systems were constructed out of galvanized pipe, making simple repairs a nightmare. Turf grasses were far more prone to disease before high-tech breeding programs. Home lawns were cut with push mowers, which was time consuming and hard work! High prices made power mowers a real luxury. Under these circumstances, you can see why groundcovers were touted as the low-maintenance salvation of the American landscape.

Although lawns are much easier to grow today, there are still many situations where they are not a good choice. Shade, steep slopes, soggy ground, poor or rocky soils are all problems that groundcovers take in stride. The key is choosing the right groundcover that will fill in quickly, be long lived, and crowd out weeds.

Dividing Up the Spoils

Before going into the specifics of choosing groundcovers, you must know how they grow. This has a strong bearing on their use in the landscape and how you water them. It also dictates whether or not they will survive on slopes or embankments. In general, woody plants tend to withstand extremes of winter and summer temperatures better than herbaceous groundcovers.

Meet Mr. Shrub

The word *shrub* is applied to plants that have hard, woody stems and branches. They can be upright in form like small trees, or very flat like lawn depending on the species and cultivars. Shrubs can be long-lived plants, and most require years to reach maturity. Once established, they take care of themselves because their root systems are deep and reach moisture trapped deep in the soil.

A Spreading Shrub Groundcover Plant

There is a group of very low-growing woody plants loosely termed spreading shrubs. Their form or habit is composed of many long, ground-hugging branches that radiate out in all directions from the central stem like spokes in a wheel. Some spreading shrubs can cover a huge area up to 15 feet in diameter.

The benefit of using spreading shrubs as groundcover is that you water just one plant. This is well adapted to drip systems because you may only need to run a tube to each of a handful of plants to serve an enormous area. For this reason, spreading shrubs have become the favorite in drought-ravaged communities. This watering technique also reduces maintenance because you don't water ground in between plants, which discourages weeds from taking up residence there.

The downside to spreading shrubs is that if just one plant dies, you have a BIG bare spot. To fill it in, you must plant a new young plant that will take months or years to reach the coverage and beauty of the original. In this sense, they are very unforgiving.

Turf Talk

The term *herbaceous* describes any plant that does not have woody parts. All stems and leaves are soft and green, and although these can toughen up when old, they are still not considered woody.

Controlled Overpopulation

The majority of our most popular groundcovers are herbaceous and behave much like turf grasses. They cover an area by sheer numbers of individual plants. They often, but not always, have a "running" growth habit, which means that they spread the way grass does, by adventurous stems or roots.

The most common example of herbaceous groundcovers is ivy. You plant one ivy plant, and it sends long tendrils out from that root as it goes. Huge areas are planted with ivy seedlings at a specific spacing, and after a short time they fill in completely.

An Herbaceous Groundcover Plant

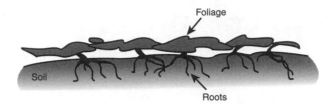

With herbaceous groundcovers, you must water the entire area, just like a lawn. Each and every plant must receive enough water to make the whole stand evenly green, and to keep it from dying out in the dry spots. But this invites weeds into your groundcover areas, and if certain species are invaded by runner grasses, control can be nearly impossible.

The downside to herbaceous groundcovers is also illustrated by ivy. If not carefully controlled, it climbs into trees and shrubs, shrouds fences, and can even cause structural damage to your house! One of the ironies of horticulture is that the plants we so appreciate for their willingness to grow under the worst circumstances prove so tenacious that they become uncontrollable pests if not maintained.

Turf Tip

Many herbaceous groundcovers can be mowed from time to time. This is done because some plants, like dwarf periwinkle or creeping Saint-John's-wort, become sparse or discolored when the stand ages. Some are mowed to remove winter damage in early spring. When you mow or cut them down manually, this renews the plants and they will grow back thick and with lovely, luxuriant new foliage. For flowering plants, this practice will stimulate more abundant bloom display. For best results, remove all the clippings when mowing, and rake up all cuttings when using hedge clippers or a string trimmer.

Top 20 American Groundcovers and Their Characteristics

When planting lawns today, we choose from about 10 major grasses, and each offers various cultivars. Groundcovers, on the other hand, come from vastly different genera adapted to vastly different climates. Each has its own exposure preferences and growth habit. This series of brief profiles shows you the 20 best and most widely grown groundcover plants on the market today.

Availability of plants is an important consideration. Many plants you read about or see in magazines are hard to find in nurseries, and if they do show up, the quantities are limited. When you choose a groundcover, availability is crucial because if you lose a few plants over the years, you must be able to get suitable replacements that are exactly the same.

The following sample shows how to read the plant profiles listed in this chapter:

Botanical Name, Common Name

➤ Type: Is it a creeping shrub or herbaceous groundcover?

➤ Climate zone: What is the coldest region of USDA climate zone map where this plant survives?

➤ Exposure: Does the plant prefer shade, part sun, or full sun?

➤ Height: How tall does the plant grow?

➤ Flowers: Does it flower and, if so, in what color?

➤ Mowable: Can it be renewed often by mowing?

➤ Buy: Container types and sizes you find for sale.

➤ Spacing: Distance from the center of one plant to that of the next one.

➤ Comment: A special tip from the author.

Ajuga reptans, Carpet Bugle

➤ Type: Herbaceous

➤ Climate zone: 4

➤ Exposure: Part sun

➤ Height: 2 to 4 inches

➤ Flowers: Blue

➤ Mowable: No

➤ Buy: Flats

➤ Spacing: 6 to 18 inches apart

➤ Comment: Look for the new, larger, flowering varieties with brighter-colored foliage.

213

Arctostaphylos uva-ursi, Bearberry, Kinnikinick

- ➤ Type: Creeping shrub
- ➤ Climate zone: 2
- ➤ Exposure: Sun
- ➤ Height: 10 inches
- ➤ Flowers: Pink
- ➤ Mowable: No
- ➤ Buy: 1-gallon containers
- ➤ Spacing: 3 feet apart
- ➤ Comment: Drought-tolerant native that requires fast drainage; best for hills and rocky sites.

Arctotheca calendula, Cape Weed

- ➤ Type: Herbaceous
- ➤ Climate zone: 9
- ➤ Exposure: Sun
- ➤ Height: 6 inches
- ➤ Flowers: Yellow
- ➤ Mowable: Yes
- ➤ Buy: Flats
- ➤ Spacing: 6 inches apart
- ➤ Comments: This one has actually replaced entire lawns in the frost-free Pacific Coast.

Campanula portenschlagiana, Serbian Bellflower

- ➤ Type: Herbaceous
- ➤ Climate zone: 6
- ➤ Exposure: Shade, part sun
- ➤ Height: 12 to 14 inches
- ➤ Flowers: Blue
- ➤ Mowable: Yes
- ➤ Buy: Flats

➤ Spacing: 8 inches

➤ Comment: A rare source of Dutch blue flowers and bright green foliage for shaded areas.

Ceanothus griseus horizontalis, Carmel Creeper

➤ Type: Spreading shrub

➤ Climate zone: 8

➤ Exposure: Sun, part shade

➤ Height: 18 inches

➤ Flowers: Blue

➤ Mowable: No

➤ Buy: 1-gallon containers

➤ Spacing: 5 feet apart

➤ Comment: An American native that needs good drainage; offers emerald foliage and blue flower spikes for drought gardens.

Cerastium tomentosum, Snow in Summer

➤ Type: Herbaceous

➤ Climate zone: 2

➤ Exposure: Sun

➤ Height: 6 inches

➤ Flowers: White

➤ Mowable: Yes

➤ Buy: Flats

➤ Spacing: 6 inches apart

➤ Comment: Best for smaller areas and offers a bonus of silvery foliage when not in bloom—a moonlight stunner!

Cotoneaster dammeri, Bearberry Cotoneaster

➤ Type: Creeping shrub

➤ Climate zone: 5

➤ Exposure: Sun

➤ Height: 12 inches

➤ Flowers: White/berries

➤ Mowable: No

➤ Buy: 1-gallon containers

➤ Spacing: 8 feet apart

➤ Comment: Bright red berries are a delight against the snow.

Euonymus fortunei, Wintercreeper

➤ Type: Herbaceous

➤ Climate zone: 4

➤ Exposure: Sun or shade

➤ Height: 12 inches

➤ Flowers: Fall color

➤ Mowable: No

➤ Buy: Flats

➤ Spacing: 4 feet apart

➤ Comment: A rare evergreen that produces fiery coloring in the fall.

Fragaria chiloensis, Wild Strawberry

➤ Type: Herbaceous

➤ Climate zone: 5

➤ Exposure: Shade, part sun

➤ Height: 10 inches

➤ Flowers: White, small red fruit

➤ Mowable: Yes

➤ Buy: Flats

➤ Spacing: 10 inches apart

➤ Comment: The true woodland groundcover for those shaded areas beneath tree groves.

Gazania leucolaena, Trailing Gazania

➤ Type: Herbaceous

➤ Climate zone: 9

➤ Exposure: Sun

➤ Height: 8 inches

➤ Flowers: Yellow

➤ Mowable: Yes

➤ Buy: Flats

➤ Spacing: 12 inches apart

➤ Comment: Very fast growth and heat tolerance makes this South African native popular in the Sun Belt.

Hedera helix, English Ivy

➤ Type: Herbaceous

➤ Climate zone: 5

➤ Exposure: Sun, part shade

➤ Height: 12 inches

➤ Flowers: No

➤ Mowable: No

➤ Buy: Flats

➤ Spacing: 12 to 16 inches apart

➤ Comment: Explore the array of dwarf ivies for small spaces with small leaves and a ground-hugging habit.

Hypericum calycinum, Creeping St.-John's-wort

➤ Type: Herbaceous

➤ Climate zone: 5

➤ Exposure: Sun, part shade

➤ Height: 24 inches

➤ Flowers: Yellow

➤ Mowable: Yes

➤ Buy: Flats

➤ Spacing: 8 inches apart

➤ Comment: So easy, it grows on freeways, and, after mowing in late winter, it springs to life and blooms like crazy.

Isotoma fluviatilis, Blue Star Creeper

➤ Type: Herbaceous

➤ Climate zone: 9

➤ Exposure: Part shade

➤ Height: 3 inches

➤ Flowers: Blue

➤ Mowable: Yes

➤ Buy: Flats

➤ Spacing: 6 inches apart

➤ Comment: As low as you can go and so charming when combined with flagstones.

Juniperus horizontalis, Creeping Juniper

➤ Type: Spreading shrub

➤ Climate zone: 3

➤ Exposure: Sun

➤ Height: 18 inches

➤ Flowers: No

➤ Mowable: No

➤ Buy: 1-gallon container

➤ Spacing: 5 feet apart

➤ Comment: Among the most rugged and reliable creeping shrubs you'll find.

Ophiopogon japonicus, Mondo Grass

➤ Type: Herbaceous

➤ Climate zone: 6

➤ Exposure: Shade, part sun

➤ Height: 10 inches

➤ Flowers: Purple

➤ Mowable: No

➤ Buy: Flats or small pots

➤ Spacing: 12 inches apart

➤ Comment: This one is the darling of Asian-inspired gardens, but unfortunately it does not spread—it stays in clumps.

Pachysandra terminalis, Japanese Spurge

➤ Type: Herbaceous

➤ Climate zone: 4

➤ Exposure: shade

➤ Height: 6 to 10 inches

➤ Flowers: No

➤ Mowable: No

➤ Buy: Flats

➤ Spacing: 12 inches

➤ Comment: The old-fashioned, favorite shade groundcover of the cooler eastern states.

Potentilla verna, Spring Cinquefoil

➤ Type: Herbaceous

➤ Climate zone: 6

➤ Exposure: Sun, part shade

➤ Height: 4 inches

➤ Flowers: Yellow

➤ Mowable: Yes

➤ Buy: Flats

➤ Spacing: 6 to 8 inches

➤ Comment: Grows so dense and flat it makes a great lawn substitute.

Rosmarinus officinalis "Prostratus," Creeping Rosemary

➤ Type: Herbaceous

➤ Climate zone: 7

➤ Exposure: Sun

➤ Height: 12 inches

➤ Flowers: Blue

➤ Mowable: No

➤ Buy: Flats

➤ Spacing: 12 inches apart

➤ Comment: Favored for hot, dry, rocky sites; not only beautiful but a culinary herb, too!

Trachelospermum jasminoides, Star Jasmine

➤ Type: Herbaceous

➤ Climate zone: 8

➤ Exposure: Sun, part shade

➤ Height: 18 inches

➤ Flowers: White-fragrant

➤ Mowable: Yes

➤ Buy: Flats

➤ Spacing: 12 inches apart

➤ Comment: Heavenly fragrant blossoms you can smell all the way down the street.

Vinca minor, Dwarf Periwinkle

➤ Type: Herbaceous

➤ Climate zone: 5

➤ Exposure: Sun or shade

➤ Height: 6 inches

➤ Flowers: Blue

➤ Mowable: Yes

➤ Buy: Flats

➤ Spacing: 10 inches apart

➤ A close relative, *Vinca major*, is nearly identical but grows to 24 inches tall.

➤ Comment: So vigorous they go wild in the countryside. The flowers are the most charming. Check out variegated ones.

Top Flowering Groundcovers

➤ *Ajuga reptans*, Carpet Bugle

➤ *Arctotheca calendula*, Cape Weed

➤ *Campanula portenschlagiana*, Serbian Bellflower

➤ *Cerastium tomentosum*, Snow in Summer

➤ *Hypericum calycinum*, Creeping St.-John's-wort

➤ *Potentilla verna*, Cinquefoil

➤ *Trachelospermum jasminoides*, Star Jasmine

➤ *Vinca major*, Periwinkle

➤ *Vinca minor*, Dwarf Periwinkle

Top Creeping Shrub Groundcovers

➤ *Arctostaphylos uva-ursi*, Kinnikinick

➤ *Ceanothus griseus "horizontalis,"* Carmel Creeper

➤ *Cotoneaster dammeri*, Bearberry Cotoneaster

➤ *Juniperus horizontalis*, Creeping Juniper

Weed Barrier Fabrics and Mulches

During the low-maintenance groundcover craze a couple of decades ago, there arose some new practices. The major ideas dealt with the problem of weeding in ground-cover patches, both right after planting and over the long term.

Black sheet plastic was suddenly cheap and widely available. The idea was to spread it out to deny weeds light, and then cover the plastic up with gravel or mulch to make it look better. The problems that arose have caused many homeowners to curse the stuff. The plastic had to be removed because:

➤ Ultraviolet light caused the plastic to break down after a few years into millions of tiny pieces that are a pain to get out of plantings and soil.

➤ When it rained, landscape plants planted in the plastic shunted runoff away from ornamental plants, which suffered from dehydration even though it was raining.

➤ Lack of air circulation caused the soils beneath to "die," and the oxygenless environment stunted plants as the earth fermented or "soured."

Geotextiles, a more recent solution, are fabrics developed to hold up under brutal conditions. One such fabric is actually woven rather than composed of one continuous membrane. The woven fabric is loose enough to allow water and air to penetrate and support landscape plants. It is also tight enough to deny light to weeds underneath and is proving to hold up very well over the long term.

Only Creeping Shrubs Need Apply

Geotextiles are great problem solvers for creeping shrubs or groundcover plants such as rosemary that do not root as they grow. Because shrubs take longer to fill in, the demand for this kind of coverage is high because nobody wants to weed those gaps for one hour, much less one year, until they fill in.

It's simple to work with these fabrics, which can be purchased at most garden centers. The best way to go about the project is to remove all weeds from the area, and then lay out the fabric, overlapping a few inches where edges meet. Cut a small hole in the fabric wherever you want a plant, and then plant them through the hole. It helps to have some newspaper or a flat plastic garbage bag laid out beside the hole so you can put the excavated soil on it. When you fill the hole back in, pull from this stockpile and carry away any leftovers.

221

After the whole area is planted, cover up the fabric with ground bark, wood chips, or gravel depending on what's available. If you use gravel, stick with round river gravel instead of the crushed kind that has sharp edges that can be hard on the fabric. Walk around and water as you would if the fabric wasn't there, and you will enjoy weed-free groundcover for years to come.

Turf Caveat

When planting shrubs and trees with weed-barrier fabrics, avoid touching the woody trunk or stem of the plant with the fabric. Doing so will cause moisture accumulation against the vulnerable bark, creating a crown rot condition that can kill the tree. In fact, this mimics the effects of planting a tree too deeply, which usually results in sure death for most species.

Groundcover Sheet Cakes

All the groundcovers in the preceding profiles are purchased in three types of containers. Herbaceous groundcovers are usually sold in *flats*, which are a lot like a sheet cake. A flat is about 2 feet square, and just 2- to 3-inches deep. The number of plants a flat holds depends on the kind of groundcover it contains. For groundcovers such as cinquefoil and blue star creeper, the entire flat may be covered solid with these matlike plants. To plant these, you must cut the flat with a knife into 2- or 3-inch squares just like a cake.

Many growers are producing groundcovers in six-packs now rather than flats. It's easier to estimate how many plants you get, and planting from these is much less damaging than dividing plants and severing roots, as is the case with traditional flats.

Spreading shrubs are best purchased in 1-gallon containers, and they are almost always sold this way. These woody plants need more root zone and are older when they reach market age. They will be more expensive per plant, but it takes fewer of these to fill an area than herbaceous species, so the cost is really about equal.

Groundcover Containers

How Many Should I Buy?

To know how many plants are needed, just measure the square footage of the area. Use a basic length × width formula to come up with an approximate square footage. Then refer to the recommended spacing in the preceding profiles, and use this handy table for your guide:

Spaced Table

Spacing	Per Square Foot
8 inches apart	2.25 plants
10 inches apart	1.44 plants
12 inches apart	1.00 plants
14 inches apart	.73 plants
16 inches apart	.56 plants
18 inches apart	.44 plants
20 inches apart	.36 plants
24 inches apart	.24 plants

Five Easy Steps to Groundcover Glory

Step 1: Get the Dirt Ready

Remove all weeds, plants, and debris from your new groundcover area. Rototill it as deeply as possible, or turn it all over thoroughly with a spading fork. Work in as much compost as possible to create a nice soft place for your new groundcover plantlets.

Step 2: Lay Out the Plants

Before you start planting, lay out all the little plants on the surface of the soil, exactly where they will be planted. This helps you get organized and makes sure that you don't run short of plants at the end. If you must adjust placement after the initial layout, go ahead. It's much easier now than later.

Step 3: Put Them in the Ground

Plant groundcovers as tenderly as you would tomatoes. Their roots need to be snugly set in the ground. The surface of the soil in their container must be level with that of the surrounding soil for best results, especially with woodier plants such as rosemary.

Step 4: Water the Plants

Use the garden hose—not the sprinklers—to water in the groundcover. Turn the flow on gently and saturate each little plant deeply so that you get its roots and the bottom of the planting hole equally wet. Pay particular attention if you're planting through weed fabric to be sure that there's enough water because your view is limited. After this first watering-in, you can switch to sprinklers.

Step 5: Mulch

If you plan to use ground bark or other wood product mulch, you may prefer to spread the mulch and then water-in to avoid a muddy planting area. Beware because this can make it difficult to tell how much water the plant is actually getting. Sometimes dry mulches suck up much of the surface moisture like sponges before it reaches the roots.

The Least You Need to Know

➤ Groundcover plants are either creeping shrubs or herbaceous perennials.

➤ Some herbaceous groundcovers can be mowed occasionally for a richer, more beautiful flowering carpet.

➤ You can reduce maintenance by using weed-barrier fabric when planting some types of groundcovers.

➤ Buy groundcovers in flats, six-packs, or pots.

Part 5
Please Feed the Grass

Bet you didn't know that lawn grass plants are 75 percent water! Your grass needs strong stems and leaves if it is to mature into a thick green carpet you can be proud of. In these chapters, you'll learn how important a regular fertilizer and watering schedule is because lawns don't look good when they're hungry or thirsty. In fact, they get rather angry and promptly turn yellow or wilt to let the whole neighborhood know of your negligence.

Your lawn takes a beating whether you know it or not. Add kids, bikes, toys, and pets into the equation, and it's a downright hostile environment. Every lawnowner should know the more subtle causes of lawn damage and how to avoid them. If they're unavoidable, you need to know how to fix them quickly so that the signs of wear go away before your guests arrive for that weekend dinner party.

Chapter 16

The Basic Food Groups

In This Chapter

➤ How fertilizer works as food for plants

➤ Choosing the fertilizer that is best for your lawn and life-style

➤ Why fertilizer schedules change according to region and grass type

➤ How to apply fertilizer safely and effectively

You can grow grass on concrete if you give it enough water and fertilizer.

—Bob Hudson, greenskeeper

Don't try this at home. Yes, you can grow turf grass hydroponically on concrete, but this is an extreme example of how far you can push turf grasses with chemical fertilizers. But don't think this is an excuse for deferred maintenance of your own lawn, because you'll turn your tired, sick grass into a genuine nitrogen junky that will ultimately spell its demise.

Many golf greens are now constructed primarily with sand rather than true soil because sand is resistant to compaction from golfers, absorbs water quickly so that the surface is free of mud and puddles, and allows a medium for the roots to travel down deeply without much resistance. But sand has little to no food for plants, so greenskeepers must fertilize often if their playing surface is to remain in top condition.

Chemical fertilizers are powerful, but like all good things, too much can be deadly. To obtain the beautiful green lawn you dream of, you must use more of an holistic program of care, where you apply a number of different techniques to meet all the needs of your grass plants.

Turf Talk

Food for plants is called *nutrients*.
They can already exist in the soil or
be added in the form of fertilizer.
Whenever we discuss plant food, it is
in terms of nutrients, which are well
defined and responsible for various
plant functions. Whenever one or
more nutrients is lacking, there is a
nutrient deficiency, evident by
symptoms such as changes in color or
growth rate.

The Macro and Micro of Nutrients

To live, plants must carry on photosynthesis, a process
that requires sunlight, oxygen, water, and some nutrients. Sunlight and oxygen are taken from the atmosphere. Water and nutrients must be taken in through
the roots and transferred to the leaves to aid in the
photosynthetic process.

Botanists have determined exactly what nutrients plant
life needs to grow at an optimal level. You can divide
these up into two basic groups. *Macronutrients* constitute
the vast majority of what plants consume daily as they
carry on photosynthesis. These are the primary components in most fertilizers. *Micronutrients* are no less
important. They are sometimes called *trace elements*
because only tiny amounts are present and needed for
plant life.

The Great Macronutrient Trilogy

Macronutrients are the meat and potatoes of a plant's
diet. These are the three most important elements of any
fertilizer program because each of them is responsible
for a different part of the growth process. Because
chemical fertilizers are often combined with inert
materials, the potency of a fertilizer is gauged by a
percentage of its total weight.

Turf Talk

You don't need a camera for
photosynthesis. This is actually a
process by which plants turn sunlight
into energy and food. *Chlorophyll*
isn't just an ingredient in breath-
freshening chewing gum, it's a
component in plants that makes
them green. Chlorophyll is essential
for photosynthesis.

N—*Nitrogen* is the primary nutrient used by grass plants.
It is responsible for the vegetative growth of leaves and
stems. It is also connected to the production of chlorophyll, a substance that makes plants green in color.
Because we're after a rich, evenly green lawn, there's
little doubt that this is the fundamental fertilizer of turf
grasses. The most visible sign of a nitrogen deficiency is
that the grass loses that emerald-green coloring and
takes on a lighter, lime-green or yellow tint. Growth rate
will also slow.

Virtually every lawn fertilizer you'll find contains a great
deal of nitrogen, but as you see from their roles in plant growth, the others are necessary, too. This is important to know, because a strict diet of nitrogen is a lot like eating
nothing but meat. An all-meat diet would provide you huge amounts of protein, but
you would suffer from a lack of vitamins, carbohydrates, and fiber, all of which are
equally important to human health.

Turf Tip

Virtually every type of fertilizer you buy is labeled with its percentage of the big three macronutrients. They are abbreviated using the initials in this order: N for nitrogen, P for phosphorous, and K for potassium. I know you're asking why potassium doesn't match its initial. Scientists decided long ago that two Ps would make for a lot of confusion between phosphorous and potassium, so they used the scientific letter for the chemical potassium, which is K_2O.

Examples of all-nitrogen chemical fertilizers and their potencies are: Urea (45%), ammonium nitrate (33%), and ammonium sulfate (20%). All potential organic gardeners should compare this with steer manure, which is only 2% nitrogen!

P—Phosphorus is connected to root formation, flowering, and seed production. Obviously, this is valuable to growing food plants such as tomatoes or peaches because these are cultivated for flowers and fruit. Phosphorus is vital to turf grasses because it stimulates a large, deep root system that makes these plants more resistant to dry spells.

A pure phosphorous fertilizer known as superphosphate is 25% phosphorous. Organic phosphate fertilizers include bone meal (30%) and rock phosphate (18%).

K—Potassium helps plants resist disease and withstand extreme cold, and helps with the photosynthetic process.

Pure potassium fertilizers are potassium chloride (62%) and potassium nitrate (44%). A common organic source is wood ashes, which contain about 5% potassium.

Micronutrients

There are many more micronutrients that exist in small amounts in most natural soils. Occasionally, there will be neighborhoods where there are specific deficiencies, or where certain micronutrients such as boron are present in abnormally large quantities. In either case, your local nursery person will probably be aware of the problem and carry special fertilizers formulated with an extra dose of the nutrient. You'll also get advice on what kinds of fertilizers may contribute to the problem and how to avoid them.

These are the most important micronutrients needed for plant growth:

➤ Sulfur

➤ Calcium

➤ Iron

➤ Magnesium

➤ Boron

➤ Manganese

➤ Copper

➤ Zinc

➤ Molybdenum

➤ Chlorine

You Are What You Eat

Every lawn needs to be fertilized on a regular basis if it is to remain healthy and beautiful. Because lawns rely so heavily on nitrogen, they require fertilizers that contain generous amounts of this nutrient. Fortunately, the demands of parks and golf courses, plus tens of millions of home lawns, have produced products specially formulated for turf grasses.

When you go to the garden center, you'll be faced with a staggering array of turf fertilizers. In recent years, many new additions have made lawn care simpler than ever before, but sorting them out can be confusing. You have to be careful and read the details carefully.

Complete Fertilizers with Trace Elements

This is the best all-around fertilizer for your lawn. You'll find it under various trade names with slightly different formulations. For example, BEST, one of the leading lawn fertilizer manufacturers, offers Turf Supreme 16-6-8. This is a true complete fertilizer because in addition to the N-P-K there is 1.5% iron, .05% zinc, and 16% sulfur.

Weed While You Feed

Some newer lawn fertilizers contain herbicides that kill unwanted plants at the same time you fertilize the lawn. This is a great labor-saving device, but there are some concerns and limitations to be aware of. Selective herbicides kill only certain kinds of plants, such as broadleaf weeds, while leaving the grasses to grow freely. Others are more specific and go after crabgrass or other grassy weeds.

Killer Fertilizers

Fertilizers that contain pesticides can be the salvation of southern lawnowners who face a huge number of pests that ravage lawns there. These can be labor saving but potentially toxic if overused or used at the wrong time of year. One of the difficulties with this kind of fertilizer is that it kills both problem pests and beneficial organisms.

But if you have a bug problem that such a fertilizer will treat, it makes for a more beautiful lawn with far less effort.

Fertilizer Forms

Fertilizers are sold as dry granules or concentrates applied in liquid forms. The granules are easiest to use because you simply distribute them over the lawn and water well. They are easily applied with a drop spreader that can be set at a certain rate that ensures you get even coverage. Plus, the wheel marks in the grass left by the previous pass of the spreader provides convenient guidelines. The granules don't start working until they gradually dissolve and enter the soil with water.

Concentrates can be either liquid or water-soluble crystals that dissolve in water. Miracle Gro is a popular example of a crystal that is applied with a special fixture that fits on the end of your garden hose. You fill its reservoir with crystals and water away. Liquid concentrates work the same way using similar proportioner devices you can buy at the garden center.

The problem with liquid concentrates is they are difficult to distribute evenly on the lawn. You can't tell where you've sprayed before, or how much you've sprayed. Lawns are real tattlers because they show light and dark color changes when fertilizers are applied unevenly.

Turf Caveat

Whenever you add toxic substances to lawn fertilizers, there is a certain degree of danger to wildlife and family life. Pesticides and herbicides are potent chemicals and should be stored and used with care. If you're growing warm-season grasses, be very careful about using an herbicide-enhanced fertilizer because some of these are designed for cool-season grasses and recognize Bermuda and others as weeds.

Chemical-Free Feeding

Organically grown home lawns appeal to many who seek to eliminate chemicals from their lives. The use of chemical fertilizers is seen as polluting and wasteful of natural resources. But beneath all these issues lies the concept of holistic plant care. This philosophy resists using chemicals that will lower the populations of beneficial small insects and microorganisms that help plants resist disease and make them more efficient growers. There is some evidence that all that nitrogen actually weakens grass plants and makes them more vulnerable to a variety of problems.

Organic lawn fertilizers do not become active very quickly. They require a variety of processes that take time for the soil and the plant to utilize. Because they are so mild, you may have to fertilize more often and use far larger amounts of material to achieve a bright green comparable to the chemical products. For many, this is a worthwhile trade-off for a more chemical-free life-style.

Many organic fertilizers such as compost and steer manure are difficult to spread on lawns, and it takes quite a bit of material to give the lawn a nitrogen boost. But interest in organic alternatives to chemical lawn fertilizers has resulted in some good dry granule products.

Turf Tip

A liquid fertilizer can help problem lawns. Years ago, I encountered a strangely discolored young lawn; the homeowner said he had fertilized it regularly. The soil, however, had not been improved properly when the lawn was planted and had settled as hard as a rock.

The granular fertilizer applied by the homeowner had dissolved to create a super–potent solution, which sat on the surface for a long time. Wherever it touched the young grass, it burned. I instructed the homeowner to aerate the lawn surface for better drainage and switch to a liquid fertilizer that would never become so potent.

Milorganite has been on the market for more than 50 years but is only now getting the widespread attention it deserves. It is truly a recycled product, made of treated sewage that has been purified so that there is no health risk. These dark brown granules will flow through most spreaders with ease. Though its nutrient content is relatively low, 6-2-0, it also contains a wealth of micronutrients well over the amounts in any fortified chemical product. Milorganite is available at most garden centers.

Lawn Restore is a newer addition to the organic lawn fertilizer family. It's made of all sorts of materials, from feather meal to soybean meal. Its nutrient content is 10-2-6 and is applied at a simple rate of about 10 pounds per 1,000 square feet. If it's an older lawn with thatch buildup, the recommendation is increased to 15 pounds per 1,000 square feet.

Nutri-Rite organic fertilizer is not specifically for lawns, but because it is granulated, it is well adapted. Formulated at 6-2-4, it also contains gypsum, sulfur, and magnesium. The recommended application rate is 2 pounds per *100* square feet.

Calories Out, Calories In

You can view fertilizer like food. Turf grasses consume the N-P-K of a soil in a certain amount of time. When they have eaten all the food, they show it by slowing growth and changing color. The idea is not to wait until the lawn shows symptoms of hunger, because it's like yo-yo dieting—it's unhealthy.

Fertilizing a lawn requires you to keep the color evenly green throughout the growing season. Yo-yo schedules allow the grass to run out of calories, and when it's that short on fuel, it can't resist pests, disease, and extremes of temperature very well. To avoid problems, fertilize consistently, regularly, and with the proper amount so that the grass enjoys a good balanced meal that will keep it growing healthily until the next scheduled feeding.

Seasons of Demand

Lawns across American experience a huge difference in climate and growing season. The grasses themselves vary, too, because some go completely dormant for months at a time. Where there is no growth, there is no need for plant food. The exception to this would be dormant warm-season lawns overseeded with annual ryegrass for a temporary crop. But in general, it's clear there are peak seasons of demand for fertilizer, and other times of the year when little or none is needed.

In cold climates, another factor comes into play. Grasses that do not have a pronounced dormancy simply slow down and get really lethargic before going to sleep under the snow. Many winter-related turf diseases and problems are fostered by the amount of dead grass that remains as winter sets in. This means that cold-weather lawnowners need to reduce the frequency of their fertilizing late in the season so that the grasses naturally go dormant without unnecessary top growth or thatch being present.

Application Rates

The experts tell us that each grass should be fed a certain number of pounds of nitrogen per 1,000 square feet. In theory, this sounds simple, but translating that to the spreader is more complex. It's made even more confusing by distributing these recommended rates over a whole season. Add climate fluctuations . . . well, you get the idea.

The key to how often you need to fertilize is related to how fast your grass is growing. You'll know that by how often you have to mow to keep it looking good. When it's growing actively, you mow more frequently, and in turn feed more frequently. When it's cooler or very hot, grass growth slows down and so does the demand for food. A good rule of thumb is to fertilize every six to eight weeks beginning in the spring.

The hard part is knowing how much fertilizer to use, which is called the application rate. This is based on the number of pounds of nitrogen recommended for a 1,000 square-foot area. Because most lawn fertilizer formulas vary from 10% to 30% nitrogen, each one will require a different application rate to achieve the same end. For example, a fertilizer that is 12% nitrogen will require twice the application rate of a fertilizer that's 24% nitrogen.

So, how do you translate fertilizer nutrient content percentages into pounds of nitrogen? No, you don't have to buy a grocery store scale, but you can work it out somewhat scientifically.

The following are some basic guidelines for determining approximately how many pounds of fertilizer are needed to reach one pound of nitrogen per 1,000 square feet:

233

➤ 16-6-8 = 6 pounds

➤ 19-3-19 = 5 pounds

➤ 32-10-10 = 3 pounds

Each turf type varies slightly in its fertilizer appetite. Most cool-season grasses need from 2 to 5 pounds of nitrogen each year for optimal health, with bluegrass and perennial rye requiring slightly more than the fescues.

Warm-season grasses vary as follows per 1,000 square feet:

➤ Bahia: 2 to 4 pounds

➤ Centipede: 1 to 2 pounds

➤ Common Bermuda: 2 to 6 pounds

➤ Hybrid Bermuda: 4 to 6 pounds

➤ St. Augustine: 4 to 5 pounds

➤ Zoysia: 3 to 4 pounds

Turf Tip

If you're like me, you don't want to turn fertilizer applications into a master course in mathematical weights and measures. It's much easier to watch a neighbor fertilize his or her lawn, see how densely the granules are distributed, and then try to match that rate with a similar potency fertilizer on your lawn. Or you can ask your local nursery person to show you the rate for a locally popular fertilizer. In terms of application frequency, it takes a few applications to get used to the needs of a particular lawn, and that sets the schedule for the future.

Money for Nitrogen

When you go shopping for fertilizer you'll find an assortment of manufacturers. Scott's and BEST are the two leading turf grass fertilizer manufacturers in America. There are also the competitors that some garden centers stock because their prices are lower. However, before you choose, it's critical that you compare apples to apples and not be blinded by the discounts.

Every bag of fertilizer carries a detailed label spelling out exactly what it contains. These are your universal guides like the labels on food products at the supermarket. Instead of looking at fat, protein, and carbohydrates, you're checking for N-P-K.

These three macronutrients are the primary listings you use to compare price. However, some of the name-brand products also contain micronutrients, which give lawns a more balanced diet, particularly if you have poor soils. Sometimes it's better to spend a few extra dollars for a high-quality turf fertilizer than to split hairs on minor differences in percentages.

Turf Tip

After you find a fertilizer you like, stick with it. Name brands will always be there, but the cheaper competitors may come and go. With a reliable fertilizer, you don't have to reinvent the wheel to compensate for more or less nutrient content.

Lawn fertilizer is sold in many different sized packages because there are many different-sized lawns. Like anything, buying in bulk saves money, but with some fertilizers, it's like buying potato chips. You can buy the large economy size, but if the chips aren't eaten quickly, they go stale. With fertilizer, it's the nitrogen that's unstable, and it can actually evaporate if the bag is left open to changes in temperature and humidity for months at a time.

Spreading the Fertilizer

In Chapter 9, "Lawn Tools and Equipment," you will find a detailed description of the various types of tools used to apply granulated fertilizer to lawns. The most widely used is the drop spreader, which you fill with fertilizer and push back and forth on the lawn. Drop spreaders are used for a variety of other tasks, from seeding to topdressing, and are one of the indispensable tools of all serious lawnowners.

If you have an abnormally small lawn where maneuvering a walk-behind drop spreader is difficult, use a small hand spreader. For huge lawns that take all day with a drop spreader, the time required can be cut in half with a whirlybird spreader, though you do sacrifice control.

Your spreader has an adjustment that regulates how much material it distributes. This is helpful when fertilizing a new seed lawn because the first couple of applications are done at half the rate of a mature lawn. After you've determined the setting for an average application, you won't have to reset it again. If you use the spreader for other functions, such as topdressing, that require a change in the setting, mark the original point so that you can go back to "fertilizer mode" without any fuss.

Spreaders also allow you to shut off the flow of fertilizer altogether with a single movement. This feature is important to use when turning to avoid overdosing parts of the lawn where you do more maneuvering.

Dead Lawns Do Tell Tales

Fertilizer is strong stuff. If it is applied too heavily, it kills the grass, which turns brown and takes weeks to recover. If it goes down unevenly, your lawn will display spots and stripes, wherever there is too much or too little fertilizer. It can be really embarrassing if you blow it on the front lawn where every passing car notices that you didn't do it right.

You can avoid all the classic problems by following a few basic practices when fertilizing. Never fill the spreader hopper when it's on the lawn. Should you overfill and it overflows, you must get those granules off the lawn immediately. Fill the spreader on the sidewalk, driveway, or other paved area where you can test and fine-tune the application rate. Afterwards, just sweep up the granules and return them to the hopper.

Know the exact pattern that your spreader delivers and try to meet the edges of each pass as accurately as possible. If you overlap at all, these strips will receive a double dose of fertilizer and show up as darker stripes later on. For whirly spreaders or hand-held ones that are less accurate, you may overlap up to $1/4$ of the spread on each side.

Apply the fertilizer in an up-and-down stripe pattern. Close the hopper as you turn and then open it again when you are all lined up for the next pass. Always walk at exactly the same pace, because speed is what makes certain parts of a drop spreader push the fertilizer out.

Fertilize the lawn when the blades of grass are dry. The granules tend to stick to wet surfaces, which will burn the grass blades on contact. Dry grass also makes it easier to sweep up any spilled granules in the grass. Water well immediately after you finish applying the fertilizer.

Applying Liquid Fertilizers

Liquid fertilizer is easy to apply by using a hose-end applicator gun. These use the pressure of water to mix a designated amount of fertilizer into the stream as you water the lawn. It's always best to use an applicator manufactured by the fertilizer company to be sure both are compatible. However, even though the proportioning action is supposed to be uniform, this is not always the case.

Turf Caveat

Beware the size of your fertilizer bags. A 50-pound bag is a very heavy, unwieldy object to get in and out of your car. Weigh the volume discount against the risk of injury before you go for the jumbo economy size. Most products are sold in smaller bags around 20 to 25 pounds, which are easier to carry and easier to pour into your spreader.

Garden-Hose Fertilizer Applicator Gun

If you place the concentrated fertilizer in the applicator reservoir, let the water fill up to the ready condition, not the color of the concentrate. This color gradually fades as you fertilize, showing that less of the fertilizer is being mixed in as you go along. Be aware of this so that if the last half of your lawn ends up slightly different in color, you know to increase applications there next time.

Turf Tip

Fertilizer spreaders are made of metal. Fertilizer left in the hopper in amounts large or small will cause the mechanism to corrode and rust. Make it a habit to wash the spreader out with the garden hose immediately after you finish a fertilizer application. Once dry, give it a quick spray with WD-40 or a similar lubricant to increase the life span of the tool and to make it much easier to use next time.

When you're finished using the product, clean out the applicator thoroughly. Fertilizer residue can be corrosive, and if it is allowed to remain, it can clog up the small holes inside the applicator. The best way to clean it is to completely empty and rinse out the reservoir, and then fill it with fresh water and operate the applicator for a few minutes so that nothing but clear water is running. That way the next time you fertilize, you won't have to worry about whether it's proportioning properly.

The Least You Need to Know

➤ Nitrogen is the most important plant food for lawns.

➤ Complete lawn fertilizer formulas provide the major nutrients and some of the most important micronutrients.

➤ The three numbers on all fertilizer bags indicate the percentages of nitrogen, phosphorus, and potassium they contain.

➤ Lawn fertilizer is potent, and mistakes in application can seriously burn your lawn.

➤ The more frequently you mow, the more frequently you need to fertilize the lawn.

➤ If you grow organically, you can still use granular fertilizer on your lawn.

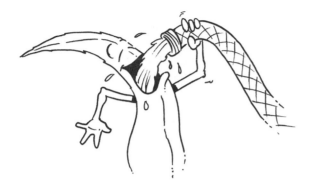

Chapter 17

Water Right, Water Deep

In This Chapter

➤ How you water influences overall health of your lawn

➤ Defining a water regime and sticking to it

➤ About in-ground sprinkler systems and how they work

➤ Strategies for water conservation on lawns

➤ Symptoms of when you water too much or too little

Because most of the water absorbed by land plants is lost by transpiration, the rate of water uptake must depend largely on the rate of transpiration.

—Leonard Bernstein, *Yearbook of Agriculture,* 1955

Transpiration is a lot like perspiration. Plants don't sweat water like humans do, but they do lose it in vapor form through little holes in their leaves, the equivalent of our skin pores. Bernstein's simple quote describes in just one sentence exactly what we are trying to do when irrigating—keep the water supply to plants balanced with the water they consume in the process of living.

The water police are watching you. Well, maybe not right now, but if you live in one of the many regions afflicted by drought recently, or perpetually for that matter, you're just a few sprinkler minutes from a citation. Although droughts are serious problems, the bigger problem with water isn't related to the weather.

Turf Talk

Plants take in carbon dioxide and release oxygen through a process called *respiration.* As the oxygen goes out, it carries with it water vapor, and this loss is *transpiration.* Humans also respire, or breathe. When we exhale, we expel carbon dioxide and water vapor, which you can see as condensation on windows or mirrors if you're breathing really close to them.

Turf Talk

Because plants don't have mouths, the respiration and transpiration process is carried on through leaf *stomata,* the equivalent of millions of little mouths all over the surface.

It has to do with the population size. It's one of those "infrastructure" issues you hear about so often from mayors and public works directors on TV. Populations in many communities are on the rise, and the water supply systems are not growing with the demand. So even though there may be plenty of water nearby, unless the water mains are large enough to move it, the end-user demand can't be met.

A Tale of Plants and Water

Plants, such as grass, that are green and juicy need water to stay upright and stiff. When they run out of water, they get soft and wilt. Plants can wilt temporarily, and after you water them, they will pull out of it. But if you deny water past the point of no return, they will stay wilted no matter how much you water them.

Most people think that the roots push water up into the leaves. It's just the opposite. The leaves suck water up out of the roots. If there isn't any water around the roots to suck up, the leaves wilt. Period.

Because grass leaves are short—because you mow them—sometimes it's difficult to see the wilt. They give us another signal, however, a color signal. In fact, this signal is related to where bluegrass got its name. When the leaves aren't getting enough water, they lose their bright green color—they become more blue or blue-gray. If you study a lawn that's drying out, you'll see the color change. It's really obvious when there are abnormally dry spots on the lawn that turn color much sooner than other places.

It's All About Roots and Dirt

Grass can only suck up as much water as the roots encounter in the soil. If the plant has a root system that goes down 2 inches, it only gets to suck water out of the 2 inches of soil. During July or August in dry climates, that water evaporates out of the soil by noon. The only way to ensure that these plants receive consistent moisture around the clock is to water around the clock.

Imagine if you were that grass plant with a deep, healthy root system that's 12-inches deep rather than just 2. You could absorb water out of a huge area of soil with constant moisture levels. This is because lower levels of soil are not influenced by surface evaporation down there. Even if it's hot and dry upstairs, you'd be a happy camper as you sucked up water like crazy. It might take a few days before you consumed all the moisture in such a large root zone, so watering would only have to be done occasionally.

Shallow Watering, Deep Watering

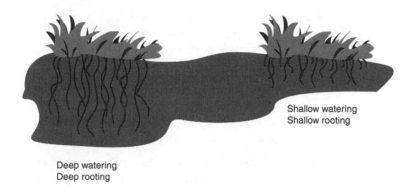

Deep watering
Deep rooting

Shallow watering
Shallow rooting

This shows you how grass with short roots suffers when it's hot and dry. Suffering plants don't look good, and they get weaker over time. Weak plants are more vulnerable to diseases and lose their natural resistance to certain bugs.

Soils Are Like Coffee

When you make coffee, hot water filters down through coffee in a strainer. When you water or when it rains, water percolates down through the soil, too. The rate at which it percolates depends on the density of the soil.

Espresso coffee is made with powdered coffee that is so fine you need a machine to push the water through. Some clay soils are so dense, they seem to resist water like espresso and percolate so slowly that they stand around in puddles waiting to enter. This density also slows the rate at which moisture evaporates from the surface of the soil. Clays are slow to get wet but stay wet deep down for a very long time.

Regular coffee is made with a more coarse grind so that the water passes through all by itself. Sandy soils are like that, and water percolates through almost immediately. The problem is that the water evaporates just as quickly. What doesn't percolate down into a bottomless pit turns to vapor easily through these big gaps. Sandy soils are easy to get wet but difficult to keep wet deeper down.

Turf Talk

The technical term for watering plants is *irrigation*. We use it in this chapter when talking about sprinkler systems and other mechanisms for watering lawns. *Gallons per minute*, or GPM, describes how much water is flowing out of a sprinkler head or flowing through an irrigation system. A standard lawn sprinkler head will put out about 2 GPM, but some heads deliver more or less.

The Rundown on Runoff

Whether a soil absorbs water quickly or slowly, every soil can eventually be saturated. Saturated soils turn into mud because they contain so much water that they turn into a semi-liquid state. Famous Los Angeles mud slides are caused by saturated soil that won't stay put on hills.

Sometimes slow-percolating soil acts like it is saturated. You'll know this is the case when water begins running away from your home, down the driveway, across the sidewalk, and into the gutter. Homeless water is not a good thing. In drought-ravaged neighborhoods, this is inappropriate behavior and can get you in a lot of trouble.

Slow-percolating soil is stubborn and only absorbs water at its own personal rate. There's not much you can do to speed things up. If you use a 2-GPM sprinkler on your soil, and it cannot absorb water at that rate, extra water will be lying around. When there's enough extra water, it gangs up and runs off together.

This illustrates an important point about watering lawns in clay or heavily compacted soil. If you turn on the sprinkler and it pumps out a lot of water but most of it runs off, you have only gotten the top inch or so of soil wet. Watering this way over time gives grass bad rooting habits.

Grass roots go only where there is water. If it's only in the top inch of soil, that's where they will congregate. The vast majority of problems in turf grass lawns comes back to this same situation: plants in dense soils with surface watering are doomed to look icky and get sick.

Aeration is the best way to speed up the percolation rate and help promote deep rooting. Complete instructions for this process are in Chapter 20, "New Life for Old Lawns."

Watering Gizmos and Systems

All lawns need blanket coverage. This means that the entire surface of the lawn should receive the same amount of water so that it all grows evenly.

In a perfect world, we'd all have in-ground sprinkler systems that guarantee blanket coverage. Unfortunately, life isn't perfect, and your home lawn may require a garden hose for watering.

It's important that you understand how each of these systems works to operate and maintain them properly. Your goal should be to provide even watering at the appropriate time and to the most beneficial depth.

Turf Tip

Buy good-quality garden hoses that don't flatten out, tear, or kink easily. Landscapers use many hoses and are particular about how to care for them. Follow these rules to extend the life and efficiency of your hoses:

➤ Don't yank on the hose—this stresses the rubber and cuts off the flow.

➤ Don't drive over the couplers—if cracked or bent, they will leak and need replacement.

➤ Coil hoses loosely to avoid kinks in the hose later on.

➤ Store your hoses carefully—away from freezing temperatures and direct sun.

➤ Immediately replace rubber washers that are lost or damaged.

In-Ground Systems

This kind of sprinkler system must be professionally designed and is a permanent underground fixture. The piping may be galvanized iron or white plastic PVC depending on how cold it gets in the winter. Plastic pipes can't take the pressures of soil freezing nearly as well as iron pipe, but they are much easier to repair.

These systems are usually divided into sections serving a certain number of sprinkler heads at a time. This is because there isn't enough city water pressure to supply a larger lawn all at once. Each section is called a station and is supplied by its own valve. To operate a manual system, you must open the valve to turn on the sprinklers in that station. With an automatic system, a time-clock controller does this for you.

Irrigation systems for lawns are different from elsewhere in the landscape because the lawn must be mowed, and it wouldn't make sense to have to work around upright sprinklers. Plus, they would look weird. Lawn heads lie below the surface of the grass and "pop up" when they water. Afterwards, they go back to a flat position. Your lawn sprinkler heads probably fall into one of these groups.

Turf Caveat

Ever since aluminum, brass, and copper recycling has become big business, there has evolved a problem with sprinkler theft. It's bad in public parks and apartment buildings with big brass valves and heads accessible to the public. If you suspect theft may occur in your neighborhood, avoid brass heads and valves in the front yard. If somebody has swiped your heads, replace them with plastic.

Brass pop-up spray heads are found on galvanized systems that are very old, or where the winter freezes are too tough for plastic heads. The orifice on these heads can be changed to alter the pattern of spray. Because brass is more expensive, these heads have been replaced by plastic wherever possible.

Plastic pop-up spray heads are tubular canisters that lie underground. They have an inner piece that pops up and is topped with a little cap that can be plastic or brass. Each cap is designed to spray in a pattern that is either a whole, half, quarter, or occasionally three-quarter, circle. If you want to change the pattern, you have to change the cap.

Pop-up Head—Impact Head

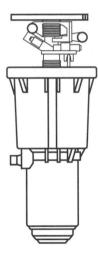

Impact heads are also called Rainbirds. They spray in one stream that depends on the water pressure to make them turn. An adjustment on this head that allows you to change the circle of spray to whatever part of a circle you want. Impact heads for lawns also pop up, but they are in a much fatter can than a spray head.

Garden-Hose Sprinklers

In many regions, it's not cost effective to put in a sprinkler system because of summer rain or other practical reasons. This leaves the garden hose and a sprinkler as the only ways to water your lawn. This isn't a bad thing; it just takes a bit more attention to be sure you get blanket coverage.

It's always a good idea to use a sprinkler that fits your lawn. If it's rectangular, choose a sprinkler that sprays a square pattern. This helps you position the sprinkler at regular places around the lawn to ensure as complete a coverage as possible. If your lawn has rounded edges, use a head that sprays in a circle.

➤ An *oscillating sprinkler*, also known as a flip-flop, sprays a neat rectangular pattern. It may be adjusted to flip on just one side or the other, which makes it handy for long, narrow spaces.

Oscillating Sprinkler

➤ An *impact sprinkler*, also known as a Rainbird, can sit on a platform or stake. It's adjustable to any percentage of a full circle. This is the most adaptable of all the circle spray heads.

➤ *Stationary spray heads* are the smallest and simplest. They are not adjustable, though you can reduce the area they cover by turning down the flow of the hose.

Stationary Spray Head

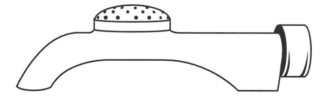

Sprinklers that turn or oscillate require water pressure to move. If you do not keep the hose on full, they may fail to turn or will do so only intermittently. Keep this in mind if you have lower-than-average water pressure, or plan to run a few heads at a time, which together can lower the overall static pressure.

How and When to Water Lawns

When do you water plants? When they need it.

Ask a simple question, get a simple answer. Unfortunately, caring for plants isn't quite that simple; but, when plants are dry, they wilt and tell us visually that they need water.

The problem is that you shouldn't wait until they show you. Plants much prefer an even level of moisture in their root zone to the yo-yo wet-dry-wet cycle. Because evaporation rates and moisture uptake through the roots consume soil moisture much faster in the heat, it makes sense to water more often when it's hot. On the other hand, if your lawn has been in the fog for the past week, chances are it may not need any more water, especially if the moss looks more vigorous than the grass.

The biggest influence on when you water is the weather. One of the set-it-and-forget-it sins of automatic lawn-watering systems is failure to adjust the timer for weather. If you water manually, this is not so often overlooked because if you step out to turn on the water and it's 110 degrees outside, you know you have to keep the water on a bit longer, and maybe give the lawn an extra drink later in the day. If it's raining outside, I guarantee you won't turn on the sprinklers, but the automatic timer will.

Day After Day

The best way to ensure that your lawn is consistently moist is to create a daily schedule. The average lawn soil needs water only every other day or every third day under normal conditions. The schedule will vary if it rains, but this is the basic framework from which you may deviate to compensate for weather. Skip days if it's wet; add a day or two if it's really dry, hot, or windy.

For problem lawns, the basic framework still applies. Lawns that are on very dense soil that is slow to absorb water can only be watered for a short time before runoff occurs. Moisture may not penetrate as deeply, so to compensate, you may need to water every day but for a short time during the peak growing season.

Fast-to-drain sandy soils need watering just as frequently, and sometimes that's every day when it's exceptionally hot and dry. But because the water goes in and out of the root zone so quickly, the plants have only a small window of opportunity to absorb it. To compensate, you may choose to water a second time in the evening now and then to avoid a yo-yo situation during weather extremes.

Time Is on Your Side

The most ideal time of day to water is before dawn in the morning. It should be early enough so that most people aren't up and in the shower yet. During this time, the municipal water supplies are flowing at peak pressure. For in-ground systems, this is a big deal because lower static pressure due to demand elsewhere can affect both efficiency and coverage.

Dew also makes early morning the most water-friendly part of the day. Watering in the heat of the day, when it is driest, makes the water from fan spray heads evaporate. Where water conservation is crucial, this daytime spray is like daytime TV: a social no-no. Unless it is abnormally hot and windy, early-morning watering ensures that nearly all the water you spray on the lawn gets there and stays there.

St. Augustine lawn.

St. Augustine lawn.

Grade change in a lawn using a low retaining wall.

Fescue lawn.

*Lawn edged by
wood benderboard.*

Bluegrass lawn with a narrow brick footpath.

Using broken concrete fragments to protect lawn against foot traffic wear and tear.

Using precast square concrete stepping stones for heavy use patterns in lawns.

Coastal lawns often require salt-resistant turf grasses because dew and salt air accumulate on leaves at night.

An alternative meadow lawn with wildflowers. Paths are mowed to allow access to the seating area.

Creative paving combined with turf grass leads down to a meadow lawn and mowed pathway.

A great shade-loving groundcover, variegated myrtle, Vinca major 'Variegata,' thrives where there is too little sunlight for turf grass. It can be mowed occasionally to renew its beauty.

As lawn dies out for lack of sun, flagstones and Irish moss make an attractive alternative.

Alternative lawn of unmowed creeping red fescue.

Cape weed,
Arctotheca calendula, is frost tender, but its drought resistance is highly valued where water supply is limited, and it rarely needs mowing. Pictured is a mature stand.

During a drought, the lawn at this old Victorian died out and was replanted with cape weed, which filled in perfectly and blooms in lovely yellow daisies.

Fresh rolls of sod as they arrive from the sod farm.

This old St. Augustine lawn illustrates what happens when it's not regularly de-thatched. The surface of the grass is a full 4 inches taller than the top of the adjacent street curb. The brown stripe is the dead thatch newly exposed by an edging machine blade. Renovating a lawn this badly neglected is a major production.

Open back yard recreational lawns are great family use areas.

Rich emerald-green lawns enhance the curb appeal of homes.

A front lawn area graded smooth with rich, dark soil ready to accept a new carpet of sod.

Measuring the lawn to calculate how much you need to order.

Sod is delivered in the driveway.

Apply preplanting fertilizer or pre-emergent herbicide prior to laying the sod.

Rake in fertilizer or herbicide.

Make sure to have the sod unloaded as close to your new lawn area as possible to cut down on time and work.

Lay out the sod one roll at a time starting on one edge.

Before you reach the opposite side, lay out a full strip of sod against the edging so that you don't end up with an abnormally narrow strip there where it's vulnerable to heat, traffic, and dryness.

Stagger each sod strip so that the joints do not line up with one another.

Water immediately after you're finished until the sod feels "squishy."

Greenskeepers at stadiums mow creatively so that the stripes reflect the lines of the sports field.

This lawn has a diamond effect because the lawn is mowed in two different directions.

Lawns are the largest and most important element in the beauty of many home landscapes.

Autumn leaves should be raked up promptly to avoid lawn diseases.

A single stationary spray head on the end of a garden hose can cover a very large area of lawn.

Trees grow better in lawns if the grass edge is set back from the trunk to reduce competition for water and fertilizer.

Lawns are a safe and comfortable recreational surface for families with young children.

Pets enjoy the natural surface lawns provide, but they can also be brutal on lawn health.

Prevailing wind influences the time of day you water. In some areas, such as inland southern California, the Santa Ana winds blowing off the desert kick up in the afternoon. The problem with watering in breezy or downright windy conditions is increased evaporation—the misted water is literally blown away from the lawn. This shorts the grass in terms of how much overall water it receives during a watering period.

Strong winds may blow water away entirely from certain parts of the lawn. You'll know by watching the effects of wind, and if you fail to get that hint, the spots will turn brown, announcing in no uncertain terms that the lawn needs water.

Turf Tip

If you live where winds are a problem with spray sprinkler heads, don't be discouraged. Special types of heads called *stream sprays* are gear driven. Stream sprays throw water out in the same pattern as a spray head, but the streams of water have more wind resistance. In most cases, you can make a direct exchange of your existing spray heads to stream sprays with the same radius and pattern of coverage. Keep in mind, this may not be perfect, but it's as good as it gets.

Duration Doesn't Always Mean Penetration

Duration of watering times has a huge impact on how much moisture reaches the root zone. "Deep watering to the depth of lawn roots" is the mantra of turf experts. "Never water lightly or frequently," they say. That may work in an ideal world, but life isn't fair.

If you're struggling with a problem lawn in the dead heat of summer, you have a special dispensation to throw all that advice out the window until you have time to aerate the lawn. Let's face it, compacted soils just can't absorb water that fast. There's no choice but to water for less time, but more frequently, until repairs can be made.

Older time clocks for sprinklers could go down to just a five-minute watering period and no less. When I worked with compacted lawns, this could be way too much for them to absorb at once. The ideal schedule was about three minutes twice a day, rather than five minutes once a day. Fortunately, new digital controllers allow a much shorter watering period. This tells us that some lawns, and it may be yours, need very short periods of watering.

Turf Tip

The question is . . . how do you deep water when there's runoff three minutes (that's only 180 seconds) after you turn on the water? The only real answer is to water for half this time, turn off the water, and wait an hour. Then turn the water back on again for the rest of the period. You can do this repeatedly to achieve a greater depth, and although it's tedious, it makes a big difference. But don't make it a habit; this is only a temporary fix.

Setting watering duration is simple if you have the luxury of an automatic system. For manual operation, the problem isn't remembering to turn the water on, it's remembering to turn the water off. Whether you have a garden-hose sprinkler or an in-ground system, it takes some effort to time your watering periods.

A good way to help time watering is to use the Pavlov's dog approach—connect watering with another activity. For example, when you get up in the morning, turn on the water sprinkler and then make coffee. When the coffee's done, turn off the water. Systematic and reliable—the association between coffee and your waking brain will soon make this connection automatic.

For the less habit-oriented lawnowner, use the timer on your stove or oven. Never turn on the water without setting the timer. A timed watering is an accurate, efficient, and conservative application.

Turf Tip

Watering with a garden hose wastes water in two ways.

#1: Bent, cracked, or otherwise damaged couplers (the screw-on parts both male and female) leak water continuously.

This one's a simple fix: Replace the couplers. You can get easy-to-install plastic replacements for original metal couplers at any garden center—don't forget the washer.

#2: Water gets left on too long.

Another easy fix: Buy a timer. This kind fits between the faucet and the hose. Turn on the faucet and set the timer, and it will automatically shut off the flow when directed.

Five Reasons Not to Overwater

➤ Oxygen-deprived roots ferment and rot off the plant.

➤ Moisture-loving turf grass diseases flourish.

➤ Runoff from the lawn drowns plants in adjacent beds.

➤ You pay for water you don't use.

➤ There is always mud on the sidewalk and patio.

Efficient Watering Practices When the Heat's On

➤ Check the lawn before you water to be sure that it's dry.

➤ Water late at night or early in the morning.

➤ Avoid watering when it's windy, if possible.

➤ Water using only one valve at a time for peak efficiency.

➤ Reduce foot and vehicle traffic on the lawn.

➤ Slow down on fertilizer applications.

➤ Mow only with a very sharp blade.

➤ Mow at a setting 25 percent higher than normal.

➤ Leave the clippings on the lawn (works like mulch).

➤ Don't overwater the entire lawn to get just a few problem dry places wet enough; use the garden hose to spot water.

➤ Make sure that all sprinkler heads are properly adjusted.

Fine-Tuning an In-Ground System

In-ground systems are more common than ever before and much easier to work with too. Because most problems relate to a lack of knowledge of how these systems work, here's a simple five-step process to become more familiar with your heads and valves. You will learn what you can change, what you can't, and how to know the difference.

Anatomy of an In-Ground System

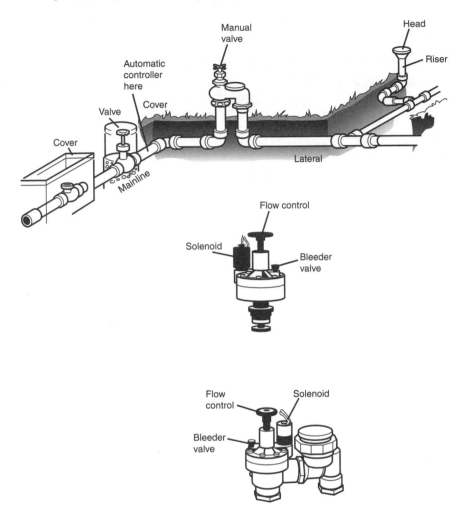

The following process assumes that you have an automatic controller. If you are working with a manual in-ground system, record your findings on paper for future reference.

Step 1: Find All Your Valves

These can be above ground and are often located together near the source of water. They may also be below ground, recessed in accessible valve boxes together, or at various locations.

Step 2: Figure Out Which Ones Belong to the Lawn

Each valve has two adjustments. The big knob on top is the flow control. It should always be fully opened on an automatic system, and when watering manually, always open the flow control completely. The second adjustment is a little knob or wing nut called a *bleeder valve*. If you turn the bleeder, it will open the valve manually so that you don't have to go back and fuss with the controller whenever you're working on the sprinklers. Be sure to turn off the bleeder before opening the next valve.

Step 3: Head Check for Each Valve

Open the first lawn valve at the bleeder, and then go out on the lawn and make sure each head is:

➤ Operating at full flow and pressure

➤ Not throwing water on pavement or shrub areas

If you must clean out a head, go back and turn off the bleeder before removing it. Failure to do so guarantees you a face full of water and sprinkler lines filled with sand that's sucked into the system when you finally get the water turned off.

Step 4: Verify Watering Times

Perform this step four times a year with the changing seasons to ensure that you are watering appropriately. Run each valve until you begin to see runoff. Note the time.

Step 5: Program the Controller

You must now designate which valve corresponds with each numbered station on the controller. Run the system through its stations, and when you know which valve each operates, program your watering times. Then designate an every-day or every-other-day frequency to start. Study the effects daily for a week or two to note whether you need to increase or decrease frequency.

Care and Repair

If you can put together a tinker-toy structure, you can make simple repairs on your PVC sprinklers. PVC is the abbreviated name for polyvinyl chloride, the material used to make white plastic water pipe. You will find PVC sold in long lengths along with little connection fittings. The pipe slides into the fittings and glues in place. In plumbing language, the fittings are usually "female" because they fit over pipe which is considered "male." You will also find PVC pipe and fittings that are prethreaded. These require you to screw them together, which is much more difficult for beginners than the unthreaded "slip" type fittings. In general, most residential sprinkler pipe and fittings are sold in $1/2$-inch or $3/4$-inch diameter sizes.

The typical tasks you may need to accomplish are:

- ➤ Clean a clogged sprinkler head.
- ➤ Change or replace a sprinkler head.
- ➤ Fix a broken riser.
- ➤ Fix a broken pipe.
- ➤ Change or replace a sprinkler head.

The most basic tools for this kind of work are:

- ➤ Small hacksaw or PVC saw
- ➤ Small pipe wrench
- ➤ Medium sandpaper
- ➤ PVC glue
- ➤ Teflon tape

This last item is used for threaded connections that occur only in conjunction with a riser and head. Because plastic is soft, sometimes these connections will leak. To seal it up without using permanent glues, simply lay this flat white tape on the threads of the male part and wrap it around two or three times, before breaking off the tape. Smooth this end down before screwing it into the fitting.

Riser and Head Assembly

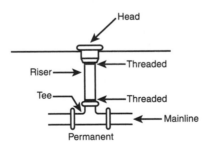

Clean a Clogged Head

A clogged head is caused by debris in the line forced into the small orifice of the sprinkler head. Use the pipe wrench to unscrew the head from the riser pipe. Inspect for big objects and then blow on the orifice where the water comes out to force any object back down where you can remove it. If this doesn't work, take the head apart and clean and replace it.

Change or Replace a Sprinkler Head

Remove the old head and purchase a new one. It must be the same size, deliver a similar gallon-per-minute output, and distribute water over the same percentage of a circle. If silt or debris got in the line when removing the old head, flush the line and then install the new head. It's that simple.

Fix a Broken Riser

Remove the head. Use the wrench to unscrew the old riser. You may be forced to uncover the underground T-fitting to reach the remaining riser base. Buy a new riser the same size and diameter and screw it in. Flush the system from the bleeder valve for a second and then replace the head.

Fix a Broken Pipe

You know when it's broken by the water and silt bubbling out of the ground. With the system off, dig out all around the pipe to expose the break plus a few inches more of good pipe on both sides. Use the hacksaw to cut out the damaged part. Buy two sleeve fittings, a piece of pipe longer than you need, and some PVC glue. Slide the sleeves on the remaining stubs and then cut a piece of pipe to fit in between, allowing for the proper insertion depth. Take it all apart, use the sandpaper to clean up the rough sawn ends, and apply glue. Then quickly assemble it before the glue dries because it dries very fast. Allow the whole thing to cure for 24 hours for a solid set and then flush out the system by removing the next sprinkler head down from the break. Backfill the hole.

Turf Caveat

Before you install your own in-ground sprinkler system, be aware that pressurized systems require a certain amount of engineering if they are to function properly and provide complete coverage. It's worth the expense to have a sprinkler expert design your system and specify the materials. Many home-improvement stores offer free or low-cost design services if you buy the materials through them.

Broken Pipe Repair

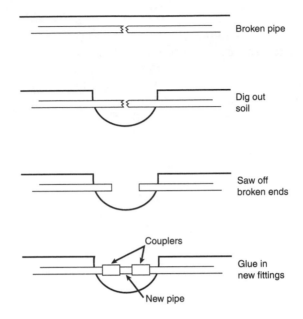

The Least You Need to Know

➤ Weather and seasons influence how and when you water.

➤ Compacted soils are the #1 cause of overwatered lawns.

➤ Water early in the morning or in late evening.

➤ You must become intimate with your sprinkler system to set proper watering times and frequency.

➤ It's simple to make basic repairs on PVC sprinkler systems.

Chapter 18

What's Eating Your Lawn

> ### In This Chapter
>
> ➤ Causes of dead or yellow patches on lawns
>
> ➤ Options in the face of drought
>
> ➤ Dealing with lawn die-out due to cars and people
>
> ➤ Reducing winter damage to lawns
>
> ➤ Repairing a wounded lawn

When elephants fight it is the grass that suffers.

—African proverb

You may not have elephants fighting in the back yard, but some days it may look that way. The perpetual use and abuse of turf grass in the process of everyday living definitely take their toll. On the bright side, it's remarkable just how much abuse some grass types will withstand and still recover. However, we must do our penance by looking at the unsightly brown or bare spots until the healing is complete.

There are many causes of lawn damage. The problems covered in this chapter are related to cultural practices. These are things that happen as a result of living on lawns, taking care of lawns, and environmental changes. Other causes, such as pests and diseases, are covered in upcoming chapters.

Assault and Battery—The Major Offenders

Lawn is like carpeting. We enjoy its beauty, but the real purpose is to keep our feet off the cold floor or dirty ground. This illustrates just how we live on carpet and lawns, day after day, year in and year out. The carpet gets worn and stained over time, and eventually it has to be replaced. But lawns are different—they have the ability to repair themselves.

The American family is by nature abusive . . . to lawns that is. The lawn is the primary outdoor play space, and it's brutalized by kids from toddlers to teenagers. It's not fair to try to take the kids off the lawn to keep it looking beautiful because this denies its fundamental function. Let the kids play and know you can repair practically any damage that results.

These are some of the most common, recurring causes of lawn damage that you may encounter. Some are due to cultural practices and are limited to certain spots. Others are environmental and more widespread, affecting the lawn as a whole. Each is treated a bit differently.

➤ Abnormally heavy foot or vehicle traffic

➤ Dry, dead spots from sprinkler malfunction

➤ Winter damage die-out

➤ Drought

➤ Increasing shade

➤ Scalping due to careless mowing practices

➤ Burns from spilled fertilizer

➤ Gouges from furniture, toys, or golf clubs

➤ Spots from liquid spills from outdoor dining and so on

The Basics of Lawn Patching

Patching bare spots in a lawn can be done in a variety of ways depending on the kind of grass you have. All can be patched with sod, but this may require you to buy a roll and use it within a matter of days. This tight time frame is inconvenient, and you can't always get such a small quantity of all grasses.

You can patch using the same methods for planting a lawn. Seed is the easiest and cheapest way. If you have a warm-season lawn type planted vegetatively, you must buy living sprigs and plugs for patching.

To patch the lawn with seed follow these simple steps:

➤ Remove all the remnants of dead grass, plants, and roots.

➤ Cultivate the soil using a hand claw or rake to a depth of at least 1 inch.

➤ Smooth the surface lightly so that it is level with that of the surrounding soil.

➤ Sprinkle the grass seed lightly and evenly over the whole area.

➤ Cover the seeded area with a ¼-inch layer of finely ground compost or sterilized steer manure.

➤ Keep evenly moist.

Patching a Lawn with Seed

Rough-up soil   Scatter seed   Cover with compost

To patch vegetatively, you can buy some sprigs or plugs from the local nursery, making sure that they are the exact same kind of grass as the rest of the lawn.

➤ Remove all the remnants of dead grass, plants, and roots.

➤ Cultivate the soil over all the area or just where the sprigs or plugs will grow.

➤ Plant the sprigs or plugs at even spacings throughout the entire area.

➤ Mulch the bare soil with a ½-inch or thicker layer of compost.

➤ Keep evenly moist.

Turf Tip

If you have a lawn planted vegetatively with warm-season grasses, you need not always buy new sprigs or plugs. Because you have an existing lawn full of "mother" plants, cut out small squares at least 2-inches deep from very dense spots and refill those holes with good topsoil with lots of compost. Transplant the squares to the bare patches, and fill these in just like store-bought plugs. The borrowed spots will disappear before you know it, and you get to patch absolutely free.

Transplanting Lawn Squares

Cut out square
from out-of-the-way spot.

Rough-up soil

Dig out bed of soil to put
patch at same level as
surrounding grade.

Patch

Burn, Baby, Burn

Everybody has done it at one point or another, and the lawn makes sure that the whole neighborhood knows. Fertilizer spills are so easy to do, and most of the time they're easy to clean up, too. But when you don't realize that it's happened, the burn comes back to haunt you days later after the damage is done.

If you spill granular fertilizer, immediately sweep it up using a whisk broom or rake and a dust pan. Try to get all the granules out of the grass at once. There will be a certain amount of residual powder there that you can't see, so use the garden hose and flood the area so that it's diluted as much as possible. If you spill liquid fertilizer concentrate, water heavily for the next few days in that place to try to leach the nitrogen down and out of the root zone.

Leaching is the best way to remove everything from fertilizer to salt out of your soil. The practice is best if done on fast-draining, rather sandy soils where water moves through quickly.

If your soils are heavy, though, it will take a lot more time, and the leaching may not be as effective. You can wet the burned area completely until water runs off and then turn off the water. Wait an hour or two and do it again. Repeat a couple more times just to be sure. In some cases, the soil may be so hard that the fertilizer fails to penetrate. A thorough flooding of the surface with the garden hose may be enough to carry off the concentrate in the runoff.

Traffic Wear Solutions

Even though turf grass is supposed to be resilient enough to withstand some light foot traffic, it does have its limitations. Some grass types, such as bluegrass, are not nearly as resistant to wear as the tall fescues. Bluegrass requires more time to repair its crushed blades, and, if it's repeatedly crushed, the grass plant as a whole will suffer.

Post-party Problems

Traffic wear can come from many sources. When it's temporary, you can repair the damage easily. For example, if you had a garden party and there's now a noticeable "trail" in the grass to where the bar was, you can help the turf heal far more quickly. The problems are that the soil underneath is compacted and that the grass on top has been crushed.

Here is a quick pick-me-up for this kind of temporary wear damage:

➤ Use a spading fork or aerating tool to poke holes in the soil all along the trail. This opens the soil up to air and water.

➤ If the grass is thin, sprinkle some new seed.

➤ Spread a ¹/₄- to ¹/₂-inch-thick layer of fine compost over the whole area.

➤ Water the grass and keep it moist for two weeks.

If the damage is really bad, you can dig out the grass along the path to an even width and depth. Then buy some sod rolls of the same type of grass and patch the whole thing. This is really the best fix if you had the lawn newly sodded for the party.

Family Patterns

Family-use patterns change as kids grow up. When toddlers turn into bike-riding, perpetual-motion machines, the lawn may be the first to suffer. It will promptly show were it's being overused and threaten to die on you if you don't take some remedial measures.

Turf Caveat

Stepping stones not "planted" deep enough into the lawn surface can become a real hazard. It's bad enough if you trip on one, but if someone else does, you may be in for a lawsuit. Stepping stones that are too high or those that wobble are litigation waiting to happen. Make sure that yours are well planted.

It's human nature and dog nature to always choose the straightest route between two points. If it's from the back door to the garage, the kids and dogs will cut across lawn, planters, and anything else to get to the bikes stored in the garage. After a few months of this, especially during summer vacation, a path of suffering grass appears where this daily pattern takes place. The combination of repeated crushing of the plants and compacted soil results in wear that's highly visible.

Instead of trying habit modification on the kids, and you know how painful that can be, it's best to accommodate this natural pattern. Choose flagstones, fragments of concrete, stepping stones, or unit pavers and install them right into the lawn along that pathway.

Any kind of stepping stone in lawns presents a hazard to you and your mower. Dig out lawn and soil so that the flagstones are recessed enough to avoid being a hazard to the mower. They don't need to be large or particularly wide, just enough to reduce the visual damage to the grass.

Stepping-Stone Pathway

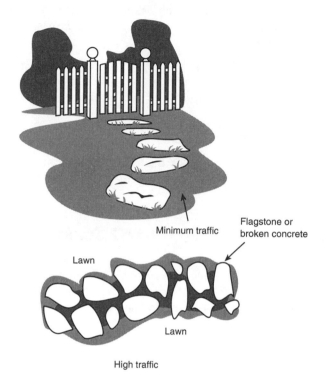

Minimum traffic

Flagstone or broken concrete

Lawn

Lawn

High traffic

Auto Phobia

Another traffic problem is caused by cars. Often, when the kids grow older, they have a car of their own. If there's no room on the street or in the driveway for parking, they often end up on the grass. This is obviously not good for the grass and really compacts soil, too.

The solution comes from products designed to allow fire trucks access over grass that is used as a fire lane in apartment complexes. Generically termed *turf block*, these square paving units are like waffles with open holes. They are laid like paving, but the holes are filled with soil and grass grows through them.

Turf block lets you convert part of your lawn to overflow parking without sacrificing its beauty. Best of all you need not redo the sprinklers, although you may have to switch to more durable heads or alter their height to protect the old ones.

The Dead Zone

When grass doesn't get enough water, it dies. No mystery here, but sometimes it can be puzzling why the grass died. If you don't solve the reason why and just patch the problem, it will happen again.

If you have an in-ground sprinkler system, consider these common reasons for dry spots and ways to fix them. Sometimes the grass will green up again on its own, but if it's been going on for some time, you'll probably have to replant the dead patch of grass.

A Clogged Sprinkler Head

When spray from a head is blocked by debris, it can alter the pattern or cut it off entirely. You must remove the head and thoroughly clean it out, and then replace, test, and adjust it.

A Broken or Out-of-Alignment Sprinkler Head

Lawn mowers, edging equipment, wheelbarrows, and a dozen other gardening tools in adjacent planters can cause heads to be pushed out of alignment. Crooked or turned heads fail to deliver water where they need to. This leaves spots in the lawn unwatered, and they turn brown. Broken heads do the same damage, but sometimes over a much larger area.

This is common on corners and lawn edges next to driveways where car tires roll over the head and either break it or bend it out of position. Repair or replace the head and check the underground riser for damage. You may replace a rigid riser with one of the new flexible rubber ones that protect the head against wayward motorists.

Sprinkler System Design Flaws

You may encounter this upon moving into a new home or after new sprinklers have been installed. Systems improperly designed may leave a dead zone that doesn't receive enough water, or maybe gets no water at all. No matter how you adjust the existing sprinklers, the spot remains dry and will not support grass.

The only solution is to add a new sprinkler head. It must match the other heads in the lawn. Adding a head is relatively simple, but makes a big mess in the lawn.

Here's how to do it step by step:

➤ Find the nearest supply line and dig down to expose it.

➤ Dig a trench to that depth in as straight a line as possible to the place where the new head will go.

➤ Cut the line and install a T-fitting.

➤ Run pipe from the T to the new head location.

➤ Install an elbow and riser.

➤ Turn on the system momentarily to flush out any debris in the line.

➤ Install the new head and adjust the riser height to make the finish position of the head equal to the others.

➤ Backfill all the trenches and patch the lawn where needed.

Adding a Head

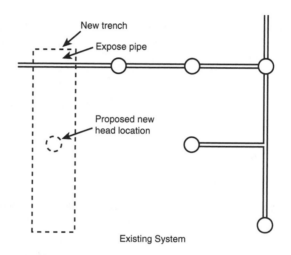

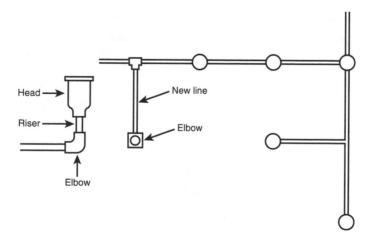

How Now Brown Mound

Water always flows downhill. This seemingly obvious statement gets ignored by many lawnowners with mounds, slopes, or undulating terrain. During the heat of the summer, yellow or brown spots suddenly appear on the high points while the rest of the lawn is evenly green. Why? Because water flows downhill, and, during normal weather conditions, enough manages to soak in to support green grass. But when temperatures soar, so does surface moisture evaporation, making the normal application inadequate.

Don't try to solve this problem by leaving the sprinklers on longer because this drowns the low spots. The best solution is to hand water the dry spots with the garden hose, or set a small sprinkler there on very low flow. It need not deliver a flood of water, just enough to supplement these areas until temperatures cool down. But don't wait until the grass dies to water; start the minute you see the high spots begin to lose their bright green color.

Turf Tip

Sprinkler-head risers are sold in various lengths to accommodate the different sizes of heads and depths of supply line. It's difficult to know ahead of time exactly how tall your riser needs to be when adding a new head. To avoid delays with ill-fitting risers, buy a *cutoff riser*. This is made out of softer plastic and threaded so that you can cut it to any length. These save time and money in the case of lawn sprinklers, where head height is crucial due to mower conflicts.

Cutoff Riser

Old Man Winter's Fingerprints

In northern states where snow, ice, and frozen soils are common, winter can leave its mark on the spring lawn. If you're on the ball and notice these problems early, you can have them repaired before it's warm enough for back yard living.

Heaving

Heaving is much like dirt that grows. It happens most often in spring when days grow warmer but nights are still well below freezing. It's not the long winter cold that hurts the lawn most, it's the repeated freeze and thaw of fluctuating temperatures that's the cause, in addition to the fact that water expands when it freezes.

With the first thaw, the soil melts and absorbs excess water. Come night when temperatures plummet, all this water freezes again. When this saturated soil freezes, the water expands, forcing the soil to actually rise to a higher level. When it melts again the next day, the soil relaxes somewhat.

This is a nasty situation for grass roots. The heaving can tear plant roots apart and expose them to drying air. Although you can mulch other kinds of plants against heaving, mulching the lawn invites turf diseases. The best hedge against the impacts of heaving is to roll the lawn gently immediately after the last ground-freezing frost has passed.

Use an empty roller at first to push grass plant crowns back firmly into the soil. If more weight is needed to smooth out the lawn, add water incrementally because a heavy roller on wet ground can cause compaction problems later on.

Snowbound Traffic

One of the biggest causes of damage is all sorts of human and vehicular traffic during periods of thaw. This can ruin the lawn at corners and along edges of pavement. If you see these dead, smashed areas, be sure to loosen up the compacted soil, seed it, and cover with a thin layer of compost. This will help it recover quickly and boost soil fertility.

You may not see winter-caused dead spots until the lawn begins to green up in spring. Sometimes they are a result of snow molds and other winter-related diseases, which are aggravated by traffic that spreads the spores. It's important to repair these diseased dead zones as soon as the soil can be worked.

➤ Remove all the remnants of dead grass and thatch completely to cut down on the number of spores left behind.

➤ Work up the surface into a fluffy seed bed and feel free to add compost to poor soil.

➤ Sprinkle with seed or plant sprigs and plugs.

➤ Cover with a light dusting of compost over seed and mulch bare soil around sprigs or plugs.

The cool, moist spring conditions will help get the seedlings well on their way before summer heat arrives.

Turf Caveat

Rock salt has been used in the past to melt ice on driveways and sidewalks. Although it works great for this, it's terrible for the adjacent lawns because all that salt ends up in the grass come spring. For a better, healthier lawn, try sand instead of salt.

Repair a Scalp

Chapter 10, "The Art of the Mow," offers more on how improperly set lawn mowers scalp the grass. But the hows and whys seem a bit inconsequential when you're looking at a butchered spot.

Scalping can mean a close crop, or the mower blade can actually scrape the top of the dirt! If you've ever shaved too close, you know what this kind of treatment does to turf grasses.

Mild scalping removes just the leaves. The white stems left behind are suddenly exposed to sunlight. Time for sunscreen, which for lawns is a nice coating of ground peat moss or fine compost. The key is to keep the stems moist so that they can heal. If the stems get dry and sunburned, they'll die back even farther, and you'll get to relish the fruits of your ill labors that much longer.

Severe scalping leaves nothing but the root systems behind on the plants. The problem here is that you can lose the whole plant to shock if it's not very healthy. There isn't much in the way of stems left to sunburn, but like a good case of road rash, you want to apply a protective bandage of compost anyway. Without stems to hold it in place, you'll have to pack the bandage down firmly.

Degrees of Scalping

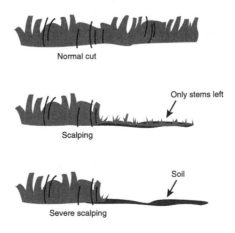

Normal cut

Only stems left

Scalping

Soil

Severe scalping

If you scalped down to bare soil, hedge your bets against die-out by overseeding just in case. It will take weeks for the grass to grow up and turn green again, and the seed makes it look better in the meantime. But either way, seed or patch, be prepared to baby it through hot spells with extra water.

Play Equipment Carnage

Swing sets always go on the lawn because, if kids fall off, they land on this moist, resilient surface. Just a few weeks after the new swing set arrives in the back yard, the wear starts to show, and over time big craters open up under each of the swings. Obviously, this kind of intensive use is rough on the grass, and no matter how many times you repair it, as long as kids still play there, you'll have craters.

Grammar schools have done away with equipment on turf, and they are even getting rid of the sand. Sand isn't that resilient, and it is attractive to every cat in the neighborhood. Instead, they have switched to ground bark because it is so spongy.

If you want to make the play area look a lot better, consider replacing that part of the lawn with bark. You can always change it back to lawn when the kids grow up and decide that bungee jumping is a lot more fun than a jungle gym. Here's how:

➤ Position the swing set so that it interferes with as few sprinkler heads as possible.

➤ Mark out a neat rectangular area just large enough to accommodate the equipment. Move the set out of the way for now.

➤ Cap off any sprinkler heads inside the bark area. Make sure that this does not cause dry spots on the lawn that remains.

➤ Dig out the existing turf to a depth of 1 inch below the soil line.

➤ Use pressure-treated wood two-by-fours along the edges and stake them in place on the inside edge.

➤ Lay out weed barrier fabric to discourage regrowth of lawn and weeds (optional).

➤ Fill with $1/2$-inch-size ground fir bark.

➤ Replace the swing set, and it's ready for play.

Worst-Case Scenario: Water Rationing During Drought

Water is a precious resource, and those who live in perpetually parched western states know that landscaping is the first casualty of over-dry years. There are really two kinds of drought:

Periodic Drought

This can strike just about anywhere from Washington state to Florida. It is the result of an unusually low rainfall, which stresses municipal water storage to the point where end-users are required to limit their consumption.

The strategy for periodic drought is to use as little water as possible and hope the lawn survives or remains alive but dormant until rains come. Follow these tips for lowering water consumption:

➤ Water only in the dark of night.

➤ Don't water unless the soil is dry deeper down.

➤ Stop fertilizing the grass altogether.

➤ Pay attention to how long you run the sprinklers.

➤ Give up and let the lawn go brown.

Persistent Drought

This condition is an ongoing problem where water supplies are not meeting demand, even in years of normal or above-average rainfall. This is typical where communities are growing more rapidly than the existing water system can serve.

When living under these conditions, it is essential to grow a lawn of the most drought-resistant turf grasses possible. You must also keep the lawn in perfect condition so that grasses root deeply, and all the water you apply goes immediately to the root zone and nowhere else.

Turf Talk

The term *xeriscape*, pronounced *zeriscape*, is used to describe landscapes that use very little water. Plants may be native or exotic; it really doesn't matter. What does count, though, is how much water it takes to keep them alive.

If you live in a low-water region, it may be worthwhile to rethink whether to have a lawn at all. Chances are, if the area is growing, the supply will continue to dwindle, forcing water prices sky high.

If you think you might want to trade in the lawn, consider these alternative landscaping options:

➤ Create a nice patio space with shade trees and attractive paving.

➤ Plant drought-tolerant groundcovers. Among those discussed in Chapter 15, "Groundcovers Where Lawns Just Won't Do," the spreading shrubs are your best bet.

➤ Plan a garden of drought-tolerant native shrubs and perennials that offer far more variety, color, and interest than lawn.

➤ Design a total xeriscape garden with lawn-substitute groundcovers, plus perennials, shrubs, and trees already adapted by nature to withstand minimal watering.

Shade, Shade Go Away

One of the few constants in this big universe is that plants grow, day in and day out, little by little. When it comes to lawns, this can spell trouble. Small trees get big and cast ever greater shadows. Shrubs grow tall, too, and cast their own shade at certain times of day. Whether a tree is in the lawn or next to the lawn doesn't matter much in terms of shade.

Here are some examples of difficult shading problems:

➤ Evergreens cast shade year round. This means that even in mild climates they cast a shadow in every season, which rules out growing grass underneath them.

➤ Wide, umbrella-shaped trees have the greatest shading potential. They can also spread out to influence lawn growth when planted many feet from the edge of the lawn.

➤ Conifers and oaks tend to make soils under them not only shady but also highly acidic, and double the conflict potential. Black walnut and eucalyptus don't change pH, but they exude natural herbicidal chemicals that make the area under their canopies hostile to plants that would compete for water.

There are really only a few options for dealing with overshaded lawns:

➤ Remove the tree. This is logical if a landscape has matured, and the trees are a bit crowded. It also helps those that remain to be healthy and disease free.

➤ Have tree trimmers thin the canopy to let more light through. Some trees, such as Chinese elm and fruitless mulberry, develop over-thick canopies. Use a certified arborist to ensure that the tree is thinned, not butchered.

➤ Abandon the lawn and turn the area into a shade garden or patio.

269

The Least You Need to Know

➤ You can fix most problems by patching and TLC.

➤ Sometimes you have to redesign new walkways and play areas into the lawn.

➤ Malfunction of sprinkler systems causes big problems often discovered when evidenced by lawn spots.

➤ Traffic over snow, rock salt, and soil heaving is the chief cold-climate winter lawn problem.

➤ Don't plant trees in lawns, and, if you have a tree cut down when appropriate, it won't spell the demise of the ozone layer.

Chapter 19

Pets and Wildlife and Your Lawn

In This Chapter

➤ Female dog spot disease and other unexplainables

➤ How to live in harmony with dog and lawn

➤ Other mammals that want to trash your lawn and why

➤ Gentle, user-friendly control measures for reducing critter damage

➤ How to get help with serious wildlife problems

What counts is not necessarily the size of the dog in the fight—it's the size of the fight in the dog.

—Dwight D. Eisenhower

Eisenhower may not have been talking about back yard dogs, but he sure got it right about lawns. A small terrier, champion of all digging breeds, can turn a gorgeous lawn into a pot-holed battlefield overnight. A good-sized retriever can un-sod a lawn in minutes. Try a mastiff for a couple of days, and you've got a lawn studded with volcano-sized land mines—personal gifts from your heavy-feeding canine friend. It's not necessarily the size of the dog, but his or her personal damage potential that counts.

Mammals that pester lawns aren't always domestic. Nobody wants to mow a lawn corrugated by mole tunnels or pocked by gopher mounds. It would curl your hair to see what a grub-hunting skunk can do to St. Augustine grass. Even field mice are a problem in winter as they rip up the grass, tunneling under a protective layer of snow.

This chapter has two parts: one dealing with dogs and cats, the other focusing on wild animals. Each part is treated differently, depending on where you live and how serious the damage can be.

Man's Best Friend

Dogs can be a beloved member of the family. They eat when we do, share the same rooms, and provide valuable home security. Most of all, they're fun for both adults and children. When conflicts arise between dogs and lawns, the solutions must respect the animal and his or her place in the household. Getting rid of the dog for the sake of the lawn is not an option.

It's important to distinguish the difference between back yard lawns and those out front on the street. What goes on in the back is directly the result of your pet. What happens in the front lawn is another matter because damage here is usually caused by other people's dogs.

Dogs love lawns, but lawns aren't really fond of dogs. The damage done to your lawn by four-legged friends falls into one of these five categories listed according to their frequency.

➤ Puppy and adult female dog urine burns the lawn and kills grass.

➤ Feces burn lawn more slowly and make it hard to mow and icky to sit on.

➤ Digging small holes or large ones for a cool damp place to lie down is common in hot weather.

➤ Puppies and young adult dogs chew off sprinkler heads and pipe.

➤ Traffic patterns of dogs can wear out trails or areas in mature lawns.

Female Dog Spot Disease

I won't beat around the bush. . . . Dog urine is devastating to lawns, and the female urine is the major offender. It's not that female urine is any different from that of a male dog. It's the delivery that varies. Females and young males squat to urinate in one spot. At about one year of age, the males start leg lifting, which occurs frequently but in shorter bursts. So instead of trashing your lawn, they start burning all your bushes! Same problem, different plane.

When dogs urinate, they are eliminating excess nitrogen from their bodies. That's right, nitrogen, the major fertilizer ingredient preferred by lawns. The difference is in potency. Dog urine contains such a huge amount of nitrogen that it's like pouring pure fertilizer on the grass. Tests have shown that as little as 1 ounce of urine on fescue is enough to cause serious burns.

Over time, the untreated concentration of nitrogen in the spot decreases, but studies show that, in most cases, even a small dose of urine can take a minimum of 30 days to neutralize. Recent studies have put to rest some notions that it is the pH of urine that does the burning. Not so. The concentration of nitrogen simply is the sole culprit.

The best way to reduce the concentration coming out of the dog is to feed moist canned food, or moisten dry food with water prior to feeding. Some vets recommend that you shake a little salt or garlic salt on the dog's food to encourage drinking of water. However, check with your veterinarian first to be sure this is right for your dog.

You can treat urine spots in your lawn if you catch them early. The problem is you usually don't know that they're there until the grass turns brown. Treat the spot like you would spilled concentrated liquid fertilizer—flood it with the garden hose, thoroughly saturating the soil in an area slightly larger than the visible spot. For best results, do this a few days in a row. Chances are, if the grass lived through the onslaught, it will come back greener and more luxuriant than the surrounding turf. What was a bare spot becomes an overly green spot as the grass is stimulated by the excess nitrogen. Eventually, this, too, will even out.

Land Mines

Dog feces are more than just a grass problem; they're a people and mower problem. These land mines vary in size with the dog, but unlike urine, they do not vary by gender. Males and females defecate exactly the same.

Just like urine, feces contain high concentrations of eliminated nitrogen and will burn lawns. But because only a portion of the mass actually contacts the grass, much of this does not burn immediately. It sheds nitrogen gradually, and latent piles often have an emerald-green ring around the edges due to nitrogen green-up. In city parks, the land mines are usually picked up frequently, which reduces the damage potential considerably.

There's another factor, though. When stepped on by dogs, kids, and unwary adults, feces are ground into the grass, and, of course, the plants suffer accordingly. If you've never mowed over a land mine and watched it spray out the discharge chute, you're missing one of the most offensive aspects of lawn care. Obviously, removing the land mines is a crucial step before mowing the lawn.

Turf Caveat

The health of your pet is essential. Do not fall for any home remedies or diet modifications that are supposed to reduce the potential for lawn damage by either urine or feces. Fruit juices and vitamin C do not change the pH. Giving the dog potassium or baking soda is no help either and can actually cause bladder stones or infections.

Here are some ways to reduce the fecal damage potential:

➤ Pick up the land mines frequently.

➤ Use the garden hose on each spot right afterwards to dilute residual nitrogen.

➤ Train the dog to do its business somewhere else.

➤ Change the dog's diet to food that provides the same nutrition but less volume.

➤ Don't step on it or mow it.

Turf Tip

Nitrogen content in feces and urine is related to food. Vets say most dogs are not very active, and dog foods contain far more protein than is necessary. Once inside the dog, the protein is not utilized and is transformed into nitrates that are later excreted. Dogs in obedience training are often fed treats that are high in protein as well, which can contribute to the potency problem. Be aware of your dog's food and try to avoid premium and super-premium pet foods. If you're in doubt, ask your vet for a good low-protein, low-volume brand.

Canine Neuroses

Dogs are a lot like people. They need friends. They don't like to be ignored. When they feel left out, they have little dog problems. When these crop up suddenly, it's time to spend more quality time with the pooch or seek out a dog shrink, or your lawn may suffer the consequences:

➤ Chewing on the fence, your house, and everything in the back yard

➤ Barking so much that you and your entire neighborhood threaten to go ballistic

➤ Strange bathroom behaviors outside of normal patterns

Some develop severe separation anxiety when you go to work, and there's no one to play with. The birth of a child, particularly the first baby, always makes you less attentive toward the dog. It can suffer from more than just a loss of intimacy; Fido may be a risk to the baby and have to stay outdoors all the time.

The solutions to these problems can be difficult. Unless they are treated, you might as well kiss your lawn good-bye. But like people, often the best remedy is quality time, your time. Take the dog for walks; spend more time with him or her. If this doesn't work, consult your veterinarian. New Prozac-like drugs for dogs are proving virtual lifesavers for anxiety-ridden canines.

Digging

Dogs dig for different reasons. In warm climates, it's common for dogs that are too hot to dig big holes and then lie in them. This is because the soil deeper down is more moist and cool than the hotter stuff on the surface. Even worse is that when the sprinklers come on, the hole will fill up with water that turns the whole thing into a mud bath.

Because your dog is deciding on its terms where the hole will be, you can turn the game around and decide where you want the hole to be. Choose an out-of-the-way place that's nice and shady for most of the day. Dig a hole about the size of the one in the lawn but 6 inches deeper. Then line the pit with coarse construction sand from 4 to 6 inches deep. This acts as a barrier between dog and mud. Some folks even line the sides of pits for large dogs with a single row of concrete block to keep them from caving in. If the sprinklers don't water the pit, keep it wet during the hottest weather and encourage the dog to lie there. Chances are he or she will prefer it over your lawn . . . or at least let's hope so.

Chewing

Puppies are the biggest source of chewing problems, but, fortunately, this is only a short-term problem. Occasionally, some adolescent and adult dogs will chew out of frustration, loneliness, or boredom. It's rare that a dog chews up the lawn. They much prefer to mangle plastic sprinklers. The M.O. is to start tugging on the head and then chew it off entirely if they can.

The best way to control chewing is to make the sprinkler head too hot to handle. Hot, peppery substances sold at pet stores can be wiped or painted on. One mouthful, and the dog may be too afraid to chomp another hot tamale. Because the material is washed off every time you water, apply the product and avoid watering for a few days. Let the animal get a taste. It may take a few applications before your pet gets the message.

Turf Tip

Horses chew on wood corrals. The traditional cowboy home remedy is cayenne pepper. Putting a dusting of the powder or a potent solution mixed with water on the wood discourages horses from chewing it. Try this on your dogs, whether they are chewing on sprinkler heads, decks, lawn furniture, or fences. Check the Mexican foods section of your supermarket for powdered cayenne, which costs a fraction of that sold in the regular spice department.

12-Volt Discouragement

The best way to keep animals off the lawn is with hot wire. It's low voltage so don't feel as though you're buying a maximum-security prison for the back yard. Although these systems don't look that great, they are problem solvers for newly seeded lawns because they can be set up temporarily. Some models run off little solar panels so they are simple to set up, and you only need one or two strands to discourage a dog. After the lawn is established, you can take it down. These are great if you have an *el destructo* puppy or want to keep the lawn part of the yard free of dogs without the prison yard look. Buy this product at home improvement stores for about $100.

Hot Wire

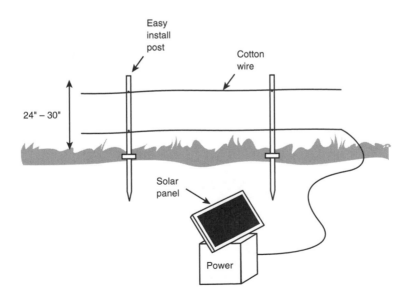

Another higher-priced deterrent is the *invisible fence*. It's simple—a main cable that's hidden in the lawn or around its edge sends up an invisible electric field. The dog wears a special collar that will give off a small electrical shock if the unit passes over the cable. Many people have found that after a few zaps, they can turn it off, and the dogs will stay away. Buy one of these systems at a full pet supply store or a feed store that caters to small animals.

Lawn and Landscapes for Dogs

There are no bad dogs.

—Penelope Woodhouse

Dogs are what we make them. The nicest dog can be made aggressive by abuse and poor handling. Conversely, a pit bull can be a pussy cat if properly loved and nurtured to be gentle when still a puppy. House training of dogs shows that we can alter their defecation behavior, and this can be extended to the yard. The key is to understand the psychology of pets to create spaces for them to use as a bathroom rather than your lawn.

Here's the process:

➤ Choose a space to be dedicated to the dog—side yards are great.

➤ Surface it in pea gravel, finely ground bark, or decomposed granite. You can plant grass there, too. The idea is to keep it well drained and free of mud.

➤ Add a post or object for marking. This can be a wood post, bird bath, boulder, or faux hydrant for kicks.

➤ Provide a "scent incentive" to show dogs it's their space.

➤ Train the dog to use the area properly.

A Side Yard Dog Yard

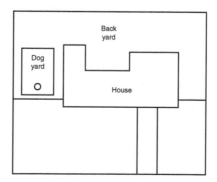

Your dog needs to know that this is a bathroom, which is indicated by scent. Vets recommend you collect dog urine in a cup to pour on and around the post, though they don't say how this is done exactly. . . . Refresh this scent frequently and distribute some feces on the dog's area as well. With luck, your dog will get the message in as short as a few weeks to a few months. If it doesn't, you can consult a trainer for a more structured behavior-modification program.

Front Yard Confrontations

Lawnowners go nuts when roaming dogs relieve themselves on the front lawn—a public lawn that's privately owned. What's worse, the damage is often done at night, or while you're gone during the day, so you never see the dog, just its gifts.

To show you just how crazy people get about this, one home remedy is to put ugly milk jugs on the front lawn. I have never found out exactly what's in the jugs, perhaps ammonia as a scent repellent. Nevertheless, I find it hysterically funny that people will destroy the beauty of their lawns with all those tacky jugs to avoid a few dog spots. What's even more weird is that there's no evidence it works!

Repellent products are not largely effective despite the promises on the label. Vets tell us that some dogs make an extra effort to over mark these scents.

Here are some other options:

➤ Fence the front yard permanently with pickets or another attractive design.

➤ Install a motion-activated sprinkler designed to frighten animals away from vegetable gardens. Be aware that squirrels, kids, and birds will set it off.

➤ Track down the offending animal's owner and remind him or her about leash laws.

➤ Find out more about the milk-jug trick.

Wildlife and Lawns

You would be surprised at how much trouble wildlife can cause in suburbs and even some cities. The more open space and undeveloped land there is, the greater the abundance of wildlife. You may at some point face a warm-blooded mammalian marauder that finds your lawn a convenient food source.

But wildlife isn't always detrimental. The whole concept of Integrated Pest Management (IPM) is based upon many of the crucial relationships between predator and prey. We like the predators that go after prey species that afflict lawns. Theoretically, we want to encourage the predators, as long as their hunting tactics don't create more damage to the lawn in the process.

These are the crown jewels of all gardens because each is capable of consuming huge numbers of pests:

➤ *Birds* are the most beautiful and effective hunters. They go after everything from grubs to grasshoppers. This is why bird baths have always been popular in lawn areas. The goal is to encourage the birds to hang out. You can try nesting boxes or bird houses approved by Audubon as suitable for bird species in your area. Bird feeders ensure that they will remain even after all the lawn pests are consumed.

➤ *Lizards* are very good pest controllers. They eat all sorts of bugs and can even keep flea populations in dog areas to a minimum. They do not bite you, nor do they sting or smell, and they are all-around good guys. Their quick movements make them a favorite prey of house cats.

➤ *Snakes* are too often misunderstood. Of the more than 200 species of snakes in North America, only 4 are venomous! Garter snakes, gopher snakes, and many other common species are excellent predators. Nothing else will so willingly disappear down a gopher hole and consume soil-dwelling pests.

➤ *Toads and frogs* are a sign of a healthy garden A single toad will consume 10,000 to 15,000 bugs in a single season! They venture out at night to gobble up all sorts of insects, larvae, and even moths and flies. Some gardeners so welcome these amphibians that they leave overturned clay pots around the garden for habitat.

➤ *Bats* can consume more than 600 mosquitoes in a single night, and they are equally as fond of dinner moths. This is important because many lawn-damaging larvae become night-flying moths after metamorphosis. Though you don't want bats in the walls, they are welcomed by all gardeners.

Belling the Cat

Domestic house cats can be great friends and highly efficient hunters. Yes, they are valuable for hunting mice and rats, but that's it. Ask any wildlife biologist about domestic cats, and you'll get some very harsh words. Why? Because cats by their very nature are killers. They kill for entertainment, not always for food. As a result, domestic cats can absolutely devastate the beneficial organism population. With the birds, lizards, and their helpful kin wiped out, there's nothing to stop the insect kingdom from multiplying unchecked.

I experienced this a few years ago. The cats had killed off the abundant population of lizards that were here when I first moved in. All of a sudden my dogs were tortured by an uncontrollable infestation of fleas. After hundreds of dollars of flea shampoo, spray, and other products, there seemed no end in sight. Something was out of balance.

I was reminded of that childhood fable *Belling the Cat*. It seemed too simple a fix, but I put a small bell on my cat's collar anyway to give the prey fair warning. The next season, the fleas were gone, and they have never returned. Now lizards and small frogs are everywhere, consuming every flea and flea larvae on the property. Balance and harmony have returned to my marriage and my dogs. I feed the cat extra to make up for his loss and my gain.

Rodenta Non Grata

Rodents comprise a group of generally undesirable pests. The two that cause the most problems in lawns are moles and gophers. They are often confused with one another, but they are very different critters in appearance and behavior. Here's how they differ:

Gophers	Moles
Eat plants and roots	Eat insects, larvae, worms
Tunnels aren't visible on surface	Visible ridges mark tunnels
Make exit-hole earth mounds	Make exit-hole earth mounds
Have big teeth that dig	Small, pink cone-shaped snout
Brown fur	Black, very fine fur
Small front feet	Big flipper front feet
Trap inside tunnels	Trap from above tunnels

Turf Caveat

The best way to control moles and gophers is to never allow them into your garden. Unlike flying pests, these guys have to dig their way in. The most common sources are neighbors' yards, vacant lots, open space, and wild lands next to you. If you see fresh mounds popping up next door, be prepared to control them there, before they get to your yard.

Once you have moles or gophers, they are difficult to control, so keeping them out is the best remedy. Underground barriers can be made of sheet metal, small mesh hardware cloth, aviary wire, or concrete. They should extend to 24 inches deep and stick up a few inches above the soil to keep the rodents from going over the top. The old-fashioned plant barriers consist of tightly planted rows of castor bean, gopher plant (*Euphorbia*), and oleander bushes. Be aware that all these plants are poison to both humans and animals.

Gopher Broke

Gophers live underground and feed on the roots and stems of most plants. In old cartoons, gophers are often depicted pulling plants down into their holes while the astounded farmer looks on in frustration. This is not far from the truth.

Here's why gophers are hard on lawns:

➤ They eat the roots off the grass, and if the plant doesn't die, it struggles until healed.

➤ Sprinkler water runs down their holes and away from the lawn before it has the opportunity saturate the root zone.

➤ Mounds destroy lawn beauty and are hard on the mower and its blade.

➤ When tunnels collapse, they leave behind unsightly depressions that must be filled and replanted.

Gophers are the worst because you never see them. They live in a network of tunnels that can be from 4 to 14 inches below the soil surface. They push all the dirt out into mounds through lateral tunnels. However, the little fellows spend most of their time in the main tunnel, and control measures must be used there. Most people make the mistake of treating at the mounds because that's the only visible part.

Gopher Tunnels

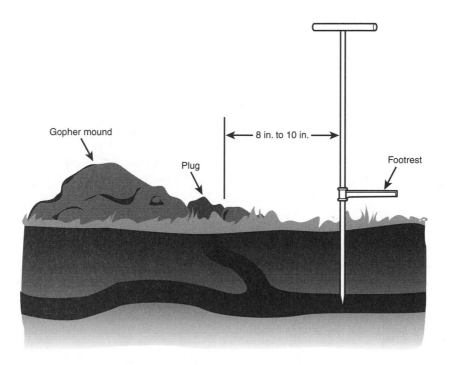

Hatred for gophers runs hot and deep. People have thought up all sorts of ingenious ways to kill them or discourage them enough to go elsewhere. You can't flood them out because burrows are designed to allow for this. Some folks smoke them out with road flares. Others pipe car exhaust into the burrow. But despite these creative ideas, there are only a few safe and hopefully effective measures:

Poison

Poison bait is the easiest choice for beginners. Poisoned grain or cakes of poisoned bait are the most common gopher products available at home improvement stores. I prefer the grain or pellets, and sometimes add some minced fresh apple and cabbage leaves to sweeten the offering.

Turf Caveat

Poison is not a selective killer. Gopher bait is toxic to pets; if the dog digs it up, it could be poisoned. Young dogs are more vulnerable because they dig and chew more. Keep all poisons out of the reach of children and always wear gloves when handling it. Wash hands and arms thoroughly with hot water and soap immediately after handling baits.

The cleanest way to get the poison to the gopher is to use a $1/4$- to $1/2$-inch-diameter metal rod or pipe. You can poke a rod down into the soil to prod for the burrow. You'll know if you got it by the lack of resistance. Remove the rod and then carefully spoon the bait into the hole. Cover it with a small stone because dirt will sift down inside and cover the bait. I do this at regular intervals along the entire network of burrows.

Cakes are more difficult because you have to make a bigger hole to get them into the burrow. Because they contain poison, you need to be careful how and where you break them up.

Traps

No matter how easy it may appear on the instructions, it's difficult to trap gophers. I have yet to catch one. But many people do have success. First, you must find the main runner tunnel, which is in itself easier said than done. Use a rod to prod the ground for its location and alignment.

Gopher traps always come in pairs. This is because you must dig a hole in the main runner to set a trap in each side tunnel. That way the gopher is forced around the traps if he wants full access. Often traps are connected with a wire and staked into place because some gophers, if not killed outright, will drag the traps away. It's advisable to wash the traps well and wear gloves when handling them to reduce the amount of human scent that lingers, because this may be a tip off.

Gopher Trap

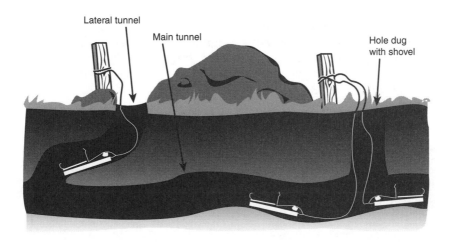

Giant Destroyers

The third kind of product you can buy for gophers is a *gasser*. It looks like a little stick of dynamite with a fuse. You light it up, and, after it starts smoking, you shove it into an open burrow. They come in packages of four, and it's common to use them in different parts of the burrow all at once. This product uses sulphur to displace oxygen in the burrow to asphyxiate the gopher. It isn't always effective.

Pollution Solution

It might surprise you that the university extension IPM experts endorse this means of fumigation. You fumigate the burrow with exhaust from your auto or tractor or small engine, and the carbon monoxide kills quickly and humanely. You need a suitable vehicle or small engine. Get some motor oil and a 10-foot length of flexible metal pipe from the auto supply store.

➤ Sprinkle a few drops of oil into one end of the pipe.

➤ Slide that end over the rigid exhaust pipe; it should fit snugly.

➤ Place the other end in the burrow and pack soil around it firmly.

➤ Turn on the engine and let it idle for 5 to 10 minutes.

The oil drops will burn and produce black smoke, which will help you see any spots where there are air leaks in the burrow. Plug these immediately. In case the gopher pops out of the ground, be prepared with a shovel and kill it immediately.

Moles' Holes

Moles are half blind, which is compensated for by their remarkable sense of smell. Moles are actually insectivores and rarely feed on plants as gophers do. This feeding habit makes them somewhat beneficial because they consume the undesirables, but in the process they create air pockets in the root zone, which is not good for plants.

The damage moles do to lawns is much more visible. Their feeding tunnels occur next to the surface of the soil where most of the grubs, larvae, and insects live. Tunnels are easy to see as ridges. If you damage or crush an active burrow, the mole will repair it quickly. If you step on the ridge or roll it, it will flatten out easily as the tunnel collapses, and the grass recovers. If the tunnel is allowed to remain, it causes the roots to dry out and die back.

Turf Caveat

Mole and gopher traps are spring loaded and have sharp tongs that can easily puncture your skin. Handle them with extreme care. Gopher traps are particularly dangerous because you must set them before inserting into the tunnel. Avoid handling these if you've been drinking alcohol.

Mole burrows include two types of runners—deeper ones that are the main travel tunnels and those on the surface, which are visible and are the feeding habitat. Moles remove soil through their doorways in "hills."

Mole Tunnels

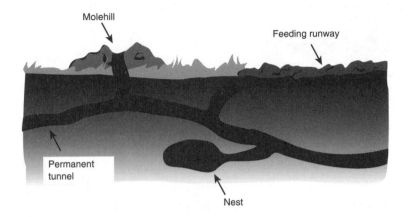

There are only two methods for control in lawns:

➤ Flood the burrows. Use the garden hose through the hill only, and, once flooded, the mole either dies or comes out, so be ready with a shovel. This is very effective in early spring when the young are in their nest.

➤ Trap moles. Use one of the three top recommended brands: Out O' Sight, Victor, or Nash. Unlike gopher traps, these do not go inside burrows but are set on top of the surface feeder runs. They crush the feeder tunnel as they are set, and when the mole comes back to repair it, he's lights out.

Mole Trap

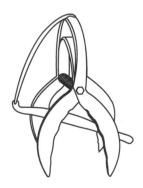

Turf Tip

If you have moles in the garden, make it a habit of stepping on every new ridge you see. This can significantly reduce root damage, and plants will be no worse for the wear.

Pepe Le Pew

You probably don't think of skunks as lawn problems, but they are much like moles. Skunks are also insectivores and are lured into lawns by the juicy grubs and other larvae that come out at night to feed on the surface of the soil. Skunks are nocturnal and are known to come into lawns and literally peel back the sod to get at the goodies. In fact, newly sodded lawns are extremely vulnerable to skunks.

Skunk scent is notorious, and, for this reason, they have no natural predators. This makes them haughty and slow to flee. They are also the most common carrier of rabies. Between the stink and the rabies, it's pretty clear that these are not nice animals to have around.

The best way to deal with skunk problems is to call your local county animal control unit. They are prepared to live trap the animals for you and take care of the problem. If you or your dogs do get sprayed by a skunk, use tomato juice, vinegar, or other highly acidic products to reduce the smell. Unfortunately, nothing gets rid of it entirely. Pee-yew!

The Least You Need to Know

➤ A nitrogen overdose causes female dog spot disease.

➤ Help spots recover by flooding with water and replanting.

➤ You can train your dog to do his business in his own bathroom area.

➤ Gophers are difficult to control once established; it's best to keep them out before they get in.

➤ Skunks and moles eat bugs, making them beneficial; but they damage lawns and stink, so they must be gotten rid of.

Part 6
Old Lawn Makeovers

Underneath every lawn there's soil, your secret treasure trove that supports a perfect lawn. But like anything else, it gets worn out and needs to be beefed up from time to time. Most gardeners don't realize that there's a direct relationship between the quality of soil and the ability of grass to resist common lawn diseases. If you get one thing right, it has to be the care and nurturing of your little patch of earth.

Just because your lawn looks old and worn out, it doesn't mean you have to replant the whole thing. After all, they don't replant golf courses because people wear out the grass. It's actually fun to renovate your lawn because of the rewards you get when it greens up and starts looking beautiful again. You'd be surprised at how many people are dissatisfied with their lawns, and if you listened in over the back fence, you'd discover they never renovated them either!

BEFORE   AFTER

Chapter 20

New Life for Old Lawns

In This Chapter

➤ Recognizing the signs of aging in your lawn

➤ An overview of the renovation processes

➤ Topdressing: the forgotten cure-all

➤ Overseeding for color and change in grass type

➤ Reconciling turf grass and lawn trees

The only remedy is a tedious and expensive one, that of constant and plentiful topdressing with a compost of manure. . . .

—Andrew Jackson Downing, 1865

Grass was grass a thousand years ago, and it will still be grass when we enter the fourth millennium. What makes grass grow well will never change. And when a stand of grass gets old, we use the same techniques as the gardener of Downing's day, but now it's a lot easier.

Turf grasses live a long time. Each type of grass has its own signs of aging that should be treated so that it doesn't impact the overall beauty and vigor of the lawn. There are regular maintenance tasks such as watering and mowing, but occasionally you need to give the grass a renewing "shot in the arm." This is like a beauty makeover for tired, worn-out turf.

Turf Talk

The term *topdressing* describes the practice of spreading material on the surface of the ground. It acts as both verb, referring to the practice, and noun, describing materials suitable to this use. Topdressing can be done with a variety of materials from manure to compost and even sand in some cases. When you apply granular fertilizer, you are topdressing it into the grass.

Turf Caveat

Any seeds brought into your lawn with topdressing materials have a good chance of germinating and growing to adulthood. You want to keep your lawn a monoculture—an environment where only one kind of plant grows. Fully composted material or material labeled as "sterilized" or "weed-seed free" is essential. Avoid using manure out of your neighbor's barn, which can bring an invasion of weeds!

Topdressing: Why We Lay It on Thick

Mulching plants is a big part of successful gardening. We put mulch around plants and shrubs as a protective layer that sits on top of the ground. It insulates roots from the heat, reduces surface evaporation from the soil, and gradually breaks down into humus. Mulches are good things for all plants.

The problem is, how do you provide these same benefits to lawn grass? By topdressing. All you do is spread the stuff around evenly over the entire surface of the lawn and then rake it down into the grass. Of course, to get it to filter down, it has to be small and finely ground in the first place.

The Hidden Organic Benefits of Topdressing

You probably learned in grammar school the importance of rotating crops in farming. Heavy feeders such as cotton and tobacco are examples of crops that deplete soil quality after just a few plantings. Can you imagine what happens to the soil underneath your lawn after 20 years?

Year after year, the same plants are consuming all the humus that exists within their root zone. Unless humus is replaced, the microorganism populations dwindle, and soil conditions become more hostile to the plants.

Topdressing is the only way to replace the valuable humus in lawn soils. This organic matter keeps microorganism populations high, and they in turn run around down there opening up the soil so that roots can penetrate more easily. If humus is never replaced, the soil becomes more sterile, and the plants suffer from deficiencies.

Topdressing also has another benefit. Some believe that the way to get rid of thatch is to topdress more often. The microorganisms move right into the thatch underneath the topdressing and start to consume it. This ideal situation might be successful with a thin thatch layer, but it's no solution for thicker ones. If we had the time and material to topdress repeatedly throughout the year, perhaps no thatch removal would be necessary at all.

But alas, time and the logistics of doing this don't make it practical. It does illustrate, however, the hidden benefits of topdressing that are not provided by synthetic fertilizers.

Qualities of Topdressing Materials

Good topdressing material must be:

➤ Available in quantity—it takes a lot of material to topdress a good-sized lawn.

➤ Affordable—don't choose Cadillac material for a Chevy lawn or budget.

➤ As weed-seed free as possible—you don't want to import noxious plants into your lawn.

➤ Finely textured—it should be easy to spread and rake in without sticking or clumping.

➤ Easy to apply with a spreader—if you use a spreader, chunks of hard stuff will clog and jam the mechanism.

> **Turf Caveat**
>
> Love thy neighbor and thyself . . . or something like that. If you choose steer manure or other types of composted manure for top-dressing, be prepared for a stink. If you or your neighbor is a super smeller and has a difficult time with potent odors, consider a different topdressing material.

How to Buy Topdressing

These are the most common materials you will find around town for topdressing. Most are sold as weed-seed free, but check the label just to be sure.

➤ Compost

➤ Sterilized steer manure

➤ Leaf mold

➤ Pine bark humus

➤ Peat humus or ground peat moss

➤ Sandy loam topsoil

➤ Worm castings

Specialty Topdressing Product

This is the black-thumb gardener's best bet because there's no chance of getting the wrong stuff. Many garden centers carry bagged material specially formulated and sold as topdressing. It will be labeled as such, and you can be sure it's suitable for use in a spreader. You will pay more for this kind of product because it is so specialized, but it consists of a combination of many of the materials recommended for topdressing in the previous list.

Turf Tip

Because you only have to topdress occasionally, do it right. If you have a big lawn, hauling dozens of bags home in the car may not be practical. For that big renovation chore you do every few years, order the material in bulk and have it delivered to your driveway. It's easier to load, there are no bags to dispose of, and it can be cheaper.

Consult your Yellow Pages for "landscape materials or supplies." Call around to find the best prices, and have it delivered just before the weekend. With luck, the job will be finished before Monday.

Turf Talk

When we add new grass seed to an existing lawn it's called *overseeding*. Overseeding is done to thicken a lawn, to grow a new kind of grass with the old, or to grow a quick grass crop to green up dormant lawns in warmer climates.

Turf Grass Health Spa Activities

Grass plants are just like other plants—they want their soil cultivated and broken up so that oxygen can reach the roots better. They also like to be nestled in soft, rich mulch to keep them insulated from the heat and to keep their roots evenly moist.

You don't do lawn renovation when you remodel or redecorate. It's a practice that should be done when the lawn is having trouble eating or drinking properly.

Lawn renovation should really be called lawn renewal because it renews the life and vigor of the grass. It's a single treatment that solves a host of problems without starting over from scratch with a new lawn.

Many lawnowners spend huge amounts of time working on common problems that can be solved by devoting one weekend to renovating the lawn.

These are the top 10 reasons to renovate a lawn:

➤ Open up compacted soil.

➤ Remove accumulations of thatch.

➤ Add new grass to increase lawn density.

➤ Sow a temporary green lawn on dormant grass.

➤ Change to a new grass type without replanting.

➤ Encourage more dense growth.

➤ Improve drought tolerance.

➤ Increase beneficial soil microorganism populations.

➤ Discourage weeds.

➤ Improve the lawn's appearance.

Opening Compacted Soils

Most soils under lawns become compacted at one time or another. The vast majority of lawn health problems lead back to compaction. Everything from drought resistance to fertilizer uptake is contingent on the texture of soil. If it gets as hard as concrete, which is more common than you might think, nothing grows well except weeds. Aeration, which is detailed in Chapter 21, "Soil Compaction—Public Enemy #1," is the only solution.

Turf Talk

Aerating is the practice of poking holes in the lawn with a hollow metal tube called a *tine.* The tine is sharp on the bottom so that it cuts, rather than tears, grass when it's forced downward. When the tine comes up, it spits out a core made of soil, roots, and grass. If you patch your lawn vegetatively, these are great for fillers!

Aerating Diagram

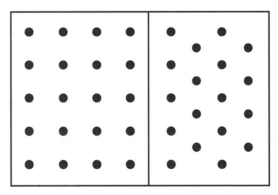

Core pattern

Thatch Removal

Thatch is the dead stems and leaves of grass plants that accumulate around grass. Thatch is more of a problem on warm-season grasses, with St. Augustine being the most notorious offender. Thatch can become so thick and dense that it blocks water and air exchange. Underneath, conditions provide a haven for diseases and pests to thrive. Frequent thatch removal, as discussed in Chapter 22, "Thatch: Not the Kind for Huts," is an essential part of warm-season grass care.

Thatch in a Lawn

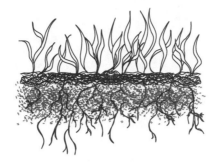

Thicker Lawns

Whereas warm-season grasses are good spreaders, cool-season species, such as the fescues, can be reluctant. These lawns require lots of individual plants to look lush and dense. Renovating provides you with an opportunity to add new plants to the lawn and thicken the stand.

Turf Caveat

Disease-resistant grasses are just that—resistant. They are not labeled disease-free or foolproof, just resistant. If conditions are extreme, and very high spore counts are combined with abominable rainfall, humidity, and high temperatures, there can be outbreaks in resistant varieties. However, whereas this situation would wipe out other grasses altogether, resistant ones would simply be injured and survive to grow again another day.

Temporary Green-Up

Warm-season grasses with long dormant periods look awful. Nobody wants to look at a brown lawn for months at a time, particularly in mild winter regions where everything else is still green and growing. The solution has been to plant a quick-sprouting annual grass that can be grown for a temporary winter green-up.

Change Grass Types

If you want to change the quality of your lawn with a new kind of grass, this can be done gradually as part of the renovation process. Thirsty bluegrass lawns may be gradually overseeded with more drought-resistant fescues over many seasons. It's a much better way of changing than ripping out the old grass and starting from scratch. Chapter 4, "Rating Top Turf Types," goes over the qualities of different turf grasses. Chapter 24, "A Fungus Among Us," lists the most disease-resistant varieties.

Efficient Water Use

Renovation is the best way to make the lawn a more efficient user of water. Disturbance of surface soils breaks up crusting and sends water deeper down where the roots are. It's essential to encouraging deep rooting in grass so that you water more effectively but less often. The importance of deep watering is discussed in Chapter 17, "Water Right, Water Deep."

Make Soil More Active

Organic lawn growers know that healthy soils make stronger plants. Topdressing is vital to encouraging these tiny critters that require organic matter to live and that in turn benefit plants. The only way to enhance their environment is healthy and frequent topdressing and aeration, both totally organic techniques. The benefits of organic matter in the soil are detailed in Chapter 8, "Dealing with Dirt," and the role of fertilizer is covered in Chapter 16, "The Basic Food Groups."

Crowd Out Weeds

Healthy, dense turf grass will naturally keep weeds from becoming established. When lawns thin out because they are stressed from different problems, the weeds invade. Regular renovation of turf pays off in eliminating most common weed problems before they start. The problem weeds found in suffering lawns are listed in Chapter 23, "Weeds."

How to Topdress Your Lawn

Topdressing is most often done after renovating a lawn by aerating it, or after thatch removal. Matlike warm-season grasses are opened up by these processes and only then will they accept topdressing. Otherwise, they are just too dense.

Cool-season grasses benefit the most from a gentle topdressing at any time. Their growth habit is more open, and the material filters down easily. It's super beneficial if your lawn is on the thin side, and the soil is not shaded by the grass as completely as it should be.

In regions with long hot summers, this organic matter reduces moisture loss from surface evaporation and helps shade the soil and keep it cooler. It actually contributes to drought and heat resistance.

A Step-by-Step Procedure

Choose whatever material you can find and afford from the list in this chapter. You'll also need a drop spreader. If you don't have one, it's worth purchasing because you'll use it in so many different lawn-care activities. You will also need a large bamboo or metal leaf rake.

Step 1: Mow the lawn and remove the clippings. If it's early in the season and temperatures are cool, you can mow a tad on the short side to make the topdressing filter down better.

Step 2: Fill the hopper of your spreader with topdressing and test it on pavement. You want to adjust it so that a layer about $1/4$-inch thick is evenly distributed. Don't worry, topdressing is mild, so you won't burn the grass if you overdo it. But avoid smothering it because topdressing applied too thickly denies light to the grass blades like a weed-stopping mulch does.

Step 3: Rake the topdressing in gently. Don't tear at the grass, just work it in slowly so that it filters down in between the grass plants.

Step 4: Topdressing is usually on the dry side to allow it to move through the spreader and down into the grass without sticking. Water the topdressed lawn thoroughly so that the material can soak up the moisture and settle down on top of the soil.

Overseeding a Dormant Lawn

All grasses turn brown with the cold winter temperatures. But grasses that go dormant when it's short-sleeve weather is a phenomenon of the deep south, Florida, and the Gulf Coast. Conditions there require certain warm-season grasses that become dormant, even though there is not a single frost. This leaves the entire landscape lush and green . . . except the lawn.

An Annual Rye Primer

Annual grasses live for one year and die. This short life span makes them sprout very quickly so that they can get on with the business of living. Annual ryegrass is the fastest-growing grass in the western world and the only annual species used for turf. It's so fast that rye has become the major component in emergency erosion-control seed mixtures for damaged land.

You can expect it to germinate and show green in as little as five or six days under ideal conditions and about a week and a half max if it's very cold or very hot. In most cases, overseed at a rate of 8 or 9 pounds per 1,000 square feet plus or minus.

Sowing It Right

Plan to sow your cover crop just after the lawn becomes fully dormant. The sooner you overseed, the sooner it will look good again.

Step 1: To make sure that the rye seed gets lots of sunshine, you need to mow the dormant grass short. Take off the leaf blades but leave the major stems, because these are a structural part of the plants. Make sure that all the clippings go into the catcher, not back on the lawn.

Step 2: Set the spreader and test it on pavement to make sure that you are getting an even distribution. Broadcast the seed using the same methods described in Chapter 11, "Seeding a Turf Grass Lawn," going back and forth in both directions.

Step 3: Reset the spreader for a more generous flow and fill the hopper with topdressing. Test this to make sure that you are getting a layer about $1/8$- to $1/4$-inch thick. Topdress the lawn evenly, going back and forth in one direction only.

Step 4: Water the lawn lightly and keep it evenly moist. Because this is a warm-climate activity, this is important because heat waves during the dormant season do occur. The plants will need progressively more water as they develop roots.

Step 5: After about a month to six weeks, you can fertilize the ryegrass with a light application. Even though it's warm, the days are short, and limited sunlight cuts down on the grass plant's demand for nutrients.

Quick-Fix Instant Rye Lawn

Nobody wants to look at bare ground or dead lawn. If you bought a new house recently, you may be faced with one of these situations. In the rainy seasons, bare ground turns to mud, which becomes a nightmare if you have kids or dogs. Plus, if you want the kids out of the kitchen for a while, they can't go outside in wet weather without some kind of covering for all that dirt.

If you don't have time to plant a new permanent lawn right away, you can make the yard look a lot better and solve a lot of mud problems by planting a quick cover crop of annual ryegrass. It's also a good practice for reducing surface erosion too.

All you need to do is till the area or use a spading fork to break up the surface. Rake out any rocks or big dirt clods to make a relatively level seed bed. Broadcast annual ryegrass seed and rake it in. You can also topdress with a good compost to help the lawn along. Water well and enjoy a grassy backyard for that first difficult season.

Repossessed homes, or those that have been vacant for a long time may end up looking like haunted houses with dead lawns and overgrown shrubbery. If you move into this situation, you can quickly green up the dead zones by treating them as a dormant lawn. Overseed the dead lawn with rye using the previous instructions, and it will green up right away. Later, after things settle down, you can replant the lawn with permanent grasses.

Trees in Lawns

There is nothing more welcome than a shade tree in the heat of summer. Few sights are as lovely as a flowering crab apple tree blooming outside your window. And above all, trees are the only things that separate your house from the view of the inquisitive neighbor's window next door. Trees make our environment more livable, more beautiful, and more private. They also wreak havoc on lawns!

Turf Tip

Some landscape designers have a strict rule concerning trees in lawns—they just don't plant them there. The eventual shading of the lawn, surface rooting, and a half-dozen other conflicts have led professionals to insist on planting trees in shrubs beds only. A tree may be very close to the edge of the lawn, but not in the lawn. If you're thinking about planting a tree in your existing lawn, or putting one on your lawn plan, think again. It's better for the lawn and the tree to keep them separate.

Turf Talk

When trees grow in lawns, or where there is bedrock and very hard soil layers, they develop a root system that is very shallow and wide. This is called *pancaked* roots because they are flat like a pancake.

Increased Shade

Lawns don't like shade. Sure, some grasses are a bit more tolerant of it, but they still suffer. Because trees are always growing larger, those in or around lawns cast an ever-larger shadow. At some point, you'll notice the lawn gets thin and spindly and eventually dies out altogether. When you get tired of fighting a losing battle, here are your options:

➤ Thin the canopy of the tree so that more light filters down through the branches to the lawn.

➤ Remove the tree. This is often the only way to get more light to the lawn.

➤ If you love the tree more than the lawn, replace the lawn with groundcover or paving.

Pancaked Tree Roots

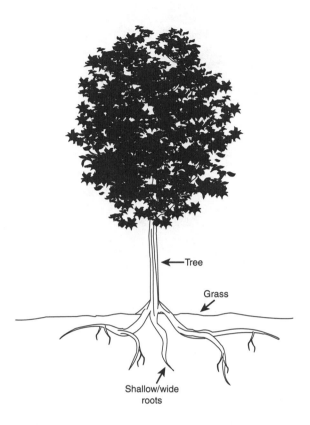

Tree

Grass

Shallow/wide
roots

Surface Rooting

Lawns are watered so that the top foot of soil gets wet. Trees growing in or around lawns go for that moisture from the very start. Rather than rooting downward to the water table, they stay up on top and become pancaked. The roots get bigger and bigger, eventually popping out of the top of the ground.

When the tree is young, the grass is the more dominant plant. When trees mature, however, they become dominant, with roots protruding out of the soil, making it difficult for you to mow the lawn. Grass just doesn't grow right there due to shade and competition. It's difficult to renovate areas around these thick, old roots. Most of all, they're ugly and break up the beauty of the lawn.

Surface Rooted Tree

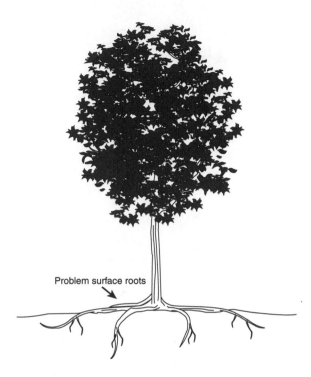

Problem surface roots

Here are your options for dealing with problem tree roots:

➤ Abandon the part of the lawn suffering with roots. Replace it with an attractive ring of ground bark, crushed walnut shells, or rock mulch. It's important to define this new edge of the lawn with benderboard or plastic bed dividers. It prevents the lawn from growing into the bark and the bark from traveling into the lawn.

Replace Lawn with a Ring of Bark

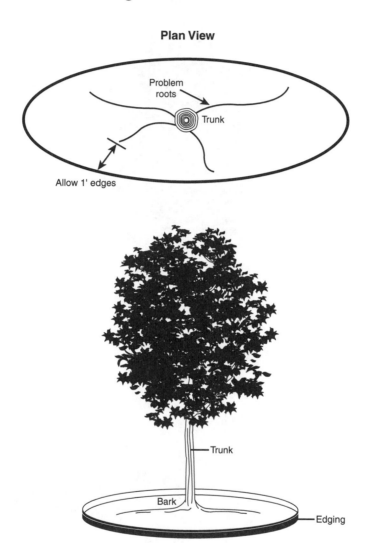

Plan View

Problem roots

Trunk

Allow 1' edges

Trunk

Bark

Edging

➤ Build up the soil around the base of the tree to cover the roots so that new grass can be planted there. Do not raise the soil elevation at the base of the trunk. Earth in contact with bark will cause crown rot and quickly kill the tree.

Build Up Soil over Exposed Roots

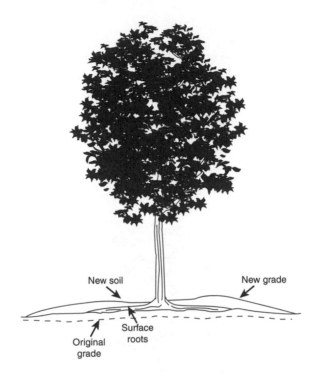

New soil

New grade

Surface roots

Original grade

➤ Remove the tree. This is appropriate if the tree has grown too large for both the lawn and the surrounding landscape.

Turf Tip

When planting trees in your lawn, don't let them start surface rooting; install a *root barrier* with the tree. These products have been proven highly effective in city parks and street tree plantings where sidewalk root damage can be hazardous.

Two rigid plastic semi-circles are placed around the root ball before you fill in the planting hole. They force the tree to root downward for about 2 feet before roots grow horizontally. The tree becomes more drought resistant and healthy, and deeper roots eliminate competition for surface moisture. Your new lawn tree will mature faster with a deep, well-anchored root system.

Tree Root Guards

Standard planter

Universal planter

Competition and Tractor Blight

Young trees in lawns always suffer from competition with the grass. To reduce this, park managers began keeping a ring of bare ground around the bases of the lawn trees. They use periodic herbicide applications to keep this ring free of unwanted weeds. This serves a number of purposes:

➤ The bare ground allows water and fertilizer to go straight down to tree roots without being intercepted by grass.

➤ Ensures trees with nice clean trunks because equipment never goes near them.

➤ Discourages leafy sucker growth that develops on wound sites of some trees at the base and where the roots are exposed.

Turf Talk

Tractor blight is not a real disease, and you won't find it in turf grass management handbooks. It was coined by farmers to describe the damage their equipment does to the bark and trunks of orchard trees. We see tractor blight in lawn-care scenarios too due to careless use of mowers and trimmers.

Wound Suckering

String trimmer damage

Exposed "knee"

Basal trunk sucker

Soil

Mowers and trimmers cause wounds that grow suckers.

The Least You Need to Know

➤ Renovation helps solve many problems in older lawns.

➤ You can use annual ryegrass to plant a quick-growing temporary lawn or green up a dormant one.

➤ Overseeding allows you to change the nature of your lawn.

➤ Topdressing is a great organic lawn-health improver.

➤ Trees in lawns root too close to the surface and cause problems.

Chapter 21

Soil Compaction— Public Enemy #1

In This Chapter

➤ Why lawns become compacted

➤ How aeration removes the effects of compacted lawns

➤ Step-by-step process of renovating a lawn

➤ Caring for a lawn after the aeration process

➤ Practices that reduce future compaction

The large machines for loosening compacted soil under a growing turf, sometimes called "aerification," are not practical for the home gardener.

—Charles E. Kellogg, 1952

Fifty years ago in Kellogg's day, you'd be stuck with rock-hard soil and pitiful grass. But now, thanks to technology and equipment rental yards, you have a homeowner-sized machine at your disposal. Whereas this practice was once exclusive to golf course greenskeepers, it's now possible for everyone to find a workable solution for the chief cause of lawn failure.

At the risk of sounding like a broken record, I'll repeat the most important fact about lawn care:

The vast majority of problems that crop up in turf grass lawns are related to soil compaction.

If you doubt this in any way, remember that a lawn is the only part of the garden designed to be walked on. Month after month, an active family abuses its lawn with

Slip-n-slides, play pools, toys, and bikes. Add lawn furniture, barbecues, and volleyball nets for the adults. Don't forget that lawn mowers spend a lot of time going back and forth on the grass. In short, lawns are the whipping boys of the landscape.

Let's Talk Dirt

When you plant a brand-new lawn, you have total access to the soil. You can put stuff in it, mix it up, rake it out, and basically change it from its original form. This is your one big chance to beef it up with juicy compost and humus of all kinds. This organic matter keeps things open and helps all those little microorganisms remain healthy and well fed.

But after the lawn is planted, you and that soil get a divorce. The grass becomes an interloper separating you from the fertile soil underneath. In fact, turf grass works that soil to death, consuming all its energy at a startling rate. What was once soft, fluffy, highly organic soil gradually becomes depleted of its fertility.

In comparison, vegetable gardeners go through this fortification process each and every year before planting. With the lawn, you have full access only once—when grass is first planted. But lawns deserve better and should receive a restoration each year.

> **Turf Talk**
>
> To *aerate* means to *air-ate,* or allow air to enter soil. Air is essential to healthy roots, but aeration has other benefits as well. When soil is *friable,* it is easy to break, crumble, or crush. When sufficient air is unavailable, an *anaerobic* condition occurs in soil. It's a lot like fermenting, and may smell like it sometimes, too.

About Disease and Microorganisms

Among one of the most important concepts of chemical-free lawn care is that soil microorganisms are there for a purpose. If we want them to hang around, we have to make the lawn a comfortable place to live.

Most lawn diseases are fungi. In many cases, the fungi and their spores are always around but don't get a foothold until conditions are right for them to grow and spread.

Healthy soil contains bacteria and other small organisms that feed on fungi. When soils become compacted, these little fellows get weak and sometimes disappear altogether. When spores blow in, there's no natural means of control, and diseases spread across lawns like wildfire. So when you aerate a lawn, it does more than make a better rooting environment, it actually encourages these beneficial organisms to be fruitful and multiply.

Doctor, Oxygen Please!

Have you ever overwatered a houseplant without adequate drainage? If so, you will probably never forget the smell of that black, slimy soil. In that case, there was so much water in the potting soil that it displaced air. Without air, the roots of the plant couldn't breathe, so they died and then rotted.

This illustrates why oxygen in the root zone of all plants is crucial. When soils get overly compacted, there are few, if any, air spaces. Because it's also connected to the happiness of your microorganism populations, compacted soil is often dead soil.

Dead soil better resembles modeling clay than real living earth. When you aerate, as the previous definition says, air or oxygen is incorporated into the soil. Rototilling does the same thing, but because you can't till a mature lawn, you have to aerate differently.

Blame It on the Clay

Most soils contain some clay. In fact, America's most fertile agricultural soils are mostly clay, with some sand and silt as well. Clay in soils is the same as potter's clay and takes on the same characteristics—it can get really hard. The only thing that separates ceramic clay from your clay is organic matter.

We know that organic matter is naturally transient because it's food for microorganisms. When it's all eaten up, your soil reverts to its basic claylike nature. Even if it's not heavy clay, soil under lawns tends to gradually become more packed down each time somebody or something presses down on it. Let's not forget Newton's Law either. Gravity takes its toll.

Normal Versus Compacted Soil Rooting

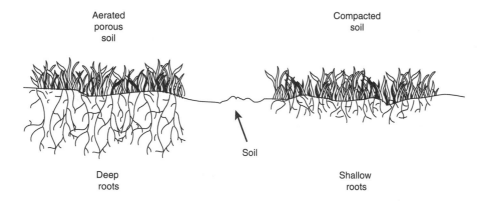

Aerated
porous
soil

Compacted
soil

Soil

Deep
roots

Shallow
roots

Compacted soil is hostile to plants in many ways:

➤ The roots of soft herbaceous plants such as grasses have a difficult time penetrating dense soil. They often stop growing altogether, or if they do develop it's right at the surface. This makes for weak plants that can't stand up against drought, bugs, or disease.

➤ Water can't percolate down through really dense soils. Water travels through the pores between soil particles, but if these are too tight, they become "bottlenecked" almost immediately. An indication of bottlenecked soils are puddles or pools of standing water and runoff.

➤ Very little oxygen exists in the spaces. Starved roots and microorganisms are sluggish and often die back.

➤ Fertilizer won't filter down into the soil to replace nutrients consumed by turf grasses. Because fertilizer is moved by water, bottlenecked soils are never penetrated enough to feed the roots.

Spots and Trails

Soil compaction in lawns may not occur consistently throughout the whole area. Irregularities in soils alone are a major cause of spot problems. It's not uncommon to find heavy clay pockets that turn rock hard while the surrounding soils are light and friable.

The process of soil compaction is also tied to traffic. Places with more traffic will suffer the worst. These are problem areas to look for:

➤ Play areas

➤ Outdoor living spaces

➤ Edges of walkways and driveways

➤ Common human and pet trails

You may not need to aerate the entire lawn if you have some spot problems due to traffic or pockets of problem soils. Try spot treatments first, using one of the smaller, inexpensive core aeration tools.

Turf Tip

Corners and edges matter. When cars and feet pack down soils beside paved areas, it's not only tough on roots, it also breeds disease. Fusarium blight is a disease that thrives on overcompacted soils. It most often crops up first in these edge conditions, partly because the traffic helps deposit fusarium spores there. Keep a close eye on corners and edges to catch this blight before it spreads to the rest of your lawn.

It's easy. Just water the area first, then perforate the mass with the tool, and follow up with a topdressing of fine compost. You can spot aerate as often as needed to keep the area healthy and keep the color consistent with that of the rest of the lawn.

Uniquely New

Newly built homesites suffer from a slew of unique peccadilloes. These often crop up even if the house was freshly landscaped because builders tend to sod the lawns over less-than-ideal soils. You may not encounter them at first but, when a heat wave sets in, they show up.

Land that has been severely graded to flatten out a building pad may leave you with subsoils on the surface. These can be heavy clay, chalky hardpan, or coarse material such as shale.

Unless they are remedied before sod is laid, they eliminate any root penetration, and the grass becomes stressed when temperatures rise. To help reduce these effects, aerate often and topdress liberally with high-quality compost, which helps the roots remain moist.

Masons clean their equipment on building sites, and these places can suffer from high concentrations of lime. When you plant a lawn on top of the area without removing these contaminated soils, the seed refuses to do well, or the sod never really becomes established. If the unnatural gray coloring tips you off to the problem, it's best to strip the sod, excavate the soil down a few inches and replace it with topsoil.

Turf Tip

If you have a new house with a barren yard, the soils probably are not in top shape. Rather than start your lawn right away, plant a temporary clover lawn. Clover roots extend deep into the soil, and clover adds nitrogen to your soil. After the first season, till the clover back into the soil for a second nitrogen boost. Clover also provides beneficial microorganisms that help prevent lawn disease.

To plant, till up the entire back yard. Add compost or sterile manures, and then sow sweet clover, genus *Melilotus*. Water as needed. This crop should grow well for a couple of years until you're ready to landscape.

Hardpan Is Deadpan

In some communities, there are special soil conditions collectively called *hardpan*. These soils can be literally the density of concrete and just as unwilling to break up. There's more to hardpan than dense clay soils. Something else is going on.

Normal soils when broken up remain open for a long time. Hardpans get hard again overnight, just as soon as they get wet. This is because they contain abnormally high concentrations of silica (they make glass out of this) or calcium carbonate (a relative of baking soda), which causes a chemical reaction. No matter how well you pulverize hardpan soils, the minute it gets wet, you're right back to square one again.

It stands to reason that if you aerate a hardpan soil, it will return to its original condition over a much shorter time than normally compacted clay. If you know there's hardpan, caliche, or other abnormally dense soils in the neighborhood, it might be a good idea to consult an expert for a more specific program to remedy compaction.

The worst case scenario is excavation and replacement of hardpan with imported topsoil.

So What's Aeration Anyway?

Aeration is a technique where you perforate your lawn with thousands of holes. These are punched with hollow tines sharpened on one end and with a hole on the other end. The tine goes down into the grass and extracts a core of grass and dirt. The roots of the grass hold it together after it comes out.

Section—Aeration of Turf

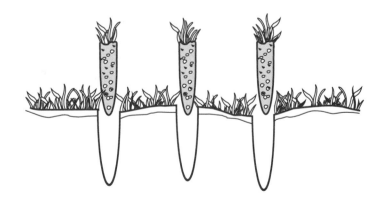

To be really effective, the tines must be inserted at least 2 to 3 inches deep. This makes sure that you get beneath the grass crown, thatch, and upper roots. What's left is a neat little passageway that allows water and air to go deep into the soil. Multiply this by a thousand, and the lawn takes its first deep breath in a long time.

After aerating, you can topdress with compost or manure, and this rich organic matter will work down into the holes. This is the only time you will ever be able to get organic matter down into that soil after the initial planting. Plus, it's a perfect time to overseed a lawn and fertilize it, with nutrients going straight down the holes to feed roots.

Heavy and Not-So-Heavy Equipment

The process of aeration is simple: poke holes in your lawn. The degree to which you do varies. Aeration is something you can do all season long on a small scale to help reduce overall compaction. You can do this by simply wearing golf shoes or cleats when you mow your lawn.

There are a few different products you can buy that work well in very small lawns or those with problem spots:

Aerating Sandals

These look like a "bed of nails" that's upside down. They fit over your regular shoes with straps, and you walk around the lawn with them on to aerate. These make small nail-sized holes. Use these for mild aeration of small lawns or spot applications.

Spading Fork

It looks like a pitch fork, but the tines are straight and much thicker—about $3/4$ inch wide. These puncture the soil but do not extract a plug. Use for spot applications.

Sod Coring Tool

This affordable tool allows you to pull actual plugs out of the lawn, from two to four with each insertion. It has a handle so that coring is as simple as inserting a spading fork or shovel. Use for spot applications or very small lawns.

Spading Fork and Coring Tool

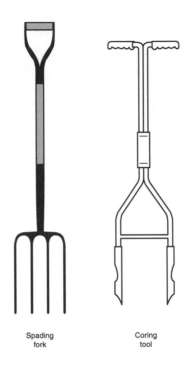

Spading
fork

Coring
tool

Aerating Roller

This large roller requires a lawn tractor to pull it. The tool is just like a hand roller but is studded with $2^{1}/_{2}$-inch-long spikes 6 inches apart. When filled with water, the weight pushes the tines down into the lawn, but they do not extract cores. Good for large areas if you already have a tractor.

Power Core

Hand-coring tools are a lot of work, and the end result will never measure up to the speed, consistency, and efficiency of a power tool. Because they are used so rarely, and are very expensive, these are always rented.

There are two kinds:

➤ *Rotating tine machines* have the punchers mounted on circular reels. These are better for very large lawns. They extract cores averaging 2 to 3 inches deep, spaced from about 4 to 6 inches apart. Sometimes these can be attached to a lawn tractor and towed. Golf courses use this kind on fairways.

Rotating Tine Aerator

➤ *Vertical punch aerators* are self propelled and punch holes to depths from 4 to 5 inches in a very tight, neat pattern just 3 inches apart. These machines are best in smaller lawns and do a more precise job than rotating tines. This is the only kind golf courses use on putting greens.

Vertical Punch Aerator

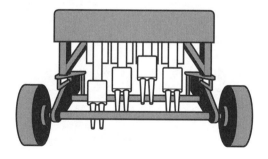

Other Stuff You Need

Punching the lawn is just one part of the aeration process. You'll have a mess to clean up, and, if you plan on some other improvements besides just aerating, that requires tools and material too. Here's the rundown:

Clean up the plugs:

➤ Iron or leaf rake

➤ Shovel

➤ Wheelbarrow

313

Overseed and topdress:

➤ Drop spreader

➤ Lawn seed

➤ Topdressing

Step-by-Step Aeration and Renovation

Renovation of a lawn can be divided into three groups of tasks:

➤ Aeration followed by topdressing is the best way to add vital organic matter into the root zone of existing lawns.

➤ Aeration followed by fertilization and topdressing adds more power to your punch and is rocket fuel for compacted lawns.

➤ Aeration followed by overseeding and topdressing allows you to add new plants or change the mix of grass varieties.

Aeration holes will not stay open forever because eventually they will collapse and fill in. In fact, they disappear a lot faster than you'd expect. If you have organic matter in there, they won't fill in so densely, making your efforts last a lot longer.

You can renovate your lawn in a weekend if you have everything ready to go ahead of time. It's important to water the lawn well the week before because the machines punch better on moist ground. You might also cut the lawn and discard the clippings to make a cleaner, more open field for accepting topdressing and seed.

Turf Tip

To avoid weed invasions, it's best to aerate lawns when the grass is vigorously growing in your climate zone.

Rent the Machine

Most rental yards carry aerating machines. Call around if you want to compare prices and to make sure that one is available. Everyone else makes this a weekend project, too, so there's big demand on Saturday and Sunday. You may be able to reserve one ahead of time.

Because rental yards charge by the hour, you save money by good planning. Have the lawn ready before you rent the machine. Then be prepared to return it as soon as the punching is done. Why rent it for a whole day at three times the cost when you may only use the machine for a couple of hours?

Punch Out Your Lawn

The aim is to aerate the entire lawn at the same rate. Avoid overdoing some spots and skipping others. These inconsistencies will show up later as uneven coloring in the grass.

Plan how you will attack your lawn. It's easiest to run the machine up and down the lawn in even stripes. When you get to the end of the stripe, shut off the tines, make the turn, and then line up the machine again before you start up the punching mechanism. When the lawn is finished, run the machine in one pass around the outside edge to finish it off.

About the Plugs

When you finish aerating, plugs of turf will be scattered all over the lawn. There are different ways to deal with them:

A Core

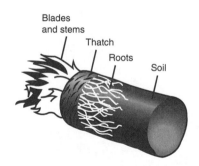

Blades and stems
Thatch
Roots
Soil

➤ *If your soil is clayey*, rake up all the plugs and dispose of them. It doesn't make sense to add clay back into a problem soil.

➤ *Mow to break them up*. Plugs can take a while to decompose, so you can mow the lawn quickly to grind them up and speed this process. Because plugs contain soil and organic matter, they make good topdressing.

Turf Caveat

Plugs are a super addition to your compost pile if they are cool-season grasses. Plugs from warm-season grasses or those contaminated by Bermuda and invasive runner grasses should not go in with your compost. These grasses can lie dormant, and, if not fully composted, they can later rise up from the grave elsewhere in your garden.

➤ *Drag them in.* This leaves the lawn looking a bit more ragged, but it's the old-time method. Use a piece of chain-link fencing or an old metal door mat and drag it by chain or rope all over the lawn. Pulling by hand is a workout, and if you're not up to it, use another method. It's ideal for large lawns where the metal fence is attached to the rear of a riding mower or lawn tractor by chains.

➤ *Save them for patching* warm-season lawns that suffer from bare spots. Each plug is like a tiny piece of sod containing everything needed to start a new plant.

➤ *Leave them alone* to decompose gradually back into the lawn. This isn't very attractive, but it's a lot lless work. Whether this is a good idea depends on your lawn. A stiff, upright fescue lawn will hide plugs much better than a closely cropped hybrid Bermuda will.

Overseed

A newly punched lawn provides an ideal environment for seed to grow. You can overseed with the same kind of grass or a different one. Use the drop spreader to distribute seed lightly and evenly over the entire lawn.

Topdress

This is the most ideal time to topdress a lawn. The aeration holes are open and ready to accept organic matter. You can tell from the size of the holes that the material needs to be very fine to filter down.

Apply a layer of topdressing evenly over the lawn in a layer from $1/4$ inch to $1/2$ inch thick. This allows enough to cover the seed and filter into the holes. It helps to use a rake leaf to rake in the topdressing so that it nestles around the seed better.

At this point, the lawn may look a little worse for the wear, but all systems are go for a spurt of new, healthy growth.

Fertilize and Microorganize

Lawn aeration gives the grass a bigger boost if it's fertilized right after aeration. Water will carry nutrients right to the bottom of the holes where roots can take it up quickly and efficiently.

Certain microorganisms feed on fungi responsible for many plant diseases. The greater the microorganism populations in your soil, the lower the chance for incidence of disease. This makes the microorganisms antagonists, and their activity makes a lawn suppressive to disease. These are some of the most beneficial antagonists:

➤ *Gliocladium*

➤ *Trichoderma*

➤ *Bacillus subtilis*

➤ *Bacillus penetrans*

Trichoderma is being used now in Europe for disease suppression, and the EPA should approve a pure form in the near future.

Many of these organisms exist in bagged, commercial organic lawn fertilizers. These are the best products for application following aerating because they reintroduce these beneficial microorganisms to the grass. The more diverse the microscopic wildlife is in your lawn, the more resistant it is to fungal diseases. Although organics don't have as high a nutrient content as chemical lawn food does, this microorganism factor more than compensates.

If you overseed the lawn after aerating, hold off a few weeks before applying chemical fertilizer.

Water

Now that you've got an expressway leading deep into the root zone, it's time to get water on the lawn in quantity. No wimpy sprays, but good deep watering. This may be the first chance you've had in a long time to deep water, so keep an eye on the system as you irrigate. Chances are you'll have to make some timing adjustments because a cored lawn can absorb a huge amount of water at once.

Those little holes won't stay open forever. Each time you water or mow, the holes fill up a little more, or their sidewalls cave in. That's why it's so essential to use fertilizer and water heavily right after you aerate.

Consider water the catalyst that makes all other things happen:

➤ Irrigation water fills the little holes, and, if you have hard soil, it will probably sit there a while and slowly seep into the ground. Monitor this to see how fast the water percolates out.

➤ Water helps to move topdressing into the holes and settle it in as deeply as possible.

➤ Water activates the dormant microorganisms in organic fertilizer to encourage them to move into the surrounding soil.

➤ Water is essential if you overseeded. Consistent, regular watering will ensure seed germinates completely and grows vigorously.

➤ Water is needed to dissolve chemical fertilizer and move the nutrients immediately into the hole and root zone.

The Least You Need to Know

➤ Soils need air to remain alive and open to plant roots.

➤ Lawn compaction can create sterile, hostile living conditions for turf grass.

➤ Aerating lawns in heavy clay is essential to health and beauty.

➤ Using organic fertilizers after aerating goes a long way to enhance microorganism activity, which helps control disease.

➤ After aerating, your lawn may behave very differently, so keep a close eye on it.

Chapter 22

Thatch: Not the Kind for Huts

In This Chapter

➤ What's bad about thatch

➤ Which lawn grasses produce the most thatch

➤ How to know when it's time to de-thatch the lawn

➤ Using a vertical mower to de-thatch your lawn

➤ Healing the wounds of the renovation process

A spade was used to cut the sod into bricks about three-feet long and carried to the building site.

—Everett Dick, 1937

Imagine your lawn cut into bricks and made into houses. Sounds weird, but that's exactly what the pioneers did because prairie sod could measure a foot thick or more. Each year, the grass sprouted, grew tall, flowered, and then died back with the first autumn frosts. Buffalo ate some of it, but they barely dented the crop.

When a grass plant that grew 3-feet tall died back, there was a lot of brown chaff composed of stem and leaf. It gradually broke up into smaller pieces and then filtered down into the grass and accumulated there.

The new year's growth rose up the following spring, and because production exceeded decomposition, the prairie sod just got thicker and thicker. Multiply this process uninterrupted over aeons, and you have quite a build up. By the time Europeans showed up, it reached the size of building blocks and had its own structural integrity.

So what does your lawn have in common with pioneers and buffalo? Thatch. That's the term for all the dead plant matter in the prairie. If you're not in the habit of building sod houses, then you have to get rid of your lawn thatch one way or another.

A Batch of Thatch

Thatch builds up in all lawns, but more so in warm-season grasses. It's a natural process that was once beneficial to wild grass but isn't so hot for turf grass. This is because our lawns are more vulnerable to various problems caused by keeping them mowed short all the time.

Thatch can be healthy for a lawn as long as it's a relatively thin layer. It functions like mulch does on other plants to preserve soil moisture and insulate roots from heat. It also acts like padding under a carpet as a shock absorber that reduces wear and tear on the living grass. But when it exceeds $1/2$ inch in thickness, it becomes a problem.

Thatch comes from a variety of sources. Some of them are related to which type of grass it is because some produce more than others. It can also be a result of mowing in wet weather and failure to bag the clippings. You may find thatch in the early spring due to winter die-back.

Measured Thatch Depth

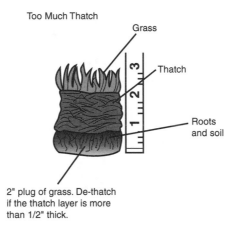

2" plug of grass. De-thatch if the thatch layer is more than 1/2" thick.

How to Know Your Thatch

The single factor that separates really good gardeners from black thumbs is time. Attentive gardeners spend more time among their plants and study them more closely than you'd think. If you get down and actually look at your grass closely, you'll see a lot of things, including whether you have thatch.

Here are some easy ways to know whether you have a problem:

➤ When you walk on the grass, it feels spongy.

➤ The level of the grass stems is at or above the sidewalk.

➤ If you pull back the blades, you don't see dirt.

➤ There's a frequent appearance of circular diseases, such as dollar spot.

➤ There are patches where the grass just lies down dead for no reason.

➤ Recurring problems persist with insects that live in the thatch such as sod webworms and chinch bugs.

Thatch has become a hotly contested part of lawn care. It's viewed differently by organic lawn growers than the rest of the turf grass crowd. There's a lot of theory flying around, but what exists in your yard is all that counts.

There is one benefit of thatch, which is why we allow it to exist up to about $1/2$ inch thick. Thatch does act like a protective, insulating mulch that keeps soil cooler and seals in moisture from surface evaporation. This is beneficial for grass in hot, dry climates where every ounce of water is precious. However, this layer should never exceed $1/2$ inch thick, with $1/4$ inch being ideal.

Roots in Thatch

Turf Caveat

Long-term thatch buildup can actually change the way your grass roots. Overseeding can be inhibited because the seeds sprout on top of the thatch instead of the soil. New surface roots of existing grass remain in the thatch rather than penetrate soil. Dry weather dehydrates the thatch, and the roots die. Cold temperatures will freeze roots that would otherwise be protected deeper in the soil.

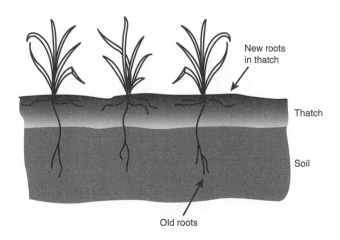

New roots in thatch

Thatch

Soil

Old roots

Thatch and Organic Lawn Gurus

Organic lawn gurus believe that the most important thing about lawn care is the holistic approach to soils and plants. They teach that the widely used granular fertilizers of the turf industry destroy the biology of soils. This, in turn, weakens plants and disturbs many natural processes.

Among those processes is the decomposition of organic matter, namely thatch. The theory is that organic lawns are naturally able to assimilate a good deal of thatch on their own. Healthy soils eat up thatch at a much faster rate, thus reducing the problems of overly thick accumulations. Only turf types that accumulate abnormally high amounts of thatch need help thinning it out.

Turf Tip

To hasten the decomposition of thinner thatch conditions without the hassle of topdressing, switch to a microbe-rich, organic lawn fertilizer. These pure organic products come bagged under various names and will introduce all sorts of organisms to the lawn that consume dead organic matter. They also help fight fungal disease, which tends to hide out in thatch.

The Grass Is Always Greener

High doses of nitrogen fertilizer are the main cause for rapid thatch buildup. It makes the grass plants grow so quickly that they shed dead material that much faster. Overloads of fungicide also contribute to the problem because this reduces or eliminates vital microorganisms that naturally break down organic matter.

Thatch According to Golf Course Greenskeepers

The gods of turf grass are golf course greenskeepers because they have to produce perfect lawns or the players get cranky. Their approach is the one preferred by most people who have a limited amount of time to spend on lawn care.

Accumulation of thatch on any lawn should never exceed $1/2$-inch maximum thickness.

Thatch causes a number of turf problems when it gets thick or when it's packed down tightly:

➤ Thatch layers present a barrier to water. Sprinkler water is either absorbed by the thatch or runs off leaving the soil underneath overdry.

➤ If water can't get to the soil through thatch, neither can water-transported fertilizer. So not only are the roots dry, but they are perpetually undernourished as well.

➤ Thatch smothers roots and soil by denying oxygen. Because oxygen is vital to soil microbes and plant roots, very dense thatch layers can literally choke it off.

➤ Insect larvae find an ideal haven in thatch where they are protected from pesticides. They are more difficult to control because they remain out of reach, and soil-borne pests are inaccessible altogether.

➤ When thatch builds up, it actually changes the finish grade of the lawn relative to adjacent surfaces. That's partly because the thatch becomes a rooting medium, and partly because the grass has to grow extra tall to reach sunlight on top of the thatch.

➤ Thatch caused by mowing in wet conditions and leaving clippings on the lawn smothers the grass in spots, where it soon dies out and mars the lawn's beauty.

The Infection Connection

There is a direct connection between thatch and lawn diseases. In short, most lawn diseases are fungi that feed on dead organic matter such as thatch. Sometimes when there's a population explosion, these fungal organisms start feeding on living plants.

Because fungi and their spores are always around, you can't eliminate them entirely. However, you can keep them from overproducing and taking over the lawn. It's all connected to the thatch. If you keep it to a minimum, less than $1/2$ inch thick, there's little chance of diseases getting out of hand.

Some common fungi use the thatch as a winter home; when the temperature warms, the fungi move out. This is the case with pythium blight, dollar spot, and melting out, all of which are detailed in Chapter 24, "A Fungus Among Us."

Turf Caveat

The quickest way to turn your thatch into a fungus nursery is to water in the evenings. This leaves the entire night for these fungi to have a big war party before they spread out and invade the healthy grass. Water in early morning so that it evaporates early in the day.

Bugs Check In, But They Don't Check Out

A host of unsavory pests just love to live in thatch. It's soft and dark and keeps them sheltered from mowers and people's feet. Sod webworms prefer to live in layers of thatch, preferably the drier part. You also find chinch bugs drawn to thatch-heavy, drought-stressed lawns.

Turf Talk

Runner grasses tend to be the major offenders because they send out really tough stolons that contain large amounts of *lignin*. Lignin is slow to decompose compared to the softer, fleshy parts of a leaf blade.

Turf Caveat

Turf experts agree that large doses of nitrogen fertilizer on lawns stimulate a lot of extra, luxuriant growth. This, in turn, stimulates proportionately more thatch accumulation. Be cautious with bluegrass and other succulent grasses and keep nitrogen levels down to earth.

When thatch layers are thick, many nontoxic controls are much less effective. Biological fixes such as milky spores and predatory nematodes must be introduced to the soil to be effective. If thatch gets in the way of these or any other chemical or botanical pesticides, your chances of heading off the problem and implementing long-lasting residual control go right out the window. More on common turf pests and how to fight them can be found in Chapter 25, "Insects—Know Thine Enemy."

So What's in It Anyway?

Dead grass, right? Yes, but there is dead grass, and there is dead grass. Thatch can come from different sources, which affects what it's composed of.

Growth habit is key. As grasses age, they naturally put out new roots and above-ground stems that will replace older, less productive ones. This is far more prevalent with runner-type grasses than bunch grasses. The abandoned dead stems at the surface and just below it become thatch.

Winter kill from either disease or frost is another big source. If the lawn goes to bed in fall while still growing, the thatch layer will be much thicker. Winter thatch is mostly stems and leaves and should be managed all at once in spring.

Mowing practices and clippings are a third source. Clippings can be left on the lawn after you mow, but for them to be healthy, the grass must be dry and short. When you mow in wet weather, long clippings tend to bunch up and smother the grass. So under ideal conditions clippings are healthy, but if not, they turn into thatch problems.

Turf Tip

Mulching mower madness can cause thatch problems. Mulching mowers are good for soil and our overburdened landfills but are a loaded gun in the hands of a novice. There are two things you can't do:

➤ Cut taller grass all at once. You have to bring it down incrementally to keep the mulched pieces small enough to be beneficial.

➤ You can't mulch well in wet grass. The chopped pieces tend to stick to one another and clump up rather than filtering down into the spaces between grass plants.

The Major Offenders

All grasses can suffer from thatch caused by mowing practices. Growth habit is the key source, though, with runner grasses leading the pack. Most of these are warm-season types that can build up thatch with incredible speed. The more coarse and broad-leafed the grass, the more thatch it produces.

All strains of Bermuda grass are the Olympic champion thatch producers. Bermuda's aggressive stolon production is the main source. Hybrid Bermuda is even faster than common Bermuda.

St. Augustine stands out because it is a big, robust grass with thick fleshy stems and broad fibrous leaves. These grasses not only produce more material due to their coarse texture; they are much slower to decompose because of a higher-than-average lignin content. This also makes them tough on hands and mowers. The mere volume of leaves and stems produced by four months' growth is huge compared to that of fine-textured Bermuda.

Lesser thatch producers are cool-season bluegrass varieties because this grass naturally forms a dense sod. Fine fescues, due to their narrow, durable leaves, are not sod producing but resist decomposition so well that they tend to accumulate thatch too.

Friday the 13th for Thatch

I'd love to tell you a great plant geek-speak term for relieving your lawn of its thatch, but there isn't one. The process is just called de-*thatching*.

De-thatching is a rather sadistic process of slashing your lawn. Cool-season grasses don't suffer as much because each plant is separate. When the slashing starts, the knives just slide down between the upright blades of grass.

Warm-season runner grasses grow differently because as they trot across the ground, the stolons of one plant become tangled up in those of another. The result is a solid carpet of stems, and to get at the thatch underneath, you have to literally rip through them.

Be prepared for the aftereffects of de-thatching, and be thankful you need only do it every other year, or less often for cool-season grasses. This cutting effect leaves a lot of loose ends, and the dense, flat lawn will appear shaggy for a while.

> **Turf Talk**
>
> A machine that removes thatch from lawns is called a *verticutter*. Break down this word, and you know how it works. *Verti* is short for vertical, and *cutter* is cutter. Hence, it's actually a lawn mower with the blades turned on end. Another name for this tool is vertical mower.

Nature's Way

We've learned from organic lawn experts that the best way to deal with thatch is to prevent it from building up. Sure, you can avoid the fungicides and nitrogen overloads that are partly to blame, but you may still have a growing thatch accumulation.

The natural solution is topdressing with sterilized manure or compost in a layer no thicker than 1/2 inch. This lays down a rich layer over the thatch, which invites microorganism activity to venture out of the soil. Their populations increase in the now cool and dark thatch, hastening their decomposition. Regular topdressing of lawns can eliminate the need for de-thatching altogether on bunch grasses that are not heavy thatch producers.

However, if the thatch is already more than 1/2 inch thick, you will have to physically de-thatch the lawn as a remedial measure. Topdressing won't solve preexisting thatch-bound lawns, but after you de-thatch, a regular program of organic topdressing may eliminate its recurrence in the future.

When to De-thatch

Obviously, the grass gets wounded. Everybody wants it to heal fast and get back to its usual beauty. The more actively growing the grass is, the faster it recovers. Unless you have a strange love of ragged lawns, it's best to de-thatch the lawn at the peak of the growing season to ensure quick and total recovery.

De-thatch warm-season grass lawns in the late spring. In the deep south, de-thatch in midspring.

De-thatch cool-season lawns in either late spring or early fall. If you de-thatch in the fall, allow a solid month of good weather before the first frost is expected.

Choose the Right Tool

De-thatching tools should fit the size of the job. They also need to fit your own capability and budget.

> **Turf Caveat**
>
> Don't, I repeat, do not de-thatch before a party, a back yard wedding, a pool party, or any other special occasion. This process tears up the grass, and it takes many weeks to return to any semblance of beauty. Do so months before or just after. It isn't pretty, but consider it tough love.

➤ A common *iron bow rake* can rip out thatch in small patches. It's best used for cool-season grasses where clippings have accumulated in small spots.

➤ A *thatching rake*, sometimes called a *cavex rake*, has a series of blades instead of the tines found in a standard rake. These blades are sharp and can be pushed or pulled through the thatch. These are a good tool for small lawns, although thick layers can make de-thatching even a limited area quite strenuous.

Thatching Rake

➤ A lawn mower *de-thatching blade* bolts onto a standard rotary mower. This is an alternative to the work of a rake and the inconvenience of rental equipment. The thatch isn't cut quite as cleanly, and healing may take longer. It may be inadequate for very thick thatch layers.

Thatching Patterns

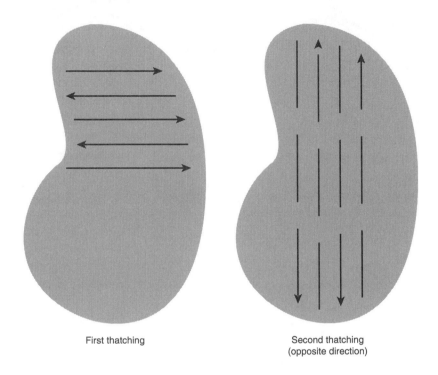

First thatching

Second thatching
(opposite direction)

➤ Lawn tractor *de-thatchers* are towed behind. Those that require power are not suitable for lawn tractors. Only the inexpensive ones that cut by dragging rigid tines through the grass are suitable. This is a wise investment if you have a large lawn of a notorious thatch-producing grass type and own a lawn tractor to pull the attachment.

➤ Rent a *verticutter*, also known as a vertical mower, if you want the best job. The machines vary in size and design. The best kind to rent is about the size of a power lawn mower that you walk behind. This machine is easy to handle, and you know that the end result will be golf course quality.

Turf Tip

If you rent a verticutter, plan to use it for a half day for a small lawn, and three-quarters to a full day for a medium-sized lawn. This applies only to the time you use the machine. Clean up and follow-up tasks will take longer.

To Aerate or Not to Aerate

A complete lawn renovation includes both de-thatching and aeration. It's not uncommon to find that neglected lawns with heavy thatch suffer from compacted soil underneath. In fact, these soils can have low oxygen content from being smothered by the thatch. Although you must rent a second machine to aerate after you de-thatch, it's worth the effort. Over the long run, it will pay off with more efficient use of water and fertilizer and make the lawn far more resistant to pests and disease.

Resurrecting Your Lawn Step by Step

Now that you understand the impact of thatch and why it should be controlled in healthy lawns, it's time to get down to business. While you're at it, consider overseeding your lawn and perhaps aerating it, too, if the soil is compacted. That way your lawn will recover all at once.

Step 1: Water and Mow

Water well and deeply. This allows the grass to become fully hydrated before it's cut to pieces. The resulting moisture loss won't stress it as badly as it would if the grass were on the dry side to begin with. Freshly mowed grass makes sure that you work on a nice, closely cropped green field. The de-thatching process will be cleaner, and there will be less material to remove when you're finished.

Step 2: De-thatch the Lawn

Have your rental de-thatching machine ready to go with the gas tank full. Set the tines to dig down $\frac{1}{2}$ inch, which will penetrate the thatch but not contact soil. Make sure that there aren't any obstacles on the lawn. Begin on a long edge and run the verticutter up and down in parallel passes. Avoid any gaps between passes. This machine makes a big mess, but don't panic—that's what it's supposed to do.

Turf Caveat

Thatch removed from your lawn is great organic matter for the compost heap if you have cool-season grasses. Beware of warm-season runner grasses such as Bermuda, though, because pieces of living root and stolon exist in the thatch. If these pieces do not fully decompose during the composting process, they will rise to life another day to contaminate other parts of your landscape.

Step 3: Rake Up the Thatch

Use a wide bamboo or metal leaf rake to gather up all the thatch ripped out by the verticutter. Gather it into piles and remove it from the lawn area altogether. Either discard it in the garbage can or add it to your compost heap.

Step 4: De-thatch Again Going the Other Way

Drop the height of the verticutter down a notch or two depending on how much thatch is left. You want the blades to sit just above the soil, but not into it, because that will dull the edges quickly. This time run the verticutter in the opposite direction over the entire lawn once again in parallel passes.

Step 5: Rake Up More Thatch

This is your final raking, so be as thorough as possible. Don't just pile it up, but rake any lingering bits out of the now-shaggy turf. Pieces of thatch left behind can reintroduce turf diseases to the newly overseeded or recovering grass.

Step 6: Aerate (Optional)

Run the aerating machine over the lawn and either dispose of the plugs or leave them on the lawn to disintegrate. You will find detailed instructions on operating an aerating machine and disposing of the cores in Chapter 21, "Soil Compaction—Public Enemy #1."

Step 7: Overseed (Optional)

Now that the soil is newly exposed and the grass is opened up, conditions are right to overseed. You may want to introduce new grasses to your lawn, or thicken up the existing one. If the lawn is dormant, you can overseed now with annual ryegrass for a quick green-up over the winter months. Either way, overseed evenly using the drop spreader.

Step 8: Topdress

Topdressing your lawn after it is de-thatched helps the grass recover better. Use sterilized manure, compost, ground peat, or a sandy topsoil. This serves as a protective mulch to help keep the wounded grass moist and cool until it heals.

If the topdressing isn't naturally sifting down into the grass, use a broad rake to gently sweep it in. You may roll the lawn with an empty roller to flatten out the ragged edges and firm the topdressing into place.

Spot Thatch Removal

If you have just a few areas where thatch has built up, you can treat these independently.

➤ Step 1: Use an iron rake or a de-thatching rake. Rake the area vigorously in one direction until you get well into the thatch.

➤ Step 2: Rake the area again in the opposite direction to a depth that encounters the soil.

➤ Step 3: Rake up all the thatch and remove it.

➤ Step 4 (optional): If the soil is compacted, use a core aerator tool or a spading fork to perforate the area to about 3 inches deep.

➤ Step 5 (optional): Sprinkle grass seed if the area is bare.

➤ Step 6: Topdress with a thin layer of manure or compost and pack down gently to firm seed into place.

➤ Step 7: Water well and keep moist if overseeded.

Coaxing Your Lawn Back to Life

Your lawn won't look great right after you de-thatch or renovate, but think of this as a work in progress. The lawn has to heal and then utilize all the goodies you provided. It takes twice as long for runner grasses such as Bermuda to recover than with bunch grasses such as fescue. Runners take a slicing but keep on growing . . . slowly.

If you were thus wounded, you would immediately try to stop the bleeding. In grass language, this means to prevent as much moisture loss as possible. When the cut ends lose moisture, they die back, which slows down the healing process. So to get a nice quick heal, water deeply and often. Compensate for very hot, dry, or windy days with extra waterings over the next few weeks until the grass is well healed.

Refer to Chapter 16, "The Basic Food Groups," for details on fertilizer options and the needs of different types of grasses. Refer to Chapter 17, "Water Right, Water Deep," for instructions on proper turf grass irrigation.

> **The Least You Need to Know**

➤ Some turf grasses such as Bermuda and St. Augustine produce a lot more thatch than others.

➤ Thatch harbors disease spores and damaging insect pests.

➤ Heavy thatch acts like a barrier, keeping out water, fertilizer, and pest control materials.

➤ You can control some thatch production with a regime of organic fertilizers and regular topdressing.

➤ Physically de-thatch your lawn if the layer is more than $1/2$ inch thick.

Part 7

In Search of Small Game and Green Invaders

Weak plants, like weak people, get sick easily. Sparse, unhealthy lawns provide the perfect haven for weeds to sprout, bugs to nest, and disease to spread through the grass at lightning speed. The best offence is the defense of keeping your lawn as strong and vigorous as you can. This in turn keeps problems at a minimum.

When problems strike, most of the time it's what you don't see that causes the biggest problems in lawns. If you watch professional turf managers in action, it's not uncommon to find them down on hands and knees to get their eyes and magnifying glass close to the plants. The early signs of disease are often easy to see, but only if you're close enough to become intimate with the grass. Actually, the key to successful gardening with any kind of plant is observation, so that you can leap on bugs or weeds before they've been around long enough to become a serious threat.

Chapter 23

Weeds—
Botanical UFOs

In This Chapter

➤ How to recognize a weed in the grass

➤ How jet-set weeds get into your yard

➤ Understanding the life cycle of weeds

➤ Using chemicals for easy weed control

➤ Chemical-free weed control

One of the most important habits of weeds is their ability to reproduce their kind very freely. If this were not so, it would be much easier to get rid of weeds.

—Walter Conrad Muenscher, 1949

What we do to make our favored plants at home also makes weeds want to come and live there. Not only do they move in, but they also have enormous families that get larger each and every year. Give your grass good soil, lots of food, and adequate sunlight, and you invite the whole neighborhood to come over and join the fun.

It's difficult enough to keep a regular garden free of weeds. There is a variety of landscape plants to begin with, but the situation gets a lot more challenging when you insist on growing just one kind of plant—grass. Even more stringent yet is a lawn composed of just one species of grass such as fescue. Carry this a step further with lawns planted in a single variety of that species such as Survivor, and all the other fescues become undesirables!

Name Calling

Would you consider a tomato plant a weed? Not in a vegetable garden. But how about a rose garden, would a tomato be a weed there? Of course, it would.

When we start calling plants bad names like "weed," it's all related to context. The official definition of a weed is "a plant out of place." Therefore, you can't call a dandelion a weed, because some urban herbalist will come along and cut off the leaves for salad. But when it sprouts up in a lawn, then its value changes from food plant to weed.

Weeds in Grass

Our context is the lawn, a turf grass lawn. Even this defies strict definitions because some lawns are blends of different grasses. Some lawns are wild and free combinations of both clovers and grasses tended by organic gardeners. There are zillions of different grasses, but all are considered weeds if they are not the exact kind designated in your lawn.

Greenskeepers' Nightmares

Golf course greenskeepers can list a handful of the most common weeds that afflict their greens and fairways. These are exceptionally prolific, reproduce at startling rates, and are nightmares to get out of established turf. Just to confuse matters, remember that to northern greenskeepers, Bermuda grass is on the major offenders' list, whereas southern greenskeepers may tend entire courses of nothing but Bermuda.

Turf Talk

When soils are disturbed, certain weeds, such as thistle, amaranth, annual grasses, and many others, are always the first to appear. Collectively called *colonizers*, they are quick to germinate and mature compared to more long-lived perennial weeds that are slower to become established.

A Grand Strategy

A mature, dense, and healthy lawn is a hostile place for weeds. The turf grass plants are so close together that they deny light to seeds that might land in their midst. Their roots deny invading seedlings the moisture and nutrients they need to mature. Mowing itself discourages many species that cannot tolerate repeated beheading.

But lawns that are not well cared for are ripe for botanical invasions. Thin grass or bare spots where there's no grass at all literally invite unwanted plants to take up residence there.

There is a direct relationship between the overall health of your lawn and the amount of weeds that will grow there. Three goals of lawn care will help keep your lawn healthy and as weed free as possible. The grand strategy to control weeds in turf also involves three practices.

Good for Grass, Bad for Weed

Make sure that conditions in your lawn are always highly favorable to the grass such as:

➤ Even moisture

➤ Consistent, balanced nutrition

➤ Aerated soils

➤ Plentiful organic matter

➤ Vigorous, well-adapted turf variety

Make conditions unfavorable to weeds:

➤ Dense turf

➤ Fierce competition for water and light

The Best Offense Is a Good Defense

If one weed is allowed to gain a foothold in the lawn, it may produce a huge number of seeds. Timing is everything. If you don't agree, consider the progeny of just one parent plant over a single season:

➤ Black mustard: 58,373 seeds

➤ Amaranth: 196,405 seeds

➤ Purslane: 193,213 seeds

Weeds such as morning glory and the clovers have extensive underground root systems. Once established, you can pull them repeatedly, but as long as the roots remain in the soil, they will return with a vengeance. Unless you use a well-timed spray with herbicide, or dig the plant out when it first appears, you will be stuck with it seemingly forever.

Don't Contaminate Your Lawn

Weeds have to get to your lawn before they can grow there. That means that seeds and bits of living root or stem should not be introduced to your turf. Here are the major sources of contamination:

➤ Seed brought in with loads of manure, compost, or topsoil

➤ Root and stolon pieces transported by lawn mower

➤ Wind-blown seed from nearby weed patches

➤ Low-quality turf grass seed containing weeds

The biggest source of contamination is from weeds allowed to go to seed near the lawn. These can spring up in forgotten corners of your own yard, or on neighboring land. Many a lawnowner has had a feud with neighbors who literally go to seed next door to their pristine turf grass lawn.

Turf Tip

A wise old garden guru told me once that he could never keep up with all the weeds in his landscape. But he also knew the danger of allowing them to go to seed. His philosophy was "if you can't pull them all, at least break off the flower heads so they can't go to seed." To this day, I am forever breaking off seed heads when I'm too busy to weed properly. For each flower head I destroy, I'm saving myself tens of thousands of weed seedlings in the future.

Weed Botany

Weeds are plants with behavior problems. They come from vastly different camps; some are highly evolved, whereas others, such as mosses, are rather primitive. You need to know their habits to control them properly. Habits and life cycle also indicate which ones are likely to be the most persistent problems.

The life cycle of a plant is the process by which it reproduces. Many reproduce by seed. Others reproduce vegetatively without flower or seed. Some do both. The secret to weed control is to attack at the most vulnerable point in the life cycle. The fact that lawns are regularly mowed has a big influence on how aggressive the weed is in turf.

Annus Horribilis

Annual weeds last for only one year, one growing season. They are quick to sprout from seed, and their life cycle is completed in the same season. The survival of the species depends on its ability to flower and make seed for the next year's crop. At the end of the year, annuals either die out on their own or are killed by winter frost.

When annual weeds sprout in the lawn, they may not set seed themselves because mowing cuts off the flower heads. The annual weed in cold climates will die out at the end of the season no matter what you do. Certain annuals in warm climates that are frost free or nearly so can act like perennials, living on for multiple seasons before they run out of gas.

Perennial Problems

Perennial weeds live a very long life. They are slow to start and may be reluctant to begin from seed. Perennial weeds do reproduce from seed, but the slow germination rates make this less crucial than with annuals.

Some perennial weeds reproduce vegetatively as well. They send up plantlets from above ground or underground stems and roots. A single individual may spread into a whole colony without ever producing a single seed. This is crucial when it comes to lawns, because mowing prevents seed heads but can actually encourage vegetative reproduction.

Turf Talk

Here's a great plant–geek speak word used to describe the body of a plant. The *morphology* of a plant is its external shape. This includes the shape of the leaves, roots, stems, and flowers.

When Weeds Sleep

Warm-season grasses often take a nap in winter. They promptly turn brown with minor drops in temperature—they don't even need a frost. If you have an evergreen cool-season lawn, consider this a heads-up warning. If warm-season grasses gain a foothold, you are destined to suffer with brown patches of dormant turf that really stand out like a sore thumb against the rest of your luxuriant lawn. This is one of the worst-case scenarios that should be avoided at all costs.

Look at and Feel the Weeds

Weeds are also divided into groups related to their shape, or morphology. This is important because it is connected to how selective herbicides work when they kill some plants in lawns but not others.

Turf Caveat

Clum or bunch grasses are easier to control than runner grasses. They are composed of a bundle of sprouts or *clums* on top of a mass of long roots. Each clum can start a new plant if separated from the mother plant. When removing bunch grasses, dig out the entire mass. If the bunch breaks apart, each clum left behind will start a new plant.

Grassy weeds are a member of the grass family, making them difficult to identify amidst turf grasses. Remember, a weed is a plant out of place, so if a grass takes up residence in your lawn, but it doesn't match your turf variety of choice, it's a weed.

There are both annual and perennial grassy weeds. Some crawl along the ground and spread out, whereas others remain in neat little clumps. Some go dormant; some don't. Some spread above ground; others do so underground.

339

Bunch Grass Clums

The *broadleaf* weeds include everything that isn't grass. They are much easier to identify by the size, shape, and color of their leaves. Growth habits may be succulent like purslane, viney as with morning glory, or leafy like dandelion.

Grassy Weed; Broadleaf Weed

Grassy

Broadleaf

Mug Shots of Lawn Criminals—Eight Notorious Grassy Weeds

You don't need to identify an unwanted plant to know it's a weed. Often they stand out in lawns so boldly there's no question what they are and that they have to go.

You will find that identification does help you understand the life cycle of the plant. That way, you know when it is most vulnerable and how to get rid of it with the least amount of hassle. Plus, you don't want it showing up again because you used a less than effective means of eradication.

The following eight grassy weeds are by no means the only grassy weeds you'll encounter, but they are the most common. Remember that identification is the key to control. The discussion will include references to chemical weed killers, but these are always optional. Should you use one of them, be sure to follow the directions exactly.

Crabgrass and Annual Bluegrasses

Crabgrass is an annual warm-season grass that resembles many other weedy grasses that live for just one season. Crabgrass, as all annuals, dies with the onset of winter frost, but seed will winter over and flourish in spring. It is so aggressive that once established, it crowds out the lawn.

Crabgrass does resemble Bermuda and other turf grasses while young. Like all annuals, it is a prolific seed producer, and its six-fingered seed heads appear in midsummer. Control crabgrass with preemergent herbicide treatments in late winter to kill any seed left over from the previous season. Some fertilizers contain crabgrass-killing additives that do virtually the same thing for much less work.

Crabgrass

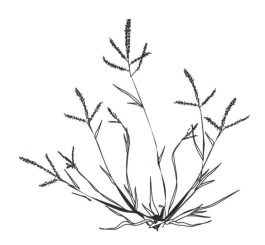

Dallisgrass

Here's a dense, clumping, coarse grass that stands out amidst finer turf grass varieties. Thick stems and fast-maturing seed heads can pop up and distribute their black seeds all over the place in just days after you mow. The best control is to pull seedlings before they make a big clump. You must dig out older plants, taking the entire crown and most of the roots. Be sure to fill in the hole left behind with clean soil.

Johnsongrass

This is similar in habit and size to Dallisgrass, but the seed heads are different. Also, Johnsongrass is not at all tolerant of the close mowing required for Bermuda lawns. This weedy grass has trouble surviving in healthy, dense turf, so it can be discouraged by extra TLC for your lawn.

Quackgrass

Quackgrass is a perennial grass identified by its large white rhizomes that travel underground. You will find this grass growing vigorously during cooler months. Here is one of the bad boys of the turf world because you can't dig it out in one piece. Low mowing does discourage it somewhat but doesn't kill it. Some lawns infested with this and other similar traveling perennial grasses are killed with herbicides and then a new lawn is planted. If you see a young plant even vaguely similar, shoot first and ask questions later.

Quackgrass

Bentgrass

Bentgrass has long been a favorite perennial turf grass on golf course greens because of its fine leaves and color. It can literally be mowed as short if not shorter than Astroturf! Though once popular for home lawns it's been phased out due to high maintenance and disease problems. Plus, new strains of more well-behaved cool-season grasses have made it obsolete. Bentgrass thrives in cool climates and loves close mowing and very moist conditions. If you find it in your lawn, dig it out immediately. To discourage it, mow high and keep the lawn on the dry side.

Bentgrass

Nutsedge

When is a grass not a grass? When it's a sedge. Sedges can seriously disfigure turf grass lawns. Although they resemble grasses, they are different in color, habit, and texture. There are a number of species, and all have pealike tubers on their roots that can run up to 4 inches underground. They can be a big problem in new sod lawns where the mother plant was removed, but the tubers send up sprouts capable of penetrating sod.

343

Sedges tend to show up in very wet lawns. Use only herbicides designated for sedges or carefully dig out new sprouts the minute you see them as well as older plants. Excavate a big root ball to make sure that you get all the tubers.

Bermuda and Other Warm-Season Grasses in Cool-Season Lawns

Here's a perfect example of how one kind of turf grass can be a weed in a lawn composed of another kind of turf grass. In this situation, Bermuda and other warm-season grasses turn brown when they go dormant in winter. This is a huge black eye in a cool-season lawn. It's easy to pick out the offenders, but if you use herbicide to control them, they must be green and actively growing. You can try to dig them out, but because they are mostly runner grasses, every little piece of root or stem left behind will reinfect the lawn.

Fescues and Other Cool-Season Grasses in Warm-Season Lawns

It's easier to spot cool-season grasses in warm-season lawns during the dormant season. The lawn will turn evenly brown except for the invaders. That's the time to control them with herbicide as long as it's still warm enough for active growth. You can pull these grasses or dig them out easily.

Bothersome Broadleafs

It's easy to ID broadleaf weeds. Even if you grew up in the heart of the city, chances are you encountered one or more of these shooting up through cracks in the pavement.

Clovers

Clovers bear that characteristic three-part leaf and can be either annual or perennial. These plants spread and will put up with close mowing, but they develop extensive root systems, which makes them difficult to pull out if already mature. Clovers aren't necessarily bad for lawns, they just disfigure them. Actually, they improve the soil, which is why the grass is always a bit greener around them. Use a broadleaf herbicide in late fall or spring to control them.

Burr Clover

Dandelion

This common perennial weed is noted for its bright yellow flowers and fluffy seed heads. This is a taprooted weed that must be dug out carefully so that the majority of the root is extracted. You can also apply herbicide in early spring.

Dandelion

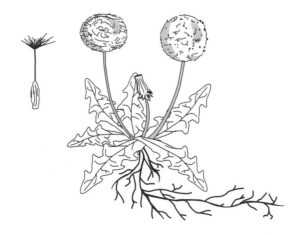

Oxalis (a.k.a. Sheep Sorrel)

This is an annual weed that bears leaves nearly identical to clover. You can tell them apart by the daisy shape of the oxalis flower, which is different from the pea-type flower of clover. Pull these by hand or spot kill with herbicide any time they are actively growing.

Broadleaf Plantain

Here's a barometer weed. If it crops up in your lawn, then chances are the lawn is not in good shape. These plants are most often found in very sparse lawns and can be discouraged by renovating the lawn and overseeding for thicker coverage. Pull by hand and try to get as much root as possible, or use herbicide.

Plantain

Spurge

This weed also crops up where turf grasses are struggling. It's really common in drought-ravaged lawns. You can pick it out because of its gray-green leaves. It's an annual that grows from a taproot, making it tricky to pull by hand. It can be controlled by herbicides.

Some Shady Characters

Turf grass does not like shade. Sure, some varieties grow in more shade than others, but overall it's not a compatible relationship. Often, certain plants will flourish along with the lawn grasses that are usually thin and spindly from lack of light.

Before you go forth into battle with these two shade lovers, decide whether you're whipping a dead horse. Is it realistic to expect turf grasses to grow there, or is Mother Nature trying to gently suggest that you give it up?

Mosses

Moss loves shady, cool, moist conditions, plus acid soil and poor drainage. If it appears to be competing with grass for territory, it's just the opposite. Turf grass is retreating, and the moss is taking up the slack.

Violets

Violets were the shade lawns of the Victorian era. They grow wild in many regions and find a new home when planted elsewhere. They make a fine lawn substitute where it's too shady. Often violets spread as the lawn declines under shade trees. Maybe you should consider pushing the limit of the lawn out to the edge of the tree canopy and encouraging the violets to fill in the gap. When they bloom in the spring, there's hardly anything more charming and fragrant!

Violet

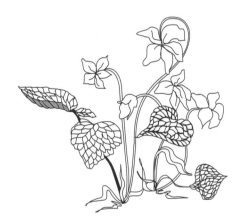

The Prevention and Eradication Program

Nobody wants to be a slave to weeds. The best way to control them on your terms is to never let them start up on their terms. One weed turns into a whole colony in a very short time, and that individual is a snap to get rid of compared to the colonial approach.

The Goal of Weed Control

➤ *Prevention* is the key to success by keeping your lawn thick, lush, and healthy.

➤ *Observation* with a keen eye helps you spot the first adventurers as they sprout in your lawn.

➤ *Identification* tells you which control method is most effective for that plant.

➤ *Immediate attention* ensures the weed is out of there before it spreads.

Manual Weed Removal

Old-fashioned turf grass weed control was done by hand. Today, many people are abandoning their chemical products in favor of a more eco-friendly means of getting the weeds out. Though it takes time and effort, the idea of sitting out on your lawn in the sunshine listening to the birds while pulling weeds is not so unattractive. It guarantees you don't need to use products that can damage the delicate flora and fauna of healthy organic soil.

Turf Tip

If you're pulling up weeds such as dandelions and plantain plants, you must get the majority of the taproot. Otherwise, these tenacious weeds will be back. It helps to buy an inexpensive tool called a *dandelion digger*. It's made of a steel blade that you stick down into the soil at an angle next to the weed, and it will sever the taproot deep down. The top part will come out cleanly and permanently with practically no effort. Be sure to buy a good sturdy model if you have hard or rocky soil because the tool will take a beating.

Dandelion Digging Tool

The real key to successful weed pulling whether it's in the lawn or flower beds is to water ahead of time. Water well and deep for a day or two before you plan to weed the lawn. This softens the soil, which gives way when you pull on the plant. Otherwise, every weed, regardless of the kind of root system it has, will break off at the soil line. They'll be back.

Herbicides—Getting Out the Big Guns

You may never need to use an herbicide on your lawn. However, when you are faced with a big infestation of crabgrass or other seriously aggressive weeds, you might change your mind. The best approach is to view these as potent tools that aren't appropriate unless you have a sizable problem.

There are many forms of herbicide, each designed to treat a different condition. They are marketed under different trade names while their purpose and effect will fall into one of the following categories. In general, these are the ones most often used in lawn care:

Fertilizer Killers

Sounds like a real oxymoron! Fertilizer herbicides are most often used because they combine fertilizing with weed control. These granular products have different formulas—some discourage crabgrass and its ilk, whereas others kill only broadleaf plants. These are easy to handle and apply with no mixing or sprayers required.

Seed Killers

Preemergent herbicides kill seeds in the soil before they emerge. These are crucial for controlling annual weeds in perennial lawns. They are also applied to soil before sod is laid to kill any existing seeds that might sprout later on. Preemergents are usually sold as granules to be spread out on bare soil.

Picky Killers

Selective herbicides kill only certain kinds of plants. For example, 2,4-D only kills broadleaf plants, so, when used on lawns, the grasses are untouched, and the broadleaf plants perish. These are mixed with water and sprayed on.

Mass Murderers

Nonselective herbicides kill all plants. They are usually applied to actively growing leaves. It takes about two weeks for them to die completely. Glyphosate is the most common nonselective herbicide on the market. This is a spray-on product.

There are some real problems with using spray-on herbicide products because of the following factors:

➤ You must dispose of excess product safely.

➤ There is a risk of killing the wrong plant.

➤ Protective clothing must be worn.

➤ You must time the application for best results.

➤ A sprayer dedicated to herbicide is required.

Sprayers and Stuff

Herbicides are sold in liquid concentrates. These are really nasty products that you mix with water in a pump sprayer. Here are some guidelines to follow:

➤ Use a plastic sprayer because some herbicides are corrosive to metals.

➤ Never use that sprayer for anything else in order to avoid costly mistakes. Mark it boldly—I use a skull and cross bones.

➤ The same applies to measuring spoons or cups used in the mixing process.

➤ Never spray herbicide when it's windy.

➤ Wear proper protective clothing.

> **Turf Caveat**
>
> WARNING! Sterilant herbicides are to be avoided at all costs. These kill everything in the soil, and the soil will not grow plants for months, sometimes years, after an application. Read labels carefully to avoid mistaking a sterilant for other herbicides.

➤ Dispose of excess product in an appropriate way.

➤ You can find more information on herbicide applications and sprayers in Chapter 11, "Seeding a Turf Grass Lawn."

The Least You Need to Know

➤ Keep your lawn healthy, and you'll prevent most weeds.

➤ Weeds can be grasses or broadleaf plants.

➤ Annual weeds die at the end of the season; perennials are forever.

➤ Identify weeds to know how to control them best.

➤ Herbicides combined with fertilizer are big time savers.

A Fungus Among Us

The air is literally charged with spores, and the soils of the whole earth are full of living spores and hyphae of different kinds of fungi.

—William W. Diehl, 1953

Diehl tells us that fungi are indeed among us all the time. The family of fungi is really unique in the world. The way they live and reproduce is truly fascinating. For example, I'll bet you didn't know that a fungus in the midwest is considered to be the largest living thing on earth?

To give you a sense of just how large and diverse the fungi are, consider these familiar examples:

➤ Penicillin

➤ Truffles

➤ Mildew

➤ Spanish moss

Turf Talk

Mycelia is the body of the fungus, which is a lot like a spider web that lives in the soil. *Hyphae* is the name for each little piece of webbing in the mycelia. *Fruiting body* is the flower of the fungus, with the most commonly recognized example being the mushroom. *Spores* aren't true seeds but act like them. These are produced inside the fruiting body.

True, you're only trying to find out what's making spots on your lawn, but in the process you'll discover a whole world of microscopic wonders you never knew existed. There are more than 400 species of fungus known to inhabit lawns. Fortunately, only about 25 percent of them are true diseases of turf grass. And less than 10 of these show up in American lawns.

Understanding Fungi

All fungus organisms are plants. When you encounter the most visible fungus, a mushroom in your lawn for example, you're looking at only the tip of the iceberg. Mushrooms themselves are just the flower or fruiting body of the plant. The plant itself is underground, composed of mycelia that spread out in the soil like a giant spider web. These fruiting bodies come and go, but the mycelia can live for a long time.

Fungi can be large like a fairy ring of mushrooms. The edge of the ring is the edge of the mycelia, which tells you how big the fungus plant is. They can also be so tiny that you can't even glimpse the fruiting bodies without a microscope. The tiny species are small enough to live inside plants that are larger than they are.

How Fungi Eat

Fungi do not need sunlight and do not carry on photosynthesis. They get their food in a different way. You can easily differentiate between them by the way they feed:

➤ Those that live in and feed on dead organic matter and hasten its decay. In plant-geek speak, these are *saprophytes*. Fairy rings are in this group because they live and reproduce in soil. Fairy rings rarely kill grass; they just make it look bad because of all the mushrooms.

➤ Those that live inside other living organisms. These are called *parasites*, and when they take up residence in living turf grasses, they become diseases. Snow mold is an example of this kind of fungus; after it feeds off the grass plant, it dies.

As we all know, parasites are not considered pleasant to their hosts and eventually kill them off. Here's where the disease connection comes in—as the fungus gets bigger, it runs out of food. So it must spread to another host plant, and another, and another. This often happens in a circle but not always. With circular diseases, the most active part is the outside edge that's moving into uninfected hosts. It's not a pretty picture.

How Fungi Travel

Remember that *the air is literally charged with spores*. This describes just how prevalent they are in our everyday environment. If you suffer from allergies, you probably know how important mold counts are to your sinuses. Spores are everywhere—in soil, in plants, and in dead organic matter. They only become a problem when these conditions are right for them to flourish:

➤ A host plant, such as grass, is present.

➤ Resistance of the host plant is compromised.

➤ Weather conditions are favorable.

Is Your Lawn a Breeding Ground?

I will repeat once again the sacred mantra of the greenskeeper: *weakened or stressed grass plants become increasingly vulnerable*. Healthy plants have a natural resistance to diseases, bugs, and the invasion of weeds. When weakened, these defenses break down, and we get problems. Healthy, happy grass equals bug-and-disease-free grass.

These factors determine whether your lawn is healthy or a breeding ground for fungal warfare. Some of these factors you can change, but others, like weather, you can't. I risk redundancy here in terms of good practices, but these fundamentals always bear repeating.

Beware the Wet

That black stuff in between your shower tiles is a fungus. It just loves that nice wet place that doesn't get any sun and rarely dries out completely. If the fungus is lucky, you don't do as much cleaning as you should either.

The reason diseases are so prevalent in the south is because it rains all summer, and it stays moist and humid all the time. Lousy for people but great for lawn fungus. When the fungi are fruiting, all the warm rain helps spread the spores even faster than normal. Bet you didn't know that some spores actually swim.

Spores like about 18 hours of continual wet weather to find a home and put down roots. Their window of opportunity is during the evening and night when there is less evaporation and the dew makes sure it stays damp. In those southern states, it's not a good idea to water in the evening—it takes a bad situation and makes it worse.

Fire and Ice

If everybody lived in the perfect northern California climate, lawn diseases wouldn't be such a serious affliction. It's not so much that fungi like bad weather; it's that the grass doesn't like bad weather.

When it's really hot, the grass dries out and starts to wilt, and in march the parasites. On the other extreme, when smothered under a foot of snow, the grass isn't too happy, and fungi such as snow mold get the upper hand. In general, though, high temperature kicks off flowering in fungus; so when all systems are go, you can get a good dose all at once.

Too Much of the Good Stuff

We know that grass likes a nice even diet of fertilizer. It doesn't like to go too long in between feedings. It also doesn't like to be underfed or overfed. Some diseases are associated with nutrient deficiencies, which make grass sluggish and unable to resist parasites. Others are more prevalent when you overdose on nitrogen, which affects grass like too many espressos in the morning affect you.

Butch Haircuts

Never forget that mowing your lawn is a process of hacking off a third or more of the plant's total volume. Mowing by itself can help disease get into plants through the wounds. If you mow too close, you aren't cutting just the leaf blades, you cut into the main stem. This weakens the plant from too much moisture loss. It's also like opening a mainline vein to parasites. This is even more important when combined with long-term damp and warm weather.

Happy Roots

Here's a no-brainer. If you have unhealthy grass because it's growing on concretelike soil, the grass gets stressed. What happens when the lawn is stressed? In come the parasites. A healthy, well-aerated lawn reduces diseases. More information on this can be found in Chapter 21, "Soil Compaction—Public Enemy #1."

Thick Thatch

Thatch is all the dead clippings, leaves, and stems that build up in the lawn. Fungi just love thatch. A thatch layer more than $3/4$ inch thick is the Beverly Hills of fungal diseases. Why give them a nice comfy home in an upscale neighborhood to start a family in? De-thatch the lawn and evict them! Sometimes these kinds of fungi can change and start becoming parasitic if they reach certain levels. Plus, thatch is not good for turf grasses. You can find more information on this in Chapter 22, "Thatch: Not the Kind for Huts."

Disease Fighters

Many organisms exist to naturally check the growth of undesirable fungi. They are often missing in neglected lawns. One strategy for nonchemical control of these diseases is to reintroduce these beneficial bacteria and other microorganisms. There are two ways to do this:

➤ Apply topdressing of compost or pulverized tree bark that contains these beneficial microorganisms. Not all compost contains them, however, so go to a quality nursery and ask for products with *Trichoderma* such as Progrow.

➤ Switch to an organic lawn fertilizer that has been inoculated with these disease-fighting microorganisms. Examples are Dis-Patch, Green Magic, Lawn Restore, or Strengthen & Renew.

A Social Disease

Diseases spread when pieces of grass or spores themselves are introduced into fresh, healthy grass. There are dozens of ways these fungi colonize a new lawn or spread across an already infected one. If you're fighting a persistent problem, be aware that these can aid in transporting diseases:

➤ Lawn mowers spread disease across your lawn, from the front lawn to the back and vice versa. Lawn services are notorious spreaders of disease.

➤ The soles of your shoes, especially if they have a lot of crevices. Smooth soles are better when fighting disease.

➤ Catcher bags can build up huge quantities of spores.

➤ Hand tools such as leaf rakes.

➤ Kids' bicycles and outdoor portable toys.

Turf Caveat

Consider disease-ridden lawns quarantined. After mowing, the clippings are highly contagious. Be cautious when emptying the catcher so that its contents don't end up blowing or being tracked on uninfected grass. For serious epidemics, bag your clippings and send them to the landfill or dispose of them far from the lawn where their spores aren't upwind from the lawn.

Keep your lawn equipment clean to reduce spreading. Diseased grass can build up on your mower, particularly the rotary kind where it cakes up under the housing.

After it has cooled, wash your mower thoroughly after each use. Disinfect it with a drench of bleach solution mixed at 1 ounce bleach per 4 gallons of water. Be sure to clean and disinfect the catcher and dip your shoe soles in it too when finished mowing. This may seem tedious, but you can quit after the disease problem is under control.

Disease Happens

Half the battle is keeping the lawn as naturally disease resistant as possible. The other half is identifying and treating whatever outbreak you find in your lawn. This is much more difficult than identification of weeds or bugs because, again, many of these organisms are microscopic.

We treat disease with the same Integrated Pest Management (IPM) least-toxic measures as we use to treat bugs. There's no need for a baseball bat when a fly swatter will do. But to choose your weapon, you need to know the behavior of the enemy, which requires accurate identification.

Many of these diseases display symptoms that closely resemble each other. If you can't find something in this rogue's gallery that you feel describes what's going on in your lawn, don't guess, because treatment for one may actually encourage others to spread. There are instructions later on in this chapter to help you get a professional diagnosis.

Brown Patch (a.k.a. *Rhizoctonia* blight) *Rhizoctoni solani*

Brown Patch

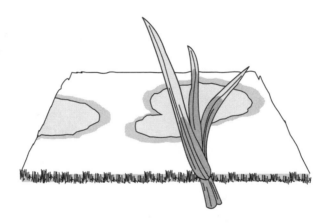

Identification: Circular brown patches with crisp edges. The fungus starts as the size of a nickel and grows outward from the center. The most active part is at the outside edge where the new host plants await infection. These plants will first turn dark like wet lettuce does after remaining too long in the crisper drawer. Sometimes the fungus smells that way, too. Then the grass dies and browns out. If the circle is large enough, you get a "doughnut hole" where the fungus has left for greener pastures, and the grass begins to recover.

Temperature Preference: 70 to 100 degrees F.

Causes: Erratic fertilization schedule and grass consecutively mowed too low.

Susceptible Grasses: Bermuda, bluegrass, fescue, ryes, St. Augustine, and zoysia.

Resistant Varieties: Perennial Rye: All star, Barry, Citation, Delray, Manhattan II, Palmer, Pennant, Prelude, Premier, and Yorktown II. Tall Fescue: Brookston, Jaguar, Mustang, and Olympic.

Least Toxic Measures:

1. Cultural practices that reduce brown patch in lawns:

   ➤ Water only in early morning and do not overirrigate.

   ➤ Reduce nitrogen and increase phosphorous and potassium in fertilizer.

   ➤ Mow less often and at a higher level with a freshly sharpened blade.

   ➤ De-thatch the lawn.

   ➤ Topdress with organic lawn fertilizers containing beneficial bacteria that attack brown patch fungus. Brands to look for include Dis-Patch or Lawn Restore.

2. Chemical controls:

   ➤ Frequent application of fungicidal soap.

   ➤ Apply neem oil botanical insecticide—it doesn't kill brown patch fungus but keeps it from reproducing.

   ➤ Sulfur-based fungicide.

   ➤ Chemical turf fungicide.

Fusarium Blight (a.k.a. Summer patch, Necrotic Ring Spot) Fusarium culmorum

Fusarium Blight

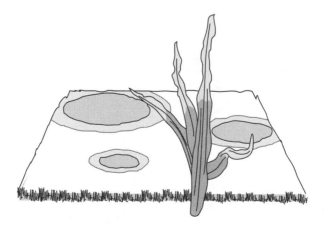

Identification: Fusarium crops up after about two dry weeks following a period of heavy rain. It thrives in areas where soils are compacted and grass roots are limited. It tends to show at edges of paving and where drainage is poor. Begins as small rings of dead grass that are not crisp like brown patch but with irregular edges. The area turns dark blue as the fungus invades host plants; then blades promptly wilt and turn a sickly yellow. One key to ID is, when the lawn is wet from dew, rain, or watering, you may see a pinkish cast, which is the fungal mycelia.

Temperature Preference: Tends to occur in warm months between June and early September.

Causes: Heavily compacted, poorly drained lawn soils. The most vulnerable grass, Kentucky bluegrass, becomes even more susceptible when overdosed on nitrogen.

Susceptible Grasses: Older strains of Kentucky bluegrass, such as Park, Flyking, and Nugget. Fine fescues.

Resistant Varieties: Kentucky Bluegrass: Columbia.

Least Toxic Measures:

1. Cultural practices that discourage fusarium and its relatives:
   - ➤ Cut back on nitrogen fertilizer, especially on bluegrass in midsummer when its growth slows down.
   - ➤ Switch to an organic lawn fertilizer containing beneficial bacteria.
   - ➤ Water more frequently.
   - ➤ Aerate problem areas or preferably the entire lawn.
   - ➤ Overseed the lawn with perennial ryegrass.
   - ➤ Plant new lawn in resistant strains of turf grass.
   - ➤ Avoid spreading fungus with infected lawn equipment.

2. Chemical controls:
   - ➤ Frequent applications of fungicidal soap.
   - ➤ Neem oil.
   - ➤ Sulfur turf fungicide.
   - ➤ Chemical turf fungicides.

Pythium Blight (a.k.a. Cottony Blight, Grease Spot) Pythium spp.

Pythium Blight

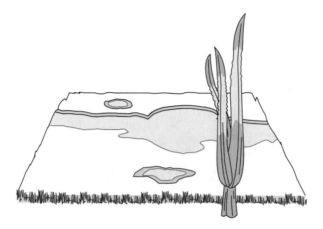

Identification: Round, brown-red spots that reach a maximum of about 6 inches in diameter. Names indicate its characteristics when wet—grass may feel greasy or look like there is a cottony, lavender-colored web material mixed in. Tends to prefer wet spots. Tendency to spread with water is illustrated in lawn drainage paths where it appears in a long stripe rather than individual spots.

Temperature Preference: When humidity levels near 100 percent, and day temperatures rise above 85 degrees F with warm nights above 68 degrees F.

Causes: Water accumulation on the lawn, excess watering, runoff, and puddles. Spreads easily on shoes, lawn equipment, mowers, and clippings. Tends to be more of a problem where soils are deficient in calcium or are alkaline.

Susceptible Grasses: All common turf grass varieties.

Least Toxic Measures:

1. Cultural practices that discourage pythium blight:
   - ➤ Water early in the day; water deeply but infrequently.
   - ➤ Fine-tune sprinkler system and check each head to be sure it's not leaking.
   - ➤ Aerate lawn to help surface water percolate into the soil more quickly.
   - ➤ Fill low spots and improve drainage in lawn to prevent water accumulation and spread.
   - ➤ Use proper mowing practices to avoid spreading the disease around the lawn.

Turf Caveat

All household bleach is not the same. Some contain additives or varying potencies. Whenever you use bleach in home remedies for plants, buy the standard kind by looking for the designation: 5.25% available chlorine.

➤ Topdress with organic lawn fertilizers containing beneficial bacteria.

➤ Overseed with resistant grasses.

➤ Replant the lawn with resistant grasses.

2. Chemical controls:

➤ Check spreading by applying a solution of 1 ounce of household bleach in 4 gallons of water.

➤ Frequent applications of fungicidal soap.

➤ Neem oil.

➤ Chemical turf fungicide.

Dollar Spot Lanzia, Moellerodiscus

Dollar Spot

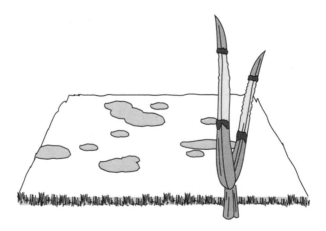

Identification: Like its name suggests, this fungus is about the size of coins. It begins about the size of a 25-cent piece and matures into the size of a silver dollar. A bunch of spots can blend into one big mess that doesn't look coin sized any more. Up close, morning dew will reveal cottony mycelia on newly infected areas. Each spot sinks into the turf like a little moon crater.

Temperature Preference: Loves great weather just like you do—warm days and nice cool nights that don't range much beyond 60 to 80 degrees F.

Causes: Underfed lawns and thatch accumulation where fungus overwinters from year to year.

Susceptible Grasses: All types.

Resistant Varieties: Fine fescue: Agram, Barfalla, Biljart, Checker, Encota, Famosa, Koket, Reliant, Scaldis, Shadow, and Tournament. Kentucky Bluegrass: Adelphi, America, Aquila, Arista, Galaxy, Geary, Majestic, Midnight, Newport, Palouse, Parade, Park, Pennstar, Prato, Primo, Sodco, and Windsor. Perennial Rye: Barry, Capper, Caravelle, Citation, Dasher, Ensporta, Exponent, Linn, Manhattan II, NK-100, NK-200, Regal, Rex, Sprinter, and Venola.

Least Toxic Measures:

1. Cultural practices that discourage dollar spot:

   ➤ Water early in the day; water deeply but infrequently.

   ➤ Use proper mowing practices to avoid spreading the disease around the lawn.

   ➤ Topdress with organic lawn fertilizers containing beneficial bacteria.

   ➤ Overseed with resistant grasses.

   ➤ Replant the lawn with resistant grasses.

2. Chemical controls:

   ➤ Check spreading by applying a solution of 1 ounce of household bleach in 4 gallons of water.

   ➤ Frequent applications of fungicidal soap.

   ➤ Neem oil.

   ➤ Chemical turf fungicides.

Melting Out (a.k.a. Leaf Spot) Drechslera

Melting Out

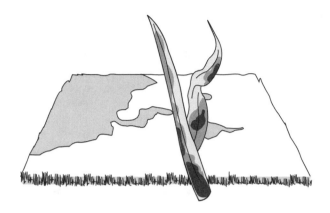

Identification: This fungus lives in thatch, and although it is a primary decomposer of dead material, in ideal conditions, it will invade living plants. When first infected, green leaf blades are marred by small black specks, followed by larger, light-brown spots before the blade turns brown altogether. Cool, wet weather can cause plants to be attacked at the crown or base and throughout the roots, causing these plants to die, which thins out the turf. The name is derived from this behavior when the grass seems to melt away.

Temperature Preference: Cooler temperatures from 40 to 75 degrees F, and wet, drizzly, or foggy weather.

Causes: Overfertilized grasses with abnormal, luxuriant growth. Watering during evening hours. Mowing too close also encourages the leaf spots to travel down into stems and roots.

Susceptible Grasses: Kentucky bluegrass.

Resistant Varieties: Kentucky Bluegrass: Bonnieblue, Challenger, Eclipse, Georgetown, Majestic, Midnight, and Nassau. Perennial Rye: Belle, Blazer, Cowboy, and Ranger. Tall Fescue: Adventure, Brookston, Houndog, Jaguar, Mustang, and Olympic.

Least Toxic Measures:

1. Cultural practices that reduce melting out:
    - ➤ Water only in early morning.
    - ➤ Use organic lawn fertilizer and keep spring nutrient levels constant.
    - ➤ Mow at a higher level with a freshly sharpened blade.
    - ➤ Keep existing thatch moist with frequent irrigation.

➤ De-thatch the lawn if needed.

➤ Topdress with organic lawn fertilizers containing beneficial bacteria.

➤ Use proper mowing practices to keep from spreading the disease around the lawn.

➤ Because melting out mainly afflicts Kentucky bluegrass, consider overseeding or replanting with another kind of turf.

2. Chemical controls:

➤ Sulfur-based fungicide.

➤ Chemical turf grass fungicide.

Pink Snow Mold, Grey Snow Mold (a.k.a. Fusarium Patch) Microdochium nivale

Snow Mold

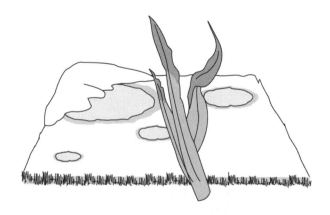

Identification: Do not confuse this with fusarium blight, which is very different. This disease is connected with conditions related to snow. While under the snow, there will be circular spots from 1 to 8 inches in diameter, which will be tan to brown in color. After the snow melts, they turn darker brown and may reach 2 feet in diameter. Right after the snow disappears, you can see a pinkish edge around the spots. This tends to be an early spring factor that goes away as grass growth rates speed up.

Temperature Preference: Between 32 and 64 degrees F; overcast, cool conditions.

Causes: Snow falling on unfrozen, poorly drained soils where there is little air movement. However, it can occur where there is no snowfall if like conditions exist. Long-term overcast weather keeps moisture levels high and enhances spread.

Susceptible Grasses: Cool-season turf types.

Resistant Varieties: Fine fescue: Barfalla, Biljart, Jade, Jamestown, Koket, and Scaldis. Kentucky Bluegrass: Adelphi, Admiral, Birka, Bonnieblue, Flyking, Glade, Lovegreen, Monopoly, Nassau, Shasta, and Victa. Perennial rye: Barenza, Diplomat, Eton, Game, Lamora, Manhattan, NK-200, Norlea, Omega, Pelo, Pennfine, Sprinter, and Wendy.

Least Toxic Measures:

1. Cultural practices that discourage fusarium patch:

   ➤ Do not fertilize late in the season because this does not allow grass growth to naturally slow enough to discourage this disease.

   ➤ Keep the lawn well aerated in late fall because poor drainage is connected to disease.

   ➤ De-thatch the lawn and do not allow clippings to remain behind in fall.

   ➤ Topdress with organic lawn fertilizers containing beneficial bacteria.

2. Chemical Controls:

   ➤ Chemical turf fungicide.

A Pathological Diagnosis

Much of the time, it's fairly easy to figure out what's making your grass look like it has chicken pox, or maybe the black plague. If the nursery can't help, consult the university extension office nearest you. They will need:

➤ A *fresh* sample of the lawn problem area.

➤ A note telling what kind of grass it is, what the symptoms are, and how long the symptoms have persisted. Include your name and phone number.

➤ You either mail it or take it to them.

➤ Sometimes they can identify the problem by sight, but if testing is required, they will get back to you with the results and recommended control measures.

The Least You Need to Know

➤ Most turf grass diseases are fungi.

➤ There are beneficial organisms in compost and organic fertilizers that naturally attack fungi.

➤ Disease outbreaks are related to mowing too closely, poor drainage, overly dense soils, and how and when you fertilize.

➤ Many diseases are related to weather and excess moisture.

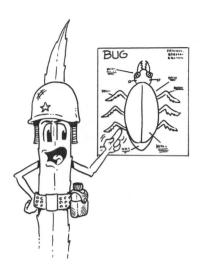

Chapter 25

Insects—Know Thine Enemy

In This Chapter

➤ Why insects live in lawns

➤ How insects differ according to life cycle

➤ The most common lawn-eating bugs

➤ Least toxic approach to pest control

➤ Pest prevention for the future

Often the number of insects runs into many millions to an acre and their large appetites more than make up for their small size.

—C. M. Packard, 1952

Insects have bugged the living daylights out of gardeners and farmers since the beginning. They used fire, poison, and any other means possible to control the populations of pests that threatened agricultural crops. When crop failure meant starvation, bug control was a real life and death affair.

Don't worry, bugs in your lawn won't cause a plague, famine, or death. They do wreak havoc with the beauty of your lawn, though. In large enough numbers, pests such as fire ants can even turn your lawn into a downright hostile place to live.

The old philosophy of "the only good bug is a dead bug" is changing. We are becoming more aware of the role of insects in ecology and realize that some bugs are actually beneficial. It's important to know which bugs are vital to the health of your lawn, your family, and your environment.

It's All in the Numbers

Lawns and all other plants are great residential neighborhoods for bugs. Insects exist in every ecosystem and range from polar mosquitoes to equatorial tsetse flies. Under normal conditions, their numbers remain fairly constant, ebbing and flowing with the changes in seasons.

You can expect a certain number of them to exist in your lawn and garden. They will do a little damage, but unless it really becomes a problem, you can pretty much ignore them.

Turf Talk

An *entomologist* is an expert on insects. Having a few bugs in the garden is normal, but when they suddenly grow to abnormal numbers, you have an *infestation*.

Natural Defenses

Plants are born with natural defenses against insects. If they didn't have them, bugs would eat them out of existence. These defenses are directly related to the health of the plant, and if they fail, the plant becomes infested with bugs.

For example, a group of broccoli plants all the same age is growing under identical conditions. For some reason, one of them is a runt and isn't growing as well as the others. The bugs will always show up on the weak plant and may never spread to the healthy ones.

This shows why healthy lawns have a lot less trouble with bugs. If well aerated, free of thatch, and adequately watered and fertilized, your lawn may never become infested. This is your best course for prevention.

Whether It's Weather

The expression "seven-year locusts" describes the fact that locust plagues don't occur every year. They are actually rare. The factor responsible for these sudden infestations is weather.

Every year has slightly different weather. When it is really unusual though, such as excessive rains or an abnormally warm winter, the insect population will be affected. In some places, weather may cause a locust plague. But normal fluctuations mean that you can't assume that last year's bug problem will happen again this year.

Shooting the Good Bugs with the Bad

Bugs live in a dog-eat-dog world. There are predators, and there are prey. The predators are the gardener's best friend because they feed on many of the pests we hate. For every bug, there is a predator species, which can be anything from bacteria to birds. Entomologists study this relationship closely to identify and harness the predators for use in agriculture.

The most common example of a predator is the ladybug, which preys on aphids. When broad spectrum chemicals are used in the garden or on fields, the ladybugs die. So do the praying mantises, the champion predators. Using chemicals may solve a short-term problem, but in the long run, it makes bigger ones. Loss of predator bugs means that the problem insects will return and do even greater damage next time.

Least Toxic

Integrated Pest Management (IPM) is a philosophy of pest control that utilizes all techniques available. The emphasis is to begin with the least toxic options, and if these aren't effective, you step up to the next choice. Only after all the nontoxic options have failed do you use the heavy artillery. Often control is as simple as changing your watering habits. It's all based on knowledge of the pests at hand and the entire array of control options available.

➤ Basic *identification* requires that you know what kind of pest you're trying to eradicate.

➤ Know the *life cycle* of the pest to apply the right control measures at the most effective time.

➤ *Understand your grass variety* and its own requirements, because how you take care of it has a lot to do with its vulnerability. Sometimes the best option is to change a vulnerable turf grass to one that is naturally resistant to persistent pests.

➤ Assess the *degree of damage* before you choose control measures. This means the amount of potential damage the bugs can do to your plants. Five bugs can have a low degree of damage compared to 500. Why use a baseball bat when a fly swatter will do?

The Rundown on Reproduction

You can divide most insects into two groups separated by their life cycle from egg to adult.

One group hatches into larvae, usually white worms, commonly called *grubs*. These have an insatiable appetite and are some of the most damaging lawn pests because they live underground. This feeding continues until they've stored enough fat to pupate. They emerge from this capsule as nearly full grown adults. Moths and butterflies, as well as many beetles, begin life this way.

Turf Talk

Larvae are the juvenile form of many insects. They *pupate* by encasing themselves in a cocoon, or capsule. While in there, they experience *metamorphosis*, which is the change from larvae to fully developed adult. A *nymph* is another juvenile form of insect that is a miniature version of the adult.

Metamorphosis Life Cycle

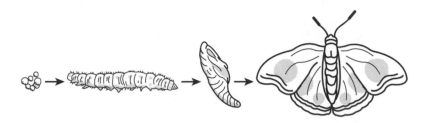

The second group hatches as a nymph. This tiny version of the adult immediately starts growing toward maturity. Flying insects often lack wings in the nymph stage, but these will develop as the insects mature. These bugs do not go through metamorphosis but shed their skins like snakes with each growth spurt.

Nymph Life Cycle

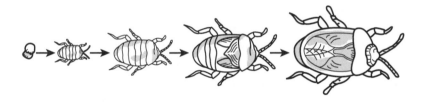

Turf Tip

Diagnosing turf takes close inspection. You won't see anything unless you kneel down and get eye to eye with the soil and grass. It helps to have a big magnifying glass on hand, too. Many bugs and the clues to their existence are small and subtle. Nobody ever identified a bad bug while still on his feet.

Underground Testing

Because we don't have x-ray vision, it's difficult to know what kind of grubs, worms, or bugs are nestled in lawn soil. You can draw them out by cutting both ends off a coffee can, or any other jumbo-sized can. Press one end firmly into the lawn soil. Fill the can up with soapy water and wait five minutes. Grubs and bugs will come to the surface of the soil for oxygen, and then float to the top of the water. This also shows the degree of damage potential by how many bugs show up.

Top Lawn Pests

Every climate zone experiences its own set of bugs. In general, hot humid climates have a much greater problem than cooler dry zones. Each lawn pest detailed here includes its cultural preferences, identification, and control measures. These measures are listed from least toxic to most toxic.

Grubs

A number of beetles lay their eggs in grass. These hatch out into white caterpillar grubs that feed on stems and roots of grass. They burrow deeper in the soil and winter over until the next season. As temperatures warm, they come back to the surface and feed like crazy for a few weeks before pupating.

Identification: Because they eat the surface roots, you can often lift up the grass like a rug. Soil may also feel soft and spongy from their tunneling underground. Use the coffee can method to draw them up for ID.

Control:

➤ Aerate the lawn in late spring when grubs are near the surface.

➤ Apply milky spore disease.

➤ Apply predatory nematodes.

➤ Apply botanical Neem insecticide.

➤ Apply synthetic pesticide designated for this insect.

Grub

The Grass Is Always Greener

There are 1.5 million different species of beetles. Scientists are discovering 7,000 to 10,000 new species each year.

Chinch Bugs

Chinch bugs are found in nearly all regions. Nymphs and adults feed on nearly all turf grasses but are a serious menace in Kentucky bluegrass and St. Augustine grass. They suck plant juices and also inject toxic substances in the process. Insect activity peaks in warm, dry conditions ranging from 70 to 80 degrees Fahrenheit.

Identification: Chinch bugs stink when you step on them! They emerge in very early spring at 45 degrees, so watch and smell for them early on. Bugs are only $\frac{1}{6}$ of an inch long. Nymphs are pinhead size and red with white, turning reddish brown as adults.

Control:

➤ Discourage heavy watering and thatching.

➤ Apply insecticidal soap products.

➤ Apply botanical pyrethrum insecticide.

➤ Apply synthetic pesticide: Diazinon, Sevin.

Chinch Bugs

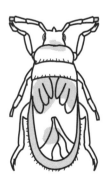

Sod Webworm

Found everywhere except the desert southwest, these caterpillars are larvae and live mostly underground. Larvae feed mostly at night, so you may never see them. They chew off leaves at the base and then drag them into silk-lined tubes where they dine in comfort. They pupate into adult moths.

Identification: They cause round, brown spots slightly bigger than a milk jug cap that resemble craters. Inspect grass blades up close for chew marks. The insects may be more prevalent in hotter, dry parts of the lawn than cool, moist ones. Web worms are similar to many other caterpillars but have rows of dark brown spots down their side.

Control: (Problematic because worms are inaccessible underground.)

➤ Prevent thatch buildup.

➤ Apply *Bacillus turingiensis* (BT), bacterial spray.

➤ Apply synthetic pesticide designated for this pest.

Sod Webworm

Billbug

Billbugs are weevil beetles around $1/2$ inch long. They often afflict bluegrass and most of the warm-season grasses. Both larvae and adults feed on grass. Adults eat the grass stems and then lay their eggs in the center of the plant. When grubs hatch, they start feeding on the most tender, new shoots and burrow down through the stem, causing massive damage and ending with the roots for dessert.

Identification: Billbugs are named for their long bill-like snout, the key to identifying them. Look for fine, sawdustlike excretions where billbugs have been feeding. You'll see adult beetles on pavement next to lawns during May and June. Pick through thatch for larvae. With this kind of structural damage, grass wilts, turns brown, and dies quickly, so time is of the essence.

Control:

➤ De-thatch, aerate, and water well.

➤ Apply predatory nematodes.

➤ Apply botanical pyrethrum insecticide.

➤ Apply synthetic insecticide: Diazinon.

Billbug

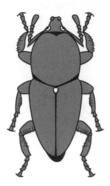

Mole Cricket

These insects measure about $1\frac{1}{2}$ inches long. They can damage grass by feeding on the roots. The chief problem with these burrowing crickets is the tunnels in young seedling lawns. The crickets dislodge seedling roots and kill the plants. One cricket can damage yards of newly seeded turf in a single night. If they are present, they must be controlled before you seed a new lawn. Mole crickets are born nymphs, so there is no larvae problem.

Identification: Mole crickets have no wings and are large enough for you to see clearly. They make sizable holes in the soil.

Control:

➤ Apply milky spore disease (*Bacillus popilliae*).

➤ Apply predatory nematodes.

➤ Apply synthetic pesticides designated for this insect.

Mole Cricket

Recognizing Beneficial Insects

It's as important to know the beneficial insects as it is the problem pests. Beneficial insects are threatened each time you use chemical pesticides and some botanical products. Whenever you work on the lawn or your garden, treasure these good guys. Their presence in large numbers indicates a healthy landscape that requires very little pest control.

➤ *Praying mantises:* These look ferocious because they get so large, but they do not harm humans and are one of the most effective problem-insect predators.

➤ *Ladybugs:* Small, red, and everybody's favorite, ladybugs have a big appetite for aphids, scale insects, and some mites that afflict lawns.

➤ *Lacewings:* Their large transparent wings distinguish these beneficial insects, which are often bright green. They prey on small larvae, ants, mites, spiders, and aphids.

The Grass Is Always Greener

Here's a great example of how important birds are to natural pest control. The mole cricket is also called the Mormon cricket because, in 1848, a plague of mole crickets devastated Utah farmlands. It was eventually ended by a flock of sea gulls that ate them out of existence. The citizens were so thankful they erected a monument in honor of the well-fed birds.

Turf Tip

If you want to make your lawn and landscape less vulnerable to pests, why not import some beneficial insects? It's easy to do by mail order, or often they are sold right at retail nurseries. Praying mantises and lacewings are sold as egg cases, which you put in the garden to allow them to hatch on their own. Ladybugs come live and raring to go in net bags. If you release these insects into your garden, avoid using pyrethrum or chemical pesticides.

Pest Control Products

For every pest, there is a pesticide. Fortunately, there are some new, relatively non-toxic products that are actually more effective in some cases than the chemicals. Most products fall into one of these three categories:

➤ Biological controls, which use organisms to kill pests

➤ Botanical pesticides, which are concentrated chemicals derived from plants

➤ Synthetic agricultural chemical pesticides

BT: Bacteria with an Attitude

Getting rid of grubs and worms used to be a lawnowner's greatest challenge. You had to literally saturate the lawn with chemicals to reach them underground. But now there's *bacillus thuringensis*, or BT, which is sold under different trade names. If caterpillars and grubs eat plants sprayed with BT, they get instant Montezuma's revenge and die. What's great is that BT need never be sprayed directly on the worms; the bacteria kill them at night as they feed and you sleep. BT is nontoxic to kids and pets, too!

Milky Spore Disease

Here's another nontoxic "eat well then die" bacterium, *Bacillus popillae*. The powdered spores are sprinkled on the soil and, when watered, come alive and take up residence in your soil. When grubs eat the roots of your grass, they ingest spores too, and these find an even better home inside the worm. They have a big party, multiply, and kill their host. It takes about two weeks to wipe out the grubs under ideal conditions. After you introduce the spores to your lawn, they keep on working for many months.

Predatory Nematodes

No, these are not related to garden toads or any other amphibian for that matter. These good predators are tiny wormlike organisms that live in the soil and attack the larval stages of more than 250 species of soil-dwelling pests, including fleas! Nematodes are sold alive, so be sure to buy very fresh dated product to ensure maximum effectiveness. They are also nontoxic.

Predatory Nematodes

Bazooka Botanicals

It may be organic, but it's awfully nasty. Most people think that botanical insecticides are perfectly safe because they are derived from plants. In nature, they may exist in plants but at much lower concentrations. Multiply that by a thousand, and that's what's in your bottle. These products are among the least toxic broad-spectrum pesticides used in lawns.

➤ *Pyrethrum* comes from African chrysanthemum petals. It gets bugs in lawn soils so irritated that they come to the surface where birds and other predators snatch them up. Pyrethrum is very toxic to fish.

➤ *Neem* is an oil extracted from the tropical margosa tree, and it shows up in some people products as well. It kicks butt on 150 different pests and also reduces some lawn diseases. It works best on bugs with a larval stage and is less damaging to beneficial insects than pyrethrum.

Chemical Warfare

With all the great new less-toxic products on the market, it's rare that you have to resort to synthetic chemicals. However, in climates where bug populations are a very serious problem, these products do have their place. In addition, they are part of some of the newer two-in-one formulas of fertilizer that include pesticide. ALL THESE PRODUCTS SHOULD BE CONSIDERED HIGHLY TOXIC TO WILDLIFE AND HUMANS IF IMPROPERLY USED.

➤ *Diazinon:* Effective on a large range of pests and one of the 10 most widely used garden pesticides. Available in easy-to-apply granules or liquid concentrate.

➤ *Dursban:* The main pesticide used on golf courses for soil-borne pests. Sold in liquid concentrate, ready-to-spray liquid, and dry granules. Kills everything.

➤ *Carbaryl:* This product rarely goes by its official name, but by Sevin, a trade name. It's been used in gardens for more than 30 years and is available in both liquid and granules. Kills almost everything. It's a frequent component of chemical flea products for dogs.

Baits

Mole crickets and fire ants are just two of the pests controlled by baits. Baits lace attractive pest food material with potent chemicals. These are especially efficient for pests that are localized or just too big to control with regular chemicals. Beware of where you use baits because they can be attractive to pets and kids.

Traps

Avoid traps that use interior bait to lure in pests. After much experimentation, it was learned that the bait is too effective! Pests from your neighbor's lawn, and sometimes from down the block, will make a bee line for your house, leaving you with a much greater problem than you started with.

Forms and Applications

Pest control products are manufactured in a variety of forms, and these influence how they are applied. The product label will indicate how much is needed per 500 or 1,000 square feet of lawn. Know the size of your lawn before you go shopping and bring a pocket calculator to do the math right in the store.

Each manufacturer offers its product in its own packaging and concentration. BT can be purchased as a powder or liquid concentrate, but because it needs water to activate the bacteria, it must be mixed and sprayed on.

Options by Type

Milky spore and nematodes can be spread dry, and then the lawn watered heavily to get these organisms down into the soil.

Botanicals are always liquid products. Some manufacturers sell their product in a concentrate that you mix and spray on. Other more expensive products have it premixed for you, and sometimes the container even has its own pump applicator.

Chemical pesticides for lawns are easiest to apply when granulated. Use your fertilizer drop spreader to distribute them evenly over the surface at the rate indicated on the package. These same chemicals are sold as liquid concentrates that you mix yourself and spray on.

Spot or Blanket

Part of the IPM strategy is to know a little bit about your bad bugs. They may be only in a small part of the lawn or throughout the whole yard. This will influence how you apply the control material.

All lawns benefit from a blanket application of BT, milky spore, or nematodes. The nontoxic quality means that you need not worry much about overdoing it.

But with botanical and chemical pesticides, use the least amount of product to get the job done. If the lawn needs a spot application, treat only that area and a little bit more to pick up any stray individuals.

Blanket applications must be done with care and precision to be sure that no untreated bugs remain behind. Your goals are:

➤ Cover the entire lawn with a consistent application rate.

➤ Do not overlap areas or stripes.

➤ Do not allow gaps of untreated lawn between stripes.

➤ Be thorough so that corners and edges are completely treated.

➤ Avoid applying materials to adjacent planters or paving.

The 10 Commandments of Pesticides

If a little is good, a lot isn't better!

Disrespect is one of the biggest causes of pesticide problems—this goes for both botanical and synthetic chemical products. All have manufacturer's directions and warnings for your protection. They also make sure that you get the right bug the right way at the right time.

These commandments are good practices for any kind of chemical, whether it's for house or garden.

1. Always follow manufacturer's instructions for application rates and concentrations.

2. Store the container in a cool, dark place that's out of the reach of children. Keep the container tightly closed. Place it on the back of the shelf where it isn't likely to be knocked over.

3. Wear protective goggles or a face shield, neoprene gloves, closed-toe shoes, and long pants when applying these products in case you spill some of it or it splashes back into your face. Do not wipe gloves on clothing.

4. Be careful. Sloppy handling can cause spills. Avoid spraying in windy conditions or just before it rains. Keep product from drifting into any natural waterways.

5. Time your applications properly. Avoid applying product when people or animals are using the lawn and allow a day or two afterwards before they are allowed to return.

6. Avoid mowing, walking, or any other use of the turf immediately after you apply. Allow liquid products to completely dry first.

Turf Caveat

It's a good idea to invest in a low-cost respirator, which is strapped on your face and filters the air. This product also provides protection when you're using anything that gives off harmful fumes. When you apply nematodes, botanical pesticides, and chemical pesticides, there's far less chance of inhaling these materials as you apply them to your lawn.

7. Wash your hands with hot water and soap before you eat, drink, or smoke after handling chemicals.

8. Avoid contaminating storm drains or sewers by pouring excess chemicals down the drain or at curbside.

9. Dispose of empty containers properly. If in doubt, call your local landfill for answers.

10. Dedicate sprayer and measuring cups and/or spoons to garden chemicals. Do not reuse these in the kitchen when you're finished. Buy a new applicator if it leaks. Store all application equipment out of the reach of children.

The Least You Need to Know

➤ Not all bugs are bad bugs.

➤ Most problem lawn pests live in the soil.

➤ The least toxic method of pest control starts with the most benign measures and works up to the heavy chemicals.

➤ You can import three kinds of natural killers into your lawn: nematodes, milky spore, and BT.

➤ Use care with all botanical and chemical pesticides and follow manufacturer's instructions to the letter.

Trees, Products, Seed, and Organic Product Guide

In This Appendix

➤ Top-25 American lawn trees

➤ Top turf grass and alternative lawn seed sources

➤ Organic lawn product sources

➤ Lawn mower makers

Top 25 American Lawn Trees

Botanical Name	Common Name	Type[*]	Zone
Acer platanoides	Norway Maple	D	3
Alnus cordata	Italian Alder	D	5
Carpinus betulus	European Hornbeam	D	5
Cedrus deodara	Deodar Cedar	E	7
Celtis australis	European Hackberry	D	6
Cinnamomum camphora	Camphor Tree	E	9
Fagus sylvatica	European Beech	D	4
Ginkgo biloba	Maidenhair Tree	D	4
Koelreuteria paniculata	Golden Rain Tree	D	5
Lagerstroemia indica	Crape Myrtle	D	7

continues

Top 25 American Lawn Trees (cont.)

Botanical Name	Common Name	Type[*]	Zone
Liquidambar styraciflua	American Sweet Gum	D	5
Liriodendron tulipifera	Tulip Tree	D	4
Magnolia grandiflora	Southern Magnolia	E	7
Nyssa sylvatica	Tupelo/Sour Gum	D	4
Pistacia chinensis	Chinese Pistache	D	9
Platanus acerifolia	London Plane Tree	D	5
Prunus cerasifera 'Atropurpurea'	Purple Leaf Plum	D	4
Pyrus calleryana 'Bradford'	Bradford Pear	D	4
Quercus palustris	Pin Oak	D	4
Quercus rubra	Red Oak	D	3
Quercus suber	Cork Oak	E	7
Sapium sebiferum	Chinese Tallow Tree	D	9
Sequoia sempervirens	Coast Redwood	E	7
Sophora japonica	Japanese Pagoda Tree	D	4
Tilia cordata	Little Leaf Linden	D	3

[*]*Evergreen (E) or Deciduous (D)*

Top Turf Grass and Alternative Lawn Seed Sources

Berlin Seeds
5371 County Road 77
Millersburg, OH 44654-9104
(330) 893-2030

Ferry-Morse Seeds
P.O. Box 520
Waterville, ME 04903
(800) 283-6400

Gurney's Seed & Nursery Co.
110 Capital St.
Yankton, SD 57079

Lockhart Seeds, Inc.
P.O. Box 1361
3 North Wilson Way
Stockton, CA 95205
(209) 466-4401

Lofts Seed, Inc.
P.O. Box 26223
Winston-Salem, NC 27114-6223
(800) 526-3890

Meyer Seed Co.
600 S. Caroline St.
Baltimore, MD 21231
(410) 342-4224

Peaceful Valley Farm Supply
P.O. Box 2209
Grass Valley, CA 95945
(916) 272-4769

Pennington Seed
P.O. Box 290
Madison, GA 30650
(800) 285-7333

P. L. Rohr & Bro., Inc.
P.O. Box 250
Smoketown, PA 17576
(717) 299-2571

The Scotts Co.
14111 Scotts Lawn Road
Marysville, OH 43041
(800) 543-TURF

Stock Seed Farms
28008 Mill Road
Murdock, NE 68407-2350
(800) 759-1520

Wetsel Seed Co.
P.O. Box 956
Kittanning, PA 16201
(800) 742-2510

Organic Lawn Product Sources

Agro-Chem Corp.
1150 Addison Avenue
Franklin Park, IL 60131
(708) 455-6900

Arbico
P.O. Box 4247-CRB
Tucson, AZ 85738-1247
(800) 827-2847
Catalog

BioLogic
P.O. Box 1777
Willow Hill, PA 17201
(717) 349-2789

Gardener's Supply Co.
128 Intervale Road
Burlington, VT 05401
(802) 863-1700
Catalog

Gardens Alive!
P.O. Box 149
Sunman, IN 47041
(812) 623-3800
Catalog

Growing Naturally
149 Pine Lane
P.O. Box 54
Pineville, PA 18946
(215) 598-7025
Catalog

Harmony Farm Supply
P.O. Box 460
Graton, CA 95444
(707) 823-9125
Catalog

IFM
333 Ohme Gardens Road
Wenatchee, WA 98801
(800) 332-3179
Catalog

Medina Agricultural Products
P.O. Box 309
Highway 90 West
Hondo, TX 78861
(512) 426-3011

Natural America
Box 7
Brentwood, NY 11717
(516) 435-2380
Catalog

Natural Farm Products, Inc.
Route 2, Box 201-A
Spencer Road SE
Kalkaska, MI 49646
(616) 369-2465
Catalog

Peaceful Valley Farm Supply
P.O. Box 2209
Grass Valley, CA 95945
(916) 272-4769
Catalog

Pest Management Supply Co.
P.O. Box 938
Amherst, MA 01004
(800) 272-7672
Catalog

Ringer Corp.
9959 Valley View Road
Eden Prairie, MN 55344-3585
(800) 654-1047
Catalog

Lawn Mower Makers

American Honda Motor Co., Inc.
Power Equipment Division
4475 River Green Parkway
Duluth, GA 30136
(800) 426-7701

Ariens Co.
655 W. Ryan Street
P.O. Box 157
Brillion, WI 54110
(920) 756-2141

Black & Decker (electric mowers)
701 E. Joppa Road
Towson, MD 21286
(800) 54-HOW-TO

Dixie Chopper
6302 E. Country Road, 100 North
Coatesville, IN 46121
(800) 233-7596

Frigidaire Home Products
P.O. Box 1569
Coffeyville, KS 67337
(800) 554-6723

Garden Way, Inc.
1 Garden Way
Troy, NY 12180
(800) 828-5500

Husqvarna Forest & Garden
9006 Perimeter Woods Dr.
Charlotte, NC 28216
(800) HUSKY-62

Ingersoll Equipment Co.
P.O. Box 5001
Winneconne, WI 54986
(920) 582-5000

John Deere
John Deere Road
Moline, IL 61265
(800) 537-8233

Murray, Inc.
P.O. Box 268
Brentwood, TN 37024
(800) 251-8007

Power King
1501 1st Ave.
Mendota, IL 61342
(800) 262-1191

Ryobi Outdoor Products, Inc.
550 North 54th St.
Chandler, AZ 85226
(800) 345-8746

Snapper, Inc.
535 Macon St.
McDonough, GA 30253
(800) 935-2967

Toro Co.
8111 Lyndale Ave.
South Bloomington, MN 55420
(800) 348-2424

Index

X–Y–Z